toys &
games

MILLER'S

toys &
games

MILLER'S TOYS & GAMES BUYER'S GUIDE

Created and designed by
Miller's Publications
The Cellars, High Street
Tenterden, Kent TN30 6BN
Telephone: 01580 766411 Fax: 01580 766100

Senior Executive Editor: Anna Sanderson
Executive Art Editor: Rhonda Fisher
Managing Editor: Valerie Lewis
Production Co-ordinator: Kari Reeves
Editorial Co-ordinator: Deborah Wanstall
Editorial Assistants: Melissa Hall, Joanna Hill, Maureen Horner, Léonie Sidgwick
Production Assistants: June Barling, Ethne Tragett
Advertising Executive: Jill Jackson
Advertising Assistant: Emma Gillingham
Advertising Co-ordinator & Administrator: Melinda Williams
Designer: Philip Hannath, Alexa Brommer
Advertisement Designer: Simon Cook
Indexer: Hilary Bird
Production: Sarah Rogers
Jacket Design: Victoria Bevan
Additional Photography: Emma Gillingham, Robin Saker

First published in Great Britain in 2004
by Miller's, a division of Mitchell Beazley,
imprints of Octopus Publishing Group Ltd,
2–4 Heron Quays, London E14 4JP

© 2004 Octopus Publishing Group Ltd

A CIP catalogue record for this book is
available from the British Library

ISBN 1 84000 956 X

Some images have appeared in previous editions of
Miller's Antiques Price Guide, *Miller's Collectables Price Guide* and
Miller's Toys & Games Antiques Checklist

Colour Origination: 1.13, Whitstable, Kent
Lab 35, Milton Keynes, Bucks
Printed and bound: L.E.G.O. SpL, Italy

Front cover illustration:
A " Robbie" robot by Nomura, c.1956 (*see p.58*)
Miller's is a registered trademark of
Octopus Publishing Group Ltd

Contents

Contributors

Wood, Games, and Puppets: Alvin Ross
Trading in London since 1989 and now on the Internet, Alvin Ross was one of the earliest dealers specializing in Pelham Puppets, as well as in vintage games and jigsaws, and is a leading source of information on these topics.
http://www.vintage-games.co.uk

Rocking Horses: Marc Stevenson
Inspired by their uncle James Bosworthick, a rocking horse maker, Marc Stevenson and his twin brother Tony established Stevenson Bros in 1982. The company specialize in making and restoring rocking horses.

Cast-iron toys and money banks: John Haley
John Haley has been a specialist dealer in moneyboxes and toys for 35 years. His shop, Collectors Old Toy Shop, is based in Halifax, West Yorkshire.

Tinplate: Nigel Mynheer
Nigel Mynheer has been an auctioneer for Christie's and Phillips and is a leading valuer in his field. He currently works for Special Auction Services as their toy expert.

Diecast: Glenn Butler
Glenn Butler is head of the Toy Department at Wallis & Wallis Auctioneers, one of the longest running toy auction houses in Europe. He has been a lifelong collector and has regularly appeared on television and radio.

Model Figures: Gerard Haley
Gerard Haley started collecting and selling toy soldiers in 1970 as a student to make some money. He now sells to clients in America, Asia, and Europe, specializing in Britains and regularly attends all the major auctions in this field.

Trains: Barry Potter
Barry Potter is an auctioneer of collectible toys and trains at Vectis Auctions (which incorporates Barry Potter Auctions) and is an organizer of toy collectors' fairs.
www.vectis.co.uk

Sci-Fi: Mick Milliard
Mick Milliard is the co-owner of Suffolk Sci-Fi of Ipswich and has been a collector of everything since the 1960s and a dealer in Sci-Fi collectibles since the late 1980s.
www.suffolksci-fi.com

Characters: Madeleine Marsh
Madeleine Marsh is a respected writer and journalist, specializing in fine and decorative arts. She started collecting at school and is the editor of the annual *Miller's Collectibles Price Guide,* and has also written other specialist books including *Miller's Collecting the 1950s* and *Collecting the 1960s.*

Soft Toys & Dolls: Barbara Ann Newman
Due to a lifelong love of dolls and juvenalia Barbara Ann Newman started dealing in the early 1990s in Kent. She now exhibits at the major doll and teddy fairs in London and the Midlands and is currently based at London House Antiques in Westerham, Kent.

General Editor: Phil Ellis
Phil Ellis has a long-standing interest in antiques and collectibles. He has worked on various magazines and publications including *Antiques Magazine,* and is the author *Miller's Corkscrews & Wine Antiques Collector's Guide, Miller's Antiques, Art, & Collectibles on the Web,* and most recently, *Miller's Sci-Fi & Fantasy Collectibles.*

How to Use

There are two key questions every collector wants to know: What to Look For and What to Pay. Both these questions are answered within these pages in the respective section. Popular collecting categories are covered in both sections of the book, which can be navigated by the colour-coded tabs. If you are looking for a particular item, turn to the contents list on p.6–7 to find the appropriate section, for example, Sci-Fi. Having located your area of interest, you will see that larger sections may be sub-divided by subject or maker. If you are looking for a particular factory, maker, or object, consult the index, which starts on p. 317. Information on the different materials, media, and other key features is included on pp.12–15.

FINDING YOUR WAY AROUND
Use these running heads to see what sub-section you are in within each collecting category.

INFORMATION BOXES
Additional historical, collecting, or practical information is included in these tint boxes.

WHAT TO LOOK FOR
Key background and collecting information is covered in this section.

Robots • Thunderbirds • SCI-FI 59

• **Astronauts** They perform similar actions to robots but they show a human face beneath the helmet. Some models are desirable, but they are generally less popular.
• **Reproductions** Robots are so popular that reproductions of classic designs are being made, often as limited edition collectibles. Look for modern parts in remote control units and differing lithographic print quality. If the feet show evidence of tampering, this could be a sign that a modern limited edition number has been removed.

TRANSFORMERS
These plastic toys which converted from robots into vehicles were launched by Hasbro, in 1984 and were an instant success. These are now becoming increasingly collectible. Although toys were retailed across the world, some objects were only produced for a particular market and as always, enthusiasts look and pay for rarities.

SCI-FI

Collecting
Some points to bear in mind when looking at robots:
• Robots were easily damaged as many were top-heavy and tended to fall over.
• Condition is always important, but damaged robots are sometimes bought for spares.
• Check for rust on tinplate models.
• Check battery compartments for signs of damage from leaking batteries.
• Switch on your robots, even if only briefly, every so often to prevent the motor from seizing up.
• Keep robots away from dust, which can get into the mechanism.

Thunderbirds

Gerry Anderson made numerous puppet series for British television from the 1950s onwards and many of them became major international hits. The biggest of them all was *Thunderbirds*, the story of International Rescue, an organization formed by a philanthropic family that carried out rescue missions using an array of hi-tech craft.

DIECASTS
Many toys based on the vehicles in the show were made, including plastic toys by Lincoln Inc. and Rosenthal.
• **Thunderbird 2** The most famous toys the Dinky diecasts of Thunderbird 2, the workhorse of the show (pictured) was made in a green diecast version from 1967 (no. 101 in the firm's catalogue). A later version (106) was made in 1973 in a metallic blue colour. The 101 version is not only in the correct colour for the actual vehicle, but was also the first and is more desirable. All versions have spring-loaded, extending legs and a detachable pod with a small Thunderbird 4 craft (a miniature submarine) contained inside.
• **FAB1** Dinky also made FAB1, a diecast version of the pink Rolls-Royce used by International Rescue's London agent Lady Penelope. It has a sliding canopy with a large missile firing from behind a radiator grille and rear firing harpoons.
• **Packaging** The Dinky Thunderbirds toys are well made, but the packaging is not that strong so boxes in good condition add considerably to the value.
• **Thunderbird 5** Rosenthal's Thunderbirds toys included a model of the space station Thunderbird 5. This plastic model recalls the tinplate style flying saucers of the 50s in its style rather than being a strictly accurate representation. The same firm made a plastic battery powered remote control Thunderbird 1.
• **Other toys** Toys of all of the Thunderbird craft were made, as were puppets and dolls of the main characters, playsuits so that children could dress up as their heroes, and various books and games. Records of the music from the series were also released, including an album to accompany the film version of the series.

Star Wars

A Palitoy *Star Wars* **Land Speeder,** 1977,
8 x 10in (20.5 x 25.5cm), boxed.
£180–200 / €260–290
$300–330 ⊞ OW

Further reading
Miller's Sci-Fi & Fantasy Collectibles,
Miller's Publications, 2003

▶ A *Star Wars* **Chewbacca action figure,**
1980, 3¾in (9.5cm) high.
£2–6 / €3–8
$4–9 ⊞ UNI

A Palitoy battery-operated
Star Wars Return of The Jedi
Millennium Falcon Vehicle, 1983,
16 x 22in (40.5 x 56cm), boxed.
£135–150 / €190–210
$220–250 ⊞ OW

A Lucasfilm *Star Wars* Episode IV
replica **Han Solo blaster,**
limited edition of 1,500, 2002,
12in (30.5cm) long.
£450–500 / €640–710
$750–830 ⊞ OW

Alien

A Hasbro Signature series *Alien
Resurrection* **call figure,** reissue, 1997,
7in (18cm) high, with original box.
£15–20 / €25–30
$30–35 ⊞ SSF

Cross Reference
See Characters (pages 228–255)

▶ A Kenner KB Toys **Aliens vs
Corp Hicks figure,** limited edition
of 25,000, American, 1997,
12in (30.5cm) high.
£180–200 / €250–280
$300–330 ⊞ SSF

Kenner produced the first
Alien toy in 1979, with the
release of the first *Alien*
movie, starring Sigourney
Weaver as Ripley. At 18in
(45.5cm) high, the figure was
deemed too scary for children
and was removed from store
shelves. Action figures have
continued to be popular
with each of the *Alien*
sequels: *Aliens, Alien 3* and
Alien Resurrection.

▶ A Hasbro Signature series
Alien Resurrection **Ripley figure,**
reissue, 1997, 7in (18cm) high.
£15–20 €25–30
$30–35 ⊞ SSF

COLOUR-CODED TABS
Each collecting category is identified
by a coloured tab allowing easy
navigation between the two
sections of the book.

SCI-FI

FURTHER READING
Suggestions about where to go
for further research are listed here.

SOURCE CODE
The codes refers to the "Key to
Illustrations" on p.313 that lists the
details of where the item was
sourced. The ✦ icon indicates the
item was sold at auction. The ⊞
icon indicates the item originated
from a dealer.

PRICE GUIDE
prices are based on actual prices
realized at auction or offered for
sale by a dealer, shown in £sterling,
€Euros and $US. Remember that
Miller's is a PRICE GUIDE not a
PRICE LIST and prices are affected
by many variables such as location,
condition, desirability, and so on.
Don't forget that if you are selling,
it is quite likely you will be offered
less than the price range. Price
ranges for items sold at auction
tend to include the buyer's
premium and VAT if applicable. The
exchange rate used in this edition is
1.66 for $ and 1.42 for €.

CROSS REFERENCES
These boxes direct the reader to
where other related items may
be found.

WHAT TO PAY
Each collecting area includes a
cross-section of items, each one
captioned with a brief description
of the item including the maker's
name, medium, date,
measurements, and in some
instances condition.

Introduction

The last five years have seen a steady growth of investors in the toy world, mainly from those traditionally investing in stocks and shares who have been looking for alternative ways of making a steady, long-term investment in a volatile stock market. With a proven track record for sustainable long-term growth, good-quality antique and collectible toys are a good area in which to invest. To purchase a product just for its investment potential is all very well, but with toys there is a great opportunity to enjoy the hunt, the find, and to create a buzz that can stay with you for life. At the end of the day, nostalgia is the number one reason people start collecting toys and games as they seek to recapture the pleasures of childhood.

The antique toy world is driven by a world-wide interest. Buyers from as far afield as Japan, Australia, South Africa, and the Americas have forced the pace of growth. Traditionally it has been the American market that has paid the higher prices but the British market has been so strong in recent years that buyers in the UK have managed to secure their desired pieces.

The Internet has become an important tool for both buyers and sellers. It has changed the way in which the world does business. Auction houses have embraced the "net" and now use its power to get the information to the customer: catalogues, pictures, and information. Although when it comes to actual purchase most people, however, still prefer to pick up and look at a toy to ascertain whether it is up to their standard.

Items sold on the Internet can achieve some high prices because they are being sold to a world-wide market, but it is certainly a case of "buyer beware". The Internet can be fraught with problems: fakes, objects not as described, damaged, or repaired, and one has to take the seller's word that the item is right. Safeguards are now in place on many sites to assist the buyer if there is a problem but one cannot emphasize enough the need to protect oneself carefully when buying online.

It is always important to research your chosen collecting areas as thoroughly as possible – read books, catalogues, visit auctions, dealers, and public collections. It is only by looking and handling as many pieces as possible that one really learns what is "right" and "wrong" and how much one should pay.

In conclusion, to be able to invest in a subject that revives cherished memories of your childhood is a wonderful thing. A good maxim to follow is always to try and buy the best example that you can find then not only will you enjoy it, you can be pretty sure that you have invested wisely and, if you can't, then just enjoy the example that you have.

what to look for

Media & Materials

When assessing a toy and its likely value, there are certain basic factors that must be considered. These include the materials from which it was made and the methods of manufacture. Toys are classified according to the medium; on the following pages you will find information on the materials you are most likely to encounter.

Cast Iron

Cast iron was especially popular with American toymakers who used it extensively to produce novelty money banks. Watch out for poor-quality Taiwanese fakes. They do not work as well as the originals and can also be recognized by the poor fit of the components and modern screws. Reproductions are often slightly smaller than the originals and the paintwork is not as thickly applied as on the originals.

For more on cast-iron toys see pp.20–21 (What to Look for) and pp.98–99 (What to Pay).

Diecast metal

Widely used for toy cars, diecast metal is a magnesium zinc alloy, also known as mazac. By the 1930s, mazac had replaced earlier alloys, which mostly contained lead and were therefore deemed unsafe.

For more on diecast toys see pp.28–35 (What to Look for) and pp.120–152 (What to Pay).

Celluloid

Celluloid was the result of a quest for a new material for making billiard balls. It was originally the trade name for the Hyatt Brothers' mix of nitro cellulose (or Pyroxylin)

and powdered camphor, which they patented in 1869. It was in the Far East in the 1940s that celluloid toys were first produced in large numbers but American and European makers soon followed suit. Celluloid toys from the 19thC are rare survivors as they are extremely fragile. Disney-related pre- and post-war celluloid toys are especially sought after.

For more on celluloid toys see pp.78–79 (What to Look for) and pp.275–276 (What to Pay)

Plastic

Modern synthetic plastics were widely used from the 1950s and became popular with toymakers as an alternative to celluloid. Plastic is not as indestructible as is often supposed; it becomes brittle and sticky with age. If it gives off a sweet smell, then this could be a sign of damage.

For more on plastic toys see p.38 and pp.78–79 (What to Look for) and pp.159–160, 285–289 (What to Pay)

Rubber

Early rubber toys were made entirely of natural material. From the mid-1950s, synthetic material was more common. This allowed the manufacture of items such as "Bendy Toys". Rubber does not last well; it is mostly used as an accessory, so beware of toy cars from the 1940s and 50s with congealed or cracked tyres – if they look perfect, they could be later replacements.

Composition

Composition is a mix of kaolin (china clay), sawdust, and glue and was widely used by the German toymakers Elastolin and Lineol in the production of toy figures. It was also used in the

manufacture of dolls. Composition figures tend to crack with age and as it is a soft material it should be handled with care to avoid damage to the surfaces.

For more on composition toys see p.36 and pp.77–78 (What to Look for) and pp.283–284 (What to Pay)

Lead

Lead was widely used in the 19thC for the production of toy soldiers. It was also used for a variety of cheap toys and for early Dinky vehicles. As a soft metal, lead is easily damaged so should be handled with care. Lead toys should be kept away from damp and acidic conditions, which can lead to a form of corrosion known as "lead rot". In severe cases, lead can be completely corroded, leaving behind a greyish-white residue.

For more on lead toys see p.31 and p.40 (What to Look for) and pp.156–157 (What to Pay)

Paper

Paper could be used on its own (in the form of card in toy theatres, board games, or puzzles) or it could be combined with wood to produce toy ships, figures, or buildings. Paper has many enemies including insects as well as damp, while sunlight causes fading. Decay as a result of the acidic content of the paper is also a problem, but ironically older paper is often better preserved than more recent items. This is because it was made from rags rather than the highly acidic wood pulp.

For more on paper toys see pp.41–46 (What to Look for) and pp.169–174, 178–184 (What to Pay)

Papier-mâché

Often used instead of wood, its big

advantage to the toymaker was that it could be moulded into various shapes without the need for carving. The disadvantage for its long term survival is that it is easily damaged, so condition is important and affects value.

For more on papier-mâché toys see p.256 (What to Pay)

Painted steel

Painted steel was and is used to make larger scale toys and vehicles, especially in the United States. It was also used by Tri-ang c.1960 to make large scale toys. Painted steel toys are not yet as collectible in Britain as in the United States.

Tinplate

Tinplated iron or steel toys were made in large quantities from the mid-19thC. Until then, most toys were wooden and home produced. It was the development of tinned sheet steel in the latter part of the 19thC that revolutionized the industry and allowed the mass production of cheap tinplate toys. These toys have survived comparatively well because of the protection afforded them by the tinplate coating.

For more on tinplate toys see pp.22–27 (What to Look for) and pp.100–119 (What to Pay)

Wood

Along with pottery and bronze, wood was one of the earliest materials used to make toys and has probably been the most widely-used of all toymaking materials. It had the advantage of being widely available and cheap. Its greatest disadvantage to this day is that it is prone to rot and damage, so it is hard to find antique wooden toys in good condition. Popular surviving wooden toys include bow rocker or safety rocking horses,

velocipedes (tricycles with horses' heads), and prams. Original British horses, made from laminated blocks of pine and beautifully carved, are sought after but beware of fakes from the Philippines. These are recognizable by their use of hardwoods and rigid poses.

For more on wooden toys see pp.17–19 (What to Look for) and pp.86–97 (What to Pay)

Techniques

Methods of toy manufacture have varied considerably over the years and have developed along with new technology and the advent of new materials. The earliest toys were made at home and the quality depended on the skill of the maker. Later factory methods using complex machines and robots gave the makers unprecedented consistency in their products. Some of the most important manufacturing methods are described on these pages.

Carving

It is not always easy to tell the difference between home- and factory-made wooden toys, but there are exceptions. Germany produced many wooden toys, especially in the Erzgebirge region of Saxony; they are quite distinctive and were mostly for export. An important difference between European and American wooden toys is that European toys are usually fully carved or turned with any decoration painted directly onto the wood. American toys use applied lithographed paper for decoration on flat surfaces. This makes American toys much more difficult to restore, so condition is always an important

consideration and affects value.

An important form of construction for wooden toys was patented in 1867 by the American toymakers Charles M. Crandall and his cousin Jesse A. Crandall. They used a unique tongue-and-groove system which allowed blocks to be interlocked. The idea could be applied to wooden figures, enabling them to have interchangeable heads and limbs, creating various movements. Other makers soon copied this idea.

For more on carved toys see pp.17–19 (What to Look for) and pp.86–97 (What to Pay)

Ring method

Animals for farmyards and arks were popular subjects, but carving them was a laborious process. The ring method, introduced in the late 19thC, used a large circle of wood, which was turned on a lathe to produce the animal in cross-section. The animals were then cut from the ring in slices and the fine detail carved in. The drawback with this method was that it created animals that were all a similar basic shape, regardless of species. Animals produced in this way have a tapered form, usually towards the front.

Cast-iron moulding

To make a cast-iron toy, it was first necessary to make a wooden pattern. This was then used to make an impression in a mould consisting of wet sand contained in a frame. Molten iron was then poured into the mould to create the form. A toy was typically cast in several parts which were then assembled with pins, bolts, or rivets. This sand-casting method allowed for the creation of various effects and detailing.

For more on cast-iron toys see

pp.20–21 (What to Look for)
and pp.98–99 (What to Pay)

Diecast

Diecast toys are made from metal cast under pressure in a mould. The process was developed in the early 20thC and the earliest diecast toys were small vehicles made in France from lead. In 1918, the American firm of Tootsie pioneered the use of the safer magnesium zinc alloy mazac.

For more on diecast toys see pp.28–35 (What to Look for) and pp.120–152 (What to Pay)

Hollow-cast

Hollow-casting involves pouring a molten mixture of lead, tin, and antimony into an engraved mould, so that a skin forms on the inside of the mould. The antimony expands as it cools, giving fine detail to the casting and the bulk of the alloy can be poured out while still molten, hence the figures are hollow and have holes in their feet or heads. The big advantage of this process, which was perfected by the American toy figure-maker William Britain Junior in 1893, is that less metal is used. This drives down both production and transport costs. Hollow-casting became the most popular method of manufacturing figures in Britain and America from the late 19thC.

For more on hollow-cast toys see p.36, 39 (What to Look for) and pp.153–160 (What to Pay)

Solid cast

The solid-cast technique was used by early makers such as Lucotte, Mignot, and Heyde. Lucotte differs from the others in that they cast the body and head of the figure individually, inserting the head into the body using a plug on the underside of the head.

For more on solid-cast toys see pp.36–40 (What to Look for) and pp.153–160 (What to Pay)

Painted tinplate

German factories used systemized production methods for their tinplate toys. Presses shaped, embossed, and stamped out components which were then soldered together. They were then painted by hand in a rich, almost enamelled finish. This style was still favoured by Märklin until around 1930, some 15 years after other makers had abandoned it.

The Nuremberg style, as used by Bing from the 1890s onwards, favoured a lighter gauge of metal with a thinner paint style. Instead of soldering, pieces were made with u-shaped tabs that could be slotted into corresponding holes in a neighbouring piece and then folded over to secure them.

Later refinements included spraying, used for Hornby trains from the 1920s, and oven baking to produce a durable, lustrous finish – this method was used for Dinky Toys.

Companies such as Tri-ang used a simple dipping process for their Minic range between 1935 and 1963.

After WWII, Japanese production of tinplate toys soared, reaching a peak c.1955–65.

For more on tinplate toys see pp.22–27 (What to Look for) and pp.100–119 (What to Pay)

Lithographed tinplate

Early decorative printing on tin used the transfer process, already used with ceramics from the 18thC. Ink was applied to a paper membrane, then transferred on to the tin surfaces and baked. This process was not durable and only worked on simple shapes.

Offset lithography, invented in 1875, printed different parts of a design on separate plates in registration, building up a colour image. Bryant & May acquired the sold rights to the process in 1877 and by 1903, the German Nuremberg factories were making full use of the intricacy and speed of production that the process allowed. It went on to dominate toy production worldwide for the next 70 years.

For more on tinplate toys see pp.22–27 (What to Look for) and pp.100–119 (What to Pay)

Tinplate restoration & fakes

Early 20thC toys were made to be played with, so it is best to be aware of this and to assume that an item in good condition has been restored unless it can be proved otherwise. Complete replicas designed to deceive are rare, but important components can be identified as replacements. Reproductions of some 1950s space toys and diecasts are on the market and some of them are of good quality; this has affected the price of the originals. The lithography is not quite as clear as on the originals, however, and the reproduction boxes have copied small creases on the original box used for duplication. As long as the collector is aware that reproductions are around and looks out for tell-tale signs, they should be easy to spot.

Additional Features

Boxes

A mint and boxed toy is the ultimate goal for many collectors.

This is especially true of diecast toys, where a box can add as much as 2,000 per cent to the value, and of lead soldiers, which should be strung on to the original insert card. It is also true of Hornby "0" Gauge trains and Hornby-Dublo, but Bassett-Lowke collectors care little for boxes. If you have original boxes, always keep them safe.

Paintwork

Original paintwork is of paramount importance to any toy whether tinplate, wooden, or diecast. With Dinky Toys, the colour shade can make a huge difference to the value – sometimes as much as 500 per cent.

Motors

Märklin motors are generally broader and more powerful than motors on other toys. Beware of tampering with them because a wound spring can be very dangerous. It is unwise to interfere with early motors unless you really know what you are doing – seek expert advice. This applies to all motors, from live steam models to early alternating current electric locomotives, as they fall far short of modern safety standards and can be extremely dangerous

Identifying marks

Most toys made after 1920 have some form of identification, usually a trademark or country of origin. Exceptions include some toy soldiers and 1940s British diecast cars. Japanese space toys are usually marked although information on the makers can be scarce.

Pre-1914 toys by the German makers including Bing and Märklin can be hard to identify. Märklin cars and trains have a bolder and plainer look than Bing or Carette

and use thicker tinplate with fewer stamped curves. Car wheels tend to be of tinplate, oversized, and using the "artillery pattern" (with convexed spokes).

Wing supports tend to be plain on Bing and Märklin cars, but of waisted form on Carette's.

Carette's tinplate cars are not usually marked, but are distinguished by their superior quality when compared with makers such as Eberl and Fischer.

Carette's railway stock for Bassett-Lowke was marked from c.1912.

Bing lithography always incorporated their mark, as do most of their painted cars and boats.

Günthermann and Issmayer lithography is very shiny, with bright and clearly lacquered gold lining; Günthermann cars sometimes incorporate painted tinplate figures.

Restoration

Generally speaking, the less restoration a toy undergoes the better, but some toys have specific problems and would be better off with some restoration. Bad restoration can cause irreversible damage and dramatically reduce the value of a toy. If in doubt, check with a specialist dealer, auction house, or museum, particularly when dealing with costly toys or trains.

Conservation

Toys and trains should only be gently dusted, preferably using a very soft brush. Clean them with water and a minute quantity of detergent; avoid commercial polishers and colour restorers.

Display

Display is a matter of personal taste, but it is best to choose a method that is appropriate to your environment. Sunlight and damp

are among the many environmental factors that can damage toys so bear this in mind if displaying them in your home. Also remember that if you have young children or pets, it might be safer to lock your collection safely in a cabinet.

MAJOR TOYMAKERS: Quick reference

WOODEN TOYS
(SEE PP.17–19, 86–97)

R. Bliss, USA	c.1835–c.95
W. S. Reed, USA	1876–97
Milton Bradley, USA	1860–present
Albert Schönhut, USA	1872–c.1935

CAST-IRON TOYS AND BANKS
(SEE PP.20–21, 98–99)

Carpenter, USA	1894–c.1945
Hubley, USA	1894–1940s
Kyser & Rex, USA	c.1875–1900
C. G. Shepard, USA	c.1865–c.1895
Stevens & Brown, USA	1843–c.1930

TINPLATE TOYS
(SEE PP.22–27, 100–119)

Alps Shoji, Japan	c.1950–present
Bing, Germany	1879–1933
George Brown, USA	1856–80
Burnett, Britain	1905–39
Carette, Germany	1886–1917
Chad Valley, Britain	1823–present
Distler, Germany	1890–1960
Francis Field & Francis, USA	1838–70s
J. M. Fallows & Son, USA	1874–1900
Ives, USA	1868–1928
Lehmann, Germany	1881–present
Lines Bros/Tri-ang, Britain	1910–71
Märklin, Germany	1859–present
Fernand Martin, France	1876–1912
Masudaya, Japan	c.1940s–present
Nomura, Japan	c.1920–present
Ernst Plank, Germany	1866–1934

DIECAST TOYS
(SEE PP.28–35, 120–152)

Corgi, Britain	1956–present
Crescent Toys, Britain	1922–81
Dinky Toys, Britain	1933–present
Lesney, Britain	1953–present
"Spot-On", Britain	1959–67
Tootsie Toys, USA	1906–present

MODEL FIGURES
(SEE PP.36–40, 153–160)

Britains, Britain	1860–present
Georg Heyde, Germany	c.1845–1949
Charbens, Britain	1920–55
Elastolin, Germany	1910–84
Grey Iron, USA	1920–39
John Hill & Co., Britain	1898–1959
Herald Miniatures, Britain	1950–83
Lineol, Germany	1920–c.41
Lucotte, France	1760–1825
C. B. G. Mignot, France	1825–1993
Pixyland, Britain	1922–32
Taylor & Barrett, Britain	1920–39

GAMES
(SEE PP.41–46, 161–185)

Waddingtons, Britain	1900–present
Parker Brothers, USA	1883–present
Hasbro, USA	1923–present

TRAINS
(SEE PP.47–56, 186–207)

Lionel, USA	1900–present
Hornby, Britain	1920–present
Rossignol, France	c.1868–1962
Radiguet, France	1875–1910

SCI-FI TOYS
(SEE PP.57–63, 208–227)

Kenner, USA	1947–2000
Masudaya, Japan	1924–present
Mego, USA	1952–82
Nomura, Japan	c.1940s–70s
Yonezawa, Japan	c.1950s–70s

PUPPETS
(SEE PP.70–71, 256–260)

Pelham, Britain	1947–92

SOFT TOYS
(SEE PP.72–76, 261–274)

Dean's, Britain	1915–present
Merrythought, Britain	1930–present
Schuco, Germany	1912–78
Steiff, Germany	1877–present

DOLLS
SEE PP.77–84, 275–304)

Mattel, USA	1945–present
Pedigree, Britain	1937–88
Marx, USA	1919–present
Hasbro, USA	1923–present

Wood

Wooden toys date back to antiquity, but the earliest surviving examples today are mostly from the 17thC. They are highly sought after and fetch high prices even though they are rarely in good condition. Wooden toys survived competition from new materials such as tinplate and were widely produced throughout the 19thC. Popular subjects included Noah's Arks (see pp.88–89), rocking horses (see pp.94–97) and wooden figures, as well as toys such as toboggans. Wooden toys were often combined with paper and/or cardboard, which could be printed with designs to add colour and realism.

EUROPE

Germany was a large producer of wooden toys throughout the 19thC and into the 20thC. The wooden swing toy pictured right is typical of the toys with movement produced from the late 18thC in Altdorf near Nuremberg, where they were known as *leyern*. Similar toys were also made in the Erzebirge region of Saxony – these tend to have more complicated mechanisms.

BRITAIN

The 20thC saw a rise in the number of British wooden toy makers, especially in the inter-war years. The firm of Forest Toys of Brockenhurst (1918–39) is particularly known for the quality of its products, which included arks, farmyard, and nativity scenes. Other major British firms included Lines Brothers and Chad Valley.

AMERICA

One of the best known American manufacturers of wooden toys, Albert Schönhut was born in Germany to a great toymaking family. His toys are European in

style and the best known is the Humpty Dumpty Circus, comprising various performers and animals, which was made between 1903–35.

State of the market

Wooden toys today can vary hugely in value; they are worth collecting not least because many are still undervalued, so they can be easily found and bought for bargain prices.

• **Top end** Wooden toys from the 18thC and 19thC such as fine dolls and Noah's Arks. These are only found at specialist auctions and achieve high prices

• **More accessible** Wooden building blocks, skittles, and various table games remain inexpensive. Look out for good quality and condition, and attractive original packaging.

• **Jigsaw puzzles** Puzzles are currently highly collectible on both sides of the Atlantic with collectors knowledgeable about each other's most treasured brands, for instance Tuck's and Holtzappfel in the UK, Pastime and Par in the United States.

• **Rocking horses** These traditional toys, particularly those which are older and sympathetically restored, can fetch five-figure sums. A rule of thumb when buying is "a good shaped head normally symbolizes a good maker". Top end makers include F. H. Ayres of London (manufacturing from the late 1800s to early 1900s). They created top end rocking horses with extra carvings and turned heads. Look out for G. & J. Lines (later became Tri-ang Toys). Collinson's of Liverpool were mass producers of rocking horses for over 100 years. Many of their horses appear at auction for mid-range prices.

Building Blocks

Building blocks are among the oldest types of toys. By the 19thC, boxes of plain wooden bricks could be found in most nurseries. By the 1860s, wooden blocks were often covered with chromolithographed coloured paper, adding educational value according to the designs used. During the 19thC, wooden building blocks became more sophisticated and boxed sets of plain wooden bricks, such as the German architectural bricks from the late 1880s pictured here, became very popular.

• **Identification** Paper-on-wood toys are rarely marked with a maker's name. They were made by numerous makers all over Europe, especially in Germany, for export. Any label is most likely to be that of the shop where the toy was sold.

Noah's Arks

Noah's Arks have been popular since the 18thC. They are often found in better condition than other wooden toys because they were often only played with on Sundays. Only toys with a religious educational theme were considered appropriate for the Sabbath in Protestant Victorian England. The arks themselves were usually simply made, decorative storage boxes for the animals; it was the latter who were the real focus of interest. However some arks are attractive in their own right.

DATING

Early arks, made up until the mid-19thC, can be recognized by their lack of a hull; a gentle curve to the base characterizes these toys, which are highly collectible. Arks can also be dated by looking at the clothing of the female figures. High waists reflect the fashions of the early 19thC.

• **Popularity** Noah's Arks remained popular toys beyond the 19thC and they are still made today, though not necessarily in wood.

• **Chad Valley** Produced colourful arks in the 1950s with a simple design and plywood figures covered with printed paper.

Puzzles

The jigsaw is the most familiar form of puzzle and up until the 1930s they were mostly made of wood. Jigsaws were originally called "dissected puzzles" and were the invention of the London map maker John Spilsbury in 1760. He applied a map to a mahogany board and cut around the countries to create a puzzle. In the Victorian era, puzzles were considered a most acceptable form of play, because of their educational potential. Puzzles were not only for children however; some were aimed at adults as after-dinner entertainment.

• **Makers** Some of the best-known 19thC makers include J. W. Barfoot, John Betts, Darton & Harvey, Milton Bradley in the United States, Raphael Tuck & Sons (1870–present), in addition to the Wallis family who were also important makers of board games.

• **Manufacturing** Making the puzzles using a hand-held saw was a laborious process, so early puzzles were expensive. The 1870s saw the invention of the power scroll saw, or jigsaw, which enabled puzzles to be made much more quickly. Dissected puzzles soon became known as jigsaw puzzles, after the tool used to make them. By the early 20thC, puzzles were no longer hand-painted and were now covered with chromolithograph-printed paper. Card began to replace wood as it was cheaper to produce and cut more than one copy at a time. Puzzles were also now sold with the puzzle reproduced on the cover of the box.

• **Subjects** Popular subjects in the 19thC included those with an educational theme (for example, telling the time), biblical scenes, as well as animals, nature, and children's stories. By the first part of the 20thC fairy stories and nursery rhymes had become popular subjects. Jigsaws often reflect the fashion of the time both in subject and look and are reminiscent of contemporary children's books in style.

• **Collecting** 19thC puzzles have been popular with collectors for many years but those made between 1900–50 have been largely overlooked and therefore this is a good place for the novice collector to start. Choose only those that have the original box and all the pieces. Jigsaws which have "cross-over" subjects will have a wider appeal beyond the puzzle collector. The puzzles illustrated on pp.89–93 could also appeal to collectors of maritime memorabilia, advertising, trains, wartime, characters (such as Noddy, James Bond, and from *The Muppets Show*), sci-fi and space memorabilia, and even *Playboy*!

Puzzle libraries

The 1920s and 30s saw a craze for jigsaws which fostered puzzle libraries and puzzle drives or parties where puzzlers competed against the clock (see detail of puzzle right, also shown on p.91, created for this purpose). Ex-library puzzles are often found in plain boxes without illustrations as they are puzzles cut by amateurs. Similarly, the boxes of popular brands often did not carry an illustration of the puzzle contained since this would have provided unwanted assistance. Such puzzles, primarily aimed at an adult market, are most keenly collected, the larger, more interestingly cut, and hence the more difficult the better.

Cast Iron

Cast-iron toys are an American phenomenon and were produced in that country from the time of the American Civil War until WWII. After the Civil War, the foundries that had produced weapons discovered that they could meet a growing demand for toys. In particular, money banks became very popular. The making of cast-iron toys enjoyed a "golden age" from the 1880s to around 1910. During this period, production was booming and competition from tinplate toys was not yet a serious problem. Cast-iron toys can be subdivided into several major categories: banks or moneyboxes, as they are known in Britain, horse drawn toys, automotive toys, cap guns, bell toys, and other novelties. However money banks are the most collectible. The main producers were American such as Stevens, Arcade, Kilgore, and Wilkins to name a few. The output was massive over a period from the 1860s to the 1940s. Few of these toys were imported into Britain therefore British collectors must source these toys directly via the Internet where bargains can be found. Good research is imperative and there are many specialist books to be found, particularly from American booksellers.

MONEY BANKS

There are basically two types of bank: still and mechanical. The former is essentially a decorative box with a slot for the money and has no mechanism. The latter has some form of mechanism to add entertainment to the task of depositing coins.

• **Key makers** J. & E. Stevens & Co. was the most prolific producer of banks, while other well known makers include Kyser & Rex and Shepard Hardware Co. John Hall of Watertown Massachusetts is credited with designing the first mechanical bank, which was patented in 1869 and manufactured by J. & .E Stevens. It was called Hall's

Excelsior and was produced in large numbers for many years, so it is not difficult to find. Charles A. Bailey was another prominent designer. His output was so prolific that he is said to have been responsible for as much as 20 per cent of all American banks.

• **Popular models** Mechanical banks could have simple or more elaborate mechanisms and there were many popular types. Well known models include Paddy and the Pig, produced by J & E Stevens (see p.98). It features a stereotypical Irishman holding a pig. A coin is placed on the pig's snout and pressing a lever makes the pig kick the coin into Paddy's opening mouth. Another famous model is the Two Frogs, which was designed by James H. Bowen and produced by J. & E. Stevens in 1882. Pressing a lever behind the large frog causes it to open its mouth, while the small frog kicks the coin inside. The lush green foliage found on the base is a typical feature of Bowen's designs.

• **European manufacturers** While cast-iron toys are an overwhelmingly American

phenomenon and remain quite scarce in Europe, some were produced in European countries. In Britain, cast-iron toys were made from the 1880s through to the 1940s by firms such as John Harper & Co. (see money box top right p.21 and p.98). Their output can look almost identical to banks made by Shepard Hardware Co.

Beware

Reproduction cast-iron banks are not difficult to make and there are far more reproductions on the market than originals. These are not always made to deceive but novice collectors can be fooled. Look out for:
• badly finished castings, particularly where sections join together
• a grainy or bumpy surface to the casting
• a poorly moulded base with a blank panel where "Taiwan" has been taken out of the mould
• pieces artificially aged in wet sand
• internal elements made of modern materials e.g. plastic.

but it is easy to tell them apart as the Harper version does not have the Shepard patent mark; there is little difference in value. Later the English manufacturers produced their own novel subjects introducing Kiltie Scotsman, Tommy the English solider, tank and canon etc. The main English manufacturers were Harpers, Sydenham & McOustra (see p.99), Chamberlin & Hill, and Starkies.

• **Repainting** Paintwork is an important feature of the cast-iron bank. Many toys have been repainted and poor restoration can result in patches where the paint remover has gone too deep. Repainting is not usually appreciated although if done well it can be hard to detect without the use of an ultra-violet light.

• **Repairs** Cast-iron banks may be easy to make, but they are also surprisingly easy to break. While cast-iron has a deserved reputation as a durable material, it is also quite brittle and can break if dropped. Repairs to cast-iron banks or other toys are acceptable to collectors, as long as they have been properly carried out. Always seek expert advice if in any doubt. Hairline cracks can appear on the base of cast-iron toys, so do inspect them carefully. Pay particular

attention to the weakest and most delicate parts of the toy, as this is where any restoration is most likely to have been carried out.

OTHER TOYS
While banks dominated cast-iron toy production, at least in the early years, many other types of cast-iron toys were also made.
• From the 1920s to the 30s, the Dent Hardware Company of Fullerton Pennsylvania produced an

outstanding range of toys (see p.99) which, although they are not marked, are recognizable by their fine casting.
• In 1921 the Arcade Manufacturing Co. produced a Yellow Cab and also made a truck that became one of its most successful lines. Vehicles of any kind were not widely produced until after about 1900, but an early example is a comical monkey riding a pull-along tricycle, which was made by J. & E. Stevens c.1890. It incorporates a ringing bell, a popular feature in American toys.
• The Gong Bell Manufacturing Company of East Hampton, Connecticut, produced cast-iron bell toys. They combined a two-wheeled base with a two-toned bell that rang when the toy was pushed or pulled. These toys have been reproduced, but the cast-iron is of a lesser quality. Look for the paint quality and smooth casting.

State of the market
• **Mechanical money banks** In Britain the largest group of cast-iron toys found are the mechanical money banks by J. & E. Stevens and Shepard Hardware Co.
  The most popular mechanical banks were the Negro bust banks and these were sold in very large numbers over a 70-year period and therefore turn up regularly. So many different variations were made, they can form a collection in their own right.
• **Still banks** Many types of still banks were made in England as these were cheaper than

mechanical banks to produce, but it was still only a fraction of the range produced in the United States. Figures, animals, clowns, tanks, etc. were popular and therefore common, as were buildings, particularly landmarks such as Blackpool Tower, and Westminster Abbey.
• **Themed collections** Money boxes and banks made of all types of materials, from different periods, and of different subjects can make a great collection.
• **Research** The importance of background reading and research cannot be underestimated.

Tinplate

New technology arising from the Industrial Revolution made the production of tinplate possible. Tinplate eventually superseded wood as the preferred material for the manufacture of toys. Early tinplate examples in particular often follow the simple folk art styling of their wooden counterparts. Tinplate is actually tinned sheet steel and it was the availability of tinplate from South Wales combined with the new methods of factory production that made it possible to produce tinplate toys relatively cheaply and in large numbers. Nevertheless tinplate toys, especially the better-quality examples, were initially too expensive for poorer families and some were the preserve only of the wealthy. Typical subjects included figures and vehicles – both horse-drawn and motor. In the United States, the first tinplate factories opened in the 1830s, but relatively few tinplate toys were made because of the American preference for cast-iron. In Europe, it was a different story and Germany was to lead the way in tinplate toy production. Tinplate toys were still produced in large numbers after WWII, but there was a gradual decline in quality and tinplate was eventually superseded by plastic. Plastic had many advantages over tinplate, not least the lack of sharp edges, as manufacturers tried to ensure that toys were safer. The late 1950s was an interesting transitional period, since many toys were produced that combined both materials.

Chad Valley

The British firm of Chad Valley was founded in 1823 in Birmingham and produced a wide variety of toys made out of different materials. In the inter-war period they produced tinplate novelty biscuit tins and by the 1940s the firm produced a range of lithographed tinplate and aluminium toys. Post WWII they became known for their tinplate vehicles and spinning tops. After WWII British firms enjoyed a renaissance due to patriotism and a growing enthusiasm for buying British. Chad Valley was particularly known for their fine buses with clockwork motors. They also made trucks and c.1947 produced a popular model advertising the company's products on the side.

BISCUIT TINS
Biscuit tins were firmly established in Britain as popular toys, and transport vehicles (see left) were particular favourites. In the inter-war period more modern and novelty designs became available (see p.112). As they were lithographed they were relatively affordable.
• **Damage** Condition of biscuit tins is crucial as they are particularly prone to damage, especially rust. They were not seen as valuable toys therefore they were not treasured or cared for properly.
• **Restoration** Lithographed tinplate is almost impossible to restore properly and poor restoration will seriously detract from value. This is an important consideration for all tinplate toys. Dents and scratches are the most obvious forms of damage; the finish of lithographed toys scratches quite easily.

Distler

Johann Distler's company, founded in 1900 in Nuremberg, became well known for small, affordable tinplate toys. Distler produced an especially appealing line in saloon cars between the wars, made from good-quality lithographed tinplate.

• **Most collectible** One of the most collectible of all Distler toys is the Electromatic 7500 Porsche from 1956 (see p.112); the quality of the motor and gearing are particularly admired by collectors.

• **Disney** The success of Mickey Mouse, created by Walt Disney in 1928, spawned a marketing phenomenon. German manufacturers, including Distler, were among the first to be licensed to make Disney toys. Distler's Disney products included the Mickey Mouse toy pictured here. Designs for early Disney toys were often created from memory after seeing the films, so they are not always accurate. The value is increased if the box confirms it was made with permission of the Walt Disney Company. Disney toys form a specialist collecting field and are always popular, look in the index, p.318, for other Disney collectibles in different media.

Günthermann

One of the most popular German makers, Günthermann was founded by Siegfried Günthermann in 1877. The company was known for the quirky humour and the detail of many of its machine-pressed tinplate toys, which ranged from a ragtime dancing couple to boys flying kites to a painted frog, c.1898, with tailcoat, bow tie, hat, and pince-nez (pictured below).

Another popular product was the "tricky ladybird" made c.1920, which moved with a random circling motion.

• **Condition** One drawback with many Günthermann toys is that they are hard to find in good condition. This is because they were inadequately primed so the paint tends to flake off very easily. The firm also made a range of Gordon Bennett racing cars. Many of Günthermann's cars have survived, partly because so many were made. However, they are easily damaged as they are quite flimsy. Condition is very important because there are so many survivors. The one above is c.1930. See p.113 for further examples.

• **Marks** Günthermann toys usually bear no marks, with the exception of the most expensive models.

Lehmann

Like the products of Günthermann, those of Ernst Lehmann were characterized by their humour. Lehmann's produced a fine range of lithographed and painted tinplate figures and while other companies tried to imitate his designs, their lack of quality makes them easy to spot and they are less sought after. The firm was founded in 1881 and by WWI was already well established as one of the most innovative of toymakers. Production of the firm's high-quality mechanical novelty toys continued after the war and many were sold abroad. Consequently, they are easy to find in most European countries as well as in the United States. Lehmann himself was known for his sharp observation and it is thought that some of his toys may have been based on people he knew. Given the quality of the toys, it is remarkable that they were retailed through high street vendors.

• **Known for** The firm made numerous animal figures, many of which were based on African animals; products included a clockwork crocodile (pictured). These crocodiles can be hard to date precisely as they were made c.1898–1945; Lehmann toys made over a long period are less valuable than those with a much shorter production run.
• **Vehicles** Lehmann's toy vehicles, unlike those of Märklin or Bing, do not aim to be accurate representations of specific vehicles. They are often based loosely on actual vehicles as was the case with the "Tut Tut" which resembled a Tonneau, a popular vehicle made c.1900. The toy version dates from 1903 and features a driver blowing a horn, which was required to warn other road users. The toy is fitted with bellows and makes a honking noise; it is perhaps the most famous of all Lehmann toys. See p.113 for some other examples of Lehmann's toy production.
• **Typical features** These include finely lithographed and painted tinplate, and spring motors. It is rare to find examples with the original box.
• **Beware** Lehmann toys are especially prone to rust.

Mettoy

Philip Ullman, former head of the German toy manufacturing company Tipp & Co. (see opposite page) founded Mettoy (which stood for metal toys) in Northampton in 1936 after he fled Germany as a refugee. The company became known for its lithographed tinplate vehicles and aircraft but, with time, their production began to focus on very simple, inexpensive toys with basic mechanisms which are prone to rust.

• **Known for** A postal delivery van made in the late 30s, which is of flimsy construction and simple design but collectible nonetheless. Products of the 50s included cars (right), a clockwork Morris traveller, and caravan. (See p.115.)

Schuco

Quality of design was one of the key features of the toys made by Nuremberg manufacturer Schreyer & Co., better known as Schuco. Their toy cars were often based on contemporary models. The shell was made from a one-piece pressing with the base plate tabbed on separately. Additional chrome parts such as bumpers were then tightly fitted to the main shell, avoiding any sharp corners. They had a high-quality finish with glossy paintwork and good-quality rubber tyres. All vehicles came with boxes.

Key features

Schuco vehicles were produced in large numbers between the two world wars but in spite of mass production methods, they retained their high quality. When buying, collectors should look out for the following features:
• Vehicles should be made from both lithographed and painted tinplate
• Vehicles should be marked "Made in Germany"
• Vehicles should use a clockwork mechanism
• Vehicles should be streamlined in design
• Vehicles should have good quality rubber tyres.

• **Known for** The ingenious Radio-Auto (pictured), from the late inter-war period, played a tune whilst driving along. The car's aerial is the on/off switch and the switch to control the driving mechanism is under the car. Two-tone colours were popular and this car was available in three versions: blue with navy blue, red with maroon and cream with maroon. (See p.115 for other items.)

POST-WAR PRODUCTION
Quality remained high and post-war toys typically have well made boxes with fitted compartments, many accessories, and excellent details. Most toys in the 1950s were still made with clockwork mechanisms, although battery power started to emerge later (see p.116).

OTHER TOYS
Schuco's range also included boats, aircraft, and a range of novelty toys. The latter include a Charlie Chaplin figure who walked along twirling his cane. They also made Disney characters, including a very collectible Donald Duck that is recognizable by his long bill.

Tipp & Co.

Nuremberg-based Tipp & Co., aka Tippco, was founded in 1912 and produced character toys, motorcycles, cars, trucks, and aeroplanes. After WWII, they made many tinplate cars based on American prototypes.

Like Distler and Schuco, Tipp & Co. was one of the German firms licensed to make Disney merchandise. Products included Mickey and Minnie on a motorcycle, which is one of the most important and rarest Disney toys today.

• **Known for** Initially for large tinplate cars (see p.116) and after 1933, military vehicles, which were accurately based on contemporary transport. This ambulance, from the late 1930s, comes with a composition driver – it is common to find such accompanying figures with tinplate vehicles.

Tonka Toys

The American firm Tonka Toys started life in 1947 in the basement of an old schoolhouse in Mound, Minnesota. It was called the Mound Metalcraft Company and the name of Tonka Toys was inspired by the nearby Lake Minnetonka. The company is best known for its range of durable, pressed steel toys including its most famous product, a dump truck, that was introduced in 1964 (see pp.117–118). However, Tonka has also produced a variety of diecast vehicles to a 1:64 scale in the 1960s and 70s. All Tonka toys have a good following among collectors, particularly in the United States and they are reasonably priced. Tonka was purchased by Hasbro in 1991.

Tri-ang

Tri-ang was founded in 1919 by William, Arthur, and Walter Lines, sons of the founders of Lines Brothers, as an offshoot of the toymaking business. In 1935 the firm began to make its Minic series of small tinplate vehicles (see below and p.119) to compete with the popular and successful diecast cars on the market. When WWII broke out, toymaking was suspended, but Tri-ang survived because its factories were turned over to arms production and so Minic toys continued to be made until 1963.

Minic series 1935–40
These cars should have the following features:
• be pocket-sized
• depict a contemporary British vehicle
• be made of painted tinplate
• have a clockwork mechanism
• still have its original key
• be solidly made
• have white tyres
• if a road vehicle, it should have a small petrol can fixed to the running board.

Post-war Minics
• are more plainly coloured than pre-war versions
• were designed to a scale enabling them to be incorporated into the popular "0" Gauge railway layouts of the day
• have a colourful, well-illustrated box
• have a clockwork mechanism, although later vehicles had a "push and go" flywheel friction drive
• have black rubber tyres (see right) – most pre-war vehicles have white.
• have diecast rather than chrome hubs.

POST-WWII
In the post-war period Minics were still produced but there are clear features which help distinguish these later products from the pre-war series (see left).
• **Popular models** Fire engines and police cars replaced military

vehicles as popular action toys. See p.119 for some examples of other models.
• **Identifying marks** Tri-ang always marked toys with a gold coloured triangle or embossed mark, representing the partnership of the three brothers.

State of the market
The past five years has seen a market shift in tinplate toys. The old traditional toys from 1900 to 1930 have stayed level or even fallen slightly in value, and post-war toys up to the mid-1960s have increased by large amounts. This change may be because the average age of new collectors is around 50, nostalgically acquiring the pieces from their late 1950s and 60s childhoods. Prices remain similar around the world as collectors know what they want and where to find it, and will pay top prices for the best pieces. The Internet can provide interesting information about the various toys, but most collectors prefer the traditional method of seeing and handling an object before buying.

Going up Transport-related toys
• 1950s German cars such as Mercedes-Benz (see p.107), Volkswagen, and Porsche, whose designs have now become classic, were all well represented by German toy makers. Toys of these marques by makers such as Tipp & Co., Neuhierl, and Schuco have almost doubled.

• 1950s and 60s German toys manufactured by Arnold and Kellerman, particularly cars, lorries, and character novelties.
• British tinplate buses by Betal, Wells (see p.108), and Chad Valley are becoming very sought after.
• 1930s Meccano Constructor and Non-Constructor cars are showing increased demand (see p.114).
• Road transport vehicles, which resemble the real vehicle as much as possible, are selling particularly well. Schuco is a classic example where a combination of fine-quality design, high paint finish, an original box, and excellent condition can make a high price.

Going down Japanese battery-operated novelty toys which have almost halved in price in some cases, and American toys by Chein and Marx which sometimes fail to attract bids at auction.
• The trend during the 1980s was toward novelty toys more than transport but this now seems to have turned the other way.

TINPLATE

Diecast

Vehicles were the most popular subjects for diecast toy makers and the production of miniature vehicles dates back to the early 20thC, when they were made of tinplate and known as "penny toys". They were also produced in lead using "slush casting", a crude form of casting in which molten metal is poured into an open mould. The improvement in casting techniques made the large-scale production of diecast toys possible at pocket money prices. Dinky were by no means the first to produce diecast toys, but Dinky's success encouraged many other makers to enter the market. One happy result of the ensuing fierce competition (apart from the wide choice for the modern collector), was that makers were keen to stamp their names on their products. Consequently, diecast toys are not usually difficult to identify. Diecast toys suffer few problems, with the possible exception of metal fatigue in some early models. They should be kept away from damp or excessively dry conditions and strong sunlight, which can cause the paintwork to fade.

MANUFACTURERS

The most important makers and their products are discussed on the following pages, but since most industrialized countries produced diecast toys (see Russian car right), it is impossible to include them all. Also look out for firms including Mebetoys, Polistil, and Mercury of Italy, Metosul from Portugal, Gamda from Israel, Lion Car from Holland, and Septoy

Gasquy from Belgium.
• **Collectibility** This can vary according to location; European collectors much prefer Dinky toys to American makes such as Tootsie, but Tootsie Toys have a large following in the United States. The Internet has made global collecting much easier.
• **Modern toys** Diecast toys today are mostly made in the Far East. They are either not of such a high quality as in the past, or they are made for the adult market.

State of the market

Recent years has seen new collectors enter the diecast toy market as an investment alternative to stocks and shares but this trend may not continue. If interest rates rise as expected some of the larger investors will probably return to their traditional markets, and exceptionally high prices for some of the rarer Dinkys will become less frequent. The more affordable toys should continue to gain in value steadily, albeit at a slower rate. This is a similar situation to the late 1980s but not as volatile. Many of the long established manufacturers have at last come into their own. Corgi, for example, has now found its place in the market with many vehicles selling for three-figure sums. They no longer have to play second fiddle to Dinky.
• **Going up:** The TV- and film-related vehicles such as *James Bond* and *The Man From Uncle*

have produced some very high-priced examples – £500–750 / €710–1,050 / $830–1,250 can be spent on rarer pieces. TV- and film-related vehicles benefit from appealing to a wider range of collectors – collectors of sci-fi or *Thunderbirds* for example, will be keen to get their hands on Lady Penelope's FAB1 (see p.215). Check out the index on p.317 for further information on diecast toys included in other collecting categories in the book.
• Prices for Matchbox Series from the late 1950s to the early 60s have shocked many a collector who discovers that the contents of their small shoe box of childhood toys are worth £2,000–3,000 / €2,900–3,400 / $3,300–5,000, somewhat more than the £2 10s 6d that they cost in total when bought new new.

Budgie

North London-based toy wholesalers Morris & Stone used the brand name of Morestone and produced toys under the name of Modern Products. From 1954–9 they produced their own range of diecast toys. From 1959, they introduced the Budgie range, which comprised a large array of vehicles including police cars, pick-up trucks, tankers, vans, and buses. Budgie even entered the TV tie-in market with a diecast model of Mike Mercury's car from the Gerry Anderson series *Supercar*. As the market became increasingly competitive, so Budgie could not compete with the major players such as Matchbox, Corgi, and Dinky. The firm eventually began to concentrate on making buses and taxis for sale to tourists through souvenir shops.

Corgi

The Corgi factory was built in Swansea, South Wales in 1948 by Mettoy, which was founded by Philip Ullman, a refugee from Nazi Germany. Corgi was chosen as a brand name because the Corgi is a typically Welsh breed of dog. The new range of diecast toys was intended to emulate the success of Dinky. The toolmakers needed to produce the dies were brought over from Germany and the resulting quality was very high. A range of small diecasts, known as "castoys", was produced in the 1950s, but they were superseded by a new series in 1956. Corgi toys made such an impact because of their quality and the number of features added to every toy (see pp.125–131).

Key features

As many extras as possible were packed into each toy.
• They boasted plastic windows, unlike Dinky whose vehicles had open windows at the time.
• Spring suspension was added to vehicles in 1959.
• From 1963, vehicles were made with opening doors and bonnets, plus folding seats.
• One of the most popular models of 1963, a Chrysler V8, even had a corgi dog on the back parcel shelf.

RALLY CARS

Rally car models became popular in Britain in the wake of British rallying successes in the 1960s.
• **Rarities** The 1965 Monte Carlo Rally set, pictured above right; is a rare group of vehicles. Corgi produced rally versions of existing vehicles by adding accessories such as lamps, transfers, and roof racks.
• **Popular models** The Hillman Hunter rally car produced to celebrate the winner of the London to Sydney rally is a popular model. It featured "golden jacks", a feature introduced in 1969 that allowed wheels to be changed. A plastic kangaroo accompanied this model. (See p.130)

TV TIE-INS

In the 1960s, Corgi pioneered film and TV tie-ins, producing vehicles based on various shows and films including *Batman, Daktari, The Saint, Chitty Chitty Bang Bang,* and the James Bond series. TV- and film-related production continued in the 70s with vehicles for *Noddy* and the *Magic Roundabout* among others. (See pp.229–238.)

• **Most successful** The Corgi Batmobile of the 1960s (see p.236), was particularly successful, selling around three million vehicles.
• **James Bond** The James Bond Aston Martin, based on the hero's car in the film *Goldfinger* is perhaps the most famous Corgi vehicle of them all and is popular with diecast collectors and James Bond fans. Its many features included an ejector seat; Corgi engineers designed a special test rig to ensure that it would operate reliably. (See pp.237–238.)

WHIZZWHEELS

"Whizzwheels" were introduced on a number of models in 1970 in response to Mattel's "Hot Wheels" range that had been introduced in 1968. Instead of using rubber tyres on cast axles, Whizzwheels were made of plastic and mounted on thin axles. While some consider them cheap and nasty, they were popular with children because the cars went much faster and further when pushed along.

DECLINE

The 70s saw a gradual decline in the quality of Corgi vehicles. In the late 70s, TV tie-ins included vehicles for shows such as *Charlie's Angels*. Mettoy, the Corgi holding company, went into receivership in 1983 and there was a management buyout. The company was taken over by Mattel in 1992. A further management buyout took place in 1995. Today Corgi produces a range of collectors' vehicles.

Crescent Toys

Crescent Toys was founded in 1922 and until 1950 sold toys produced for them by DCMT (Diecast Casting Machine Tools Ltd) of London. DCMT later achieved success as Lone Star, making a range of diecast toys including toy guns, soldiers, and military vehicles. Crescent moved production to Wales in 1950 and produced various diecast toys of which the most sought after are its racing cars (right). Ten different Grand Prix racing cars were made c.1956–60 and they are admired for their quality which makes them more valuable than the equivalent Dinky Toy 23/230 series.

Dinky Toys

Dinky is one of the best-known names in the collectible toy world. The firm was founded by Frank Hornby, the founder of Meccano, who was encouraged to produce diecast vehicles by the example of Tootsie Toys in the United States. His first pocket-sized vehicles were issued in 1933 and were initially marketed as "Modelled Miniatures" to go with the figures and other accessories the firm was making for model railway sets. Products were made in sets or series. The early models included a motor truck and delivery van in what was known as the 22 series. This series also included a colourful tractor and a military tank which are sought after by collectors.

EARLY DINKYS

The diecast models became known as Dinky Toys in April 1934. The name probably comes from the Scottish word "dink", meaning neat or fine. From the early days, Dinky Toys were made in both Britain and France.

• **24 series of saloon cars** This series typifies early Dinky toys. They have a stylish contemporary design and attractive colours.

• **Pre-war Dinky production** Included a fine range of delivery vans in the 28 and 280 series. Pictured right is a Dinky Toy part set of 28/1 series delivery vans in original trade box, c.1934.

• **Rarities** One of the most valuable of all Dinky toys is a "Bentalls" van, which was produced as a promotion for a department store. Other Dinky vans bore advertisements for products such as Hartley's Jam and Bisto gravy. The transfers should be

Look for

The most sought-after pre-war Dinkys are the following:
• 28 and 280 series vans
• 24 series saloon cars
• 23 series racing cars
• 25 series lorries
• 30 series saloon and sports cars
• 36 series saloon and sports cars
• 38 series British sports cars
• 39 series American cars.

original and in good condition.
• **Lead** Early Dinky toys were made of lead, but its use was discontinued in 1934 in favour of the magnesium-zinc alloy mazac. Although the new alloy was safer, impurities could result in metal fatigue – there were complaints from some retailers in the 1930s about this. Early lead Dinky toys are particularly rare and collectible.

POST-WAR TOYS
Production was halted during WWII. After the war, there was initially no time to develop new models so some of the pre-war range was re-issued, in particular the 23 series racing cars, 25 series lorries, 30 and 36 series saloons, 38 series sports cars, and 39 series American cars. Each series had minor variations in detail and was slightly upgraded during the years of production.

The differences between pre- and post-war production include the following:
• Post-war models used an improved alloy that was less prone to fatigue.
• Later models have thicker axles than pre-war models.
• Colours are drab when compared with pre-war models.
• Pre-war vehicles have smooth wheel hubs and white tyres. However, changes did not take place overnight, so some early post-war production may still have some typically pre-war features.

SUPERTOY RANGE
In 1947, Dinky introduced its Supertoy range of larger vehicles. (See pp.133–143.) The first model was the No. 501 Foden diesel 8 wheel wagon, which measured 7½in (19cms) long.
• **Guy range** A series of Supertoy commercial vehicles known as the Guy range was introduced in 1947. Like the pre-war 28 series vans, they had advertising transfers – the first model was a Slumberland van, which is among the most commonly found today. Products and companies advertised on these vans included Spratts, Lyons Swiss Rolls, Ever Ready, and Weetabix. The Weetabix van was only produced from 1952–3 and is the most rare.

SALOON CARS
In 1947, Dinky also introduced its 40 series of saloon cars. The Riley Saloon was the first, with the Hillman Minx, Morris Oxford, Austin Taxi, and Austin Somerset to follow by 1954. They are good replicas and each model had its own range of colours such as grey, black, pale blue, green, and red. Sometimes though, a model is found in a different colour from

the norm. Such variations are of great interest to collectors as they are rare. The reason they exist is probably simply because the correct colour of paint was used up before a batch was completed, so another colour was used to finish the remaining few.

"GOLDEN AGE"
The period from 1958–64 is considered the "Golden Age" of Dinky Toys. In the mid-late 50s, Dinky began to upgrade its range. Initially, this meant a new paint job for ageing models as in the two-tone 161 Austin Somerset from 1956 pictured below left. New and brighter colours were introduced, taking Dinky back to the paint styles of the pre-war era.
• **Commercial vehicles** New models were introduced, including a BBC Television van, part of a range of BBC vehicles produced in 1959. In 1962 a set of ABC TV vehicles was introduced – they are rarer than the BBC versions.
• **Rarities** Another rarity is the Guy Warrior Heinz van from 1960, produced with and without plastic windows. Combining a Guy Warrior chassis and box van from the earlier Guy Otter lorry, fewer than 1,000 were made. It should not be confused with the larger "Big Bedford" van, which is more common and was made from a different casting.
• **Buses** One of the most successful of the models produced

from new castings during this period were the buses. The Dinky AEC or Leyland-type double decker buses had been more or less unchanged in appearance since 1938, but in 1962 a new model was introduced. This was the revolutionary rear-engined Leyland Atlantean Bus, which had a front entrance with concertina doors.

OTHER DINKY DIECASTS

Dinky's diecast production was by no means confined to cars, vans, and buses and also included military vehicles and even aircraft (see pp.132–142). Commonly found Dinky aircraft include the Tempest II fighter and the Viking airliner. One of the rarest is the Avro Vulcan delta wing bomber, whose shape made it difficult to maintain consistent quality when casting. It was therefore only made for a short time.

LATER DINKYS

Dinky Toy production was taken over by Airfix in 1971, but the quality began to suffer and toys from this later period are not very collectible, with the exception of certain TV-related toys produced at this time. Dinky's French factory continued independently and continued to produce some fine vehicles (see pp.143–144), the most collectible of which is the

Citroen Presidentielle. Production was transferred to Spain in 1977 and the French factory at Bobigny closed in 1981. Dinky's factory in Binns Road, Liverpool, had closed two years earlier. The Dinky name now belongs to Matchbox Toys, which is owned by Mattel and toys are made in China.

VARIATIONS

Part of the reason for the popularity of Dinky toys is that numerous variations were produced, giving plenty of scope for the collector. The variations have been well documented, so they can be traced. Numerous contemporary retailers' catalogues, magazines, and books are available to aid identification.

MECCANO

Dinky Toys had the model vehicle market covered for its parent Meccano, but it is worth mentioning that Meccano itself produced cars (as well as aircraft) in the Constructor Sets range for many years. Meccano in general ranks among the most collectible of British toys. The quality was very high and the kits included everything needed to make the models. Complete boxed sets with all the tools and instructions are especially sought after while Meccano magazines, catalogues, and other ephemera are all collectible. Meccano came in sturdy boxes but although they were strong, they seldom survive. This is because the owners, having assembled the models, were unlikely to dismantle them and return them to the box which then would get misplaced. (For more Meccano see p.114.)

Ertl

Ertl was founded in Iowa by a German immigrant in 1945 and soon developed a reputation for quality diecast toys. The company is still based in Iowa, but its toys are mostly manufactured in China. Ertl initially produced farm-related toys such as cattle trucks and tractors but the range soon expanded to include cars and motor vehicles of all kinds Later products included TV and film tie-ins; Ertl made vehicles based on popular television programmes such as *The Dukes of Hazzard*, *Knight Rider,* and *Smokey and the Bandit*. They are mostly found in the United States.

Märklin

Prompted by the success of Dinky, the German maker Märklin, best known for its tinplate toys, began to produce diecasts in 1935. Many pre-war models are very scarce but production resumed after the war and mostly concentrated on German vehicles such as Mercedes-Benz, Volkswagen, and Porsche as well as trucks by Krupp and Magirus. Crisp detail and an excellent quality of casting are hallmarks of Märklin diecasts, but during the 1960s more features were added to models, which then lost their finely cast appearance. Production finally ceased in 1972.

Matchbox

Matchbox toys were made by Lesney, a company founded in 1947 by two old school friends, Leslie Smith and Rodney Smith, who had just left the Royal Navy. The name comes from a combination of their first names. Rodney had previously worked for DCMT (see p.30). Their first diecast toys appeared the following year; their first model was a 4in (10cm) long crawler tractor. From 1950–59 the name "Moko" appears alongside Lesney on their toys. This refers to the Anglo-German firm of Moses Kohnstam Ltd., which was given the exclusive right to sell them alongside other toys.

• **Prime Mover set** Lesney's first diecast model mentioned above developed into a Bulldozer, which was part of the 1950 Prime Mover Set (12in/30cm long) seen here.

THE MATCHBOX RANGE
This was created in 1953 by Jack Odell, on the back of the success of the company's Coronation

Coach model. His idea of making affordable, pocket-sized toys with packaging to resemble a matchbox is said to have been inspired by his daughter, whose school would only allow pupils to bring in toys no bigger than a matchbox. The Matchbox range was an instant success.
• **Typical models** The Commer Pick-Up (pictured left) is typical of the range. It is a commercial version of the Hillman Minx from 1958. It has metal wheels and a plain "Moko" box. The two-colour version of this model, made four years later and sporting plastic wheels and a more elaborate box is worth five times as much as the model shown, since relatively few were ever made.
• **Models of Yesteryear** In 1956, Lesney added this range, which was aimed at the adult collector.
• **Production** By 1962, total production was running at the rate of one million models a week.
• **Most collectible** The early 60s marked the zenith of Matchbox production for many collectors and examples from both the Matchbox and Yesteryear ranges from this era are among the most collectible. (See pp.145–148.)

"SUPERFAST" RANGE
In common with Dinky and Corgi, Matchbox was forced to react to the introduction of Mattel's "Hot Wheels" range. The resulting "Superfast" range with its thinner axles and garish colours marked a decline in quality that continued through the 70s.
  In 1982, Matchbox was taken over by Universal Holdings and in 1996, the Matchbox brand was taken over by American Mattel.

DIECAST

Schuco

The German firm of Schuco, which became renowned for the quality of its tinplate cars from the 1930s onwards, is equally admired for its diecasts. In the 1960s, they produced a fine range of diecast vehicles, largely in response to the declining interest in tinplate toys. Packaged in plastic cases, many were popular European (and mostly German) production cars, but Schuco's range also included racing cars. (See pp.149–150.) Schuco's diecast work was exceptional, but its decision to concentrate on diecast came too late and the firm eventually filed for bankruptcy in 1976. The firm was initially bought by the British firm DCMT but was then taken over by a succession of different owners. The firm still exists and concentrates on the classic and collectors' market.

Shackleton Toys

Shackleton Toys only operated a few years, (1948–52) and produced a range of large-scale diecast Foden FG lorries. The first issues were flatbed lorries, with a Dyson trailer added in 1949, and a rarer tipper lorry in 1950, (pictured). They were more expensive than Dinky Toys and Shackleton suffered from a shortage of materials during the Korean War of the early 50s. This, coupled with low sales, led to the company's closure.

Solido

Founded in 1932 Solido is the most famous of the French diecast companies. The firm produced a variety of diecast vehicles before WWII. Of Solido's post-war production, the 100 Series vehicles, launched in 1957, are admired for their quality which rivals and even exceeds that of Corgi. Solido is best known for its military vehicles, produced from 1961. Other French manufacturers include JRD, CIJ-Europarc, and Norev.

Tekno

Founded in Denmark in the 1930s, Tekno first produced tinplate toys. One of its most collectible diecast products is the Mercedes-Benz 230SL (pictured) which has a fingertip steering action. Commercial vehicles in unusual liveries are especially sought after.

Tootsie Toys

American firm Tootsie Toys created the first diecast toys in 1906 and went on to produce a fine range of diecasts in the 1930s. Their most famous models are of Graham and La Salle cars but Tootsie also made diecast versions of cars by Ford, Lincoln, De Soto, and Auburn. They were both attractive and affordable and from the mid-1920s included detail such as recessed lines around the engine compartment and doors. After WWII quality declined and products became cruder in appearance. By the 1970s, their toys had become very simple in design and were made of plastic

Tri-ang

Founded in 1919 by William, Arthur, and Walter Lines, sons of the founders of Lines Brothers. Tri-ang had noted the success of diecast toys for some time and had created its Minic series of small tinplate vehicles (see pp.26–27) to compete with diecasts in 1935. With the rise of Matchbox and Corgi alongside Dinky, Tri-ang entered the diecast market with a range called "Spot-On", produced at a factory in Northern Ireland.

"SPOT-ON" RANGE

These were modelled to a 1:42 scale, slightly larger than Dinky and much larger than Matchbox. Like many Corgi models, they boasted numerous features, some of which were highly innovative. They came with fully fitted interiors and windows as well as "Flexomatic suspension", which was probably the most convincing suspension found on any diecast model. Electric headlamps were added from 1961–62 and Spot-On vehicles came in a wide variety of colours.

• **Boxes** Spot-On boxes were not as robust as the vehicles, so examples complete with their box are rare and consequently sought after by collectors.

• **Models** The range of cars comprised many contemporary vehicles such as the Austin A60, Vauxhall Cresta, Morris 1000, and Ford Zephyr 6 (the latter featured a poodle on the back seat). They also produced gift sets (see right, and p.152).

• **Commercial vehicles** A range of haulage vehicles was introduced in 1960, (see p.151) but it was short-lived and due to high overheads the series was axed in 1963.

• **Buses** The most famous of all Spot-On models is probably the London "Routemaster" bus of 1963 (pictured) which, apart from its stock wheels, is a very accurate representation of the vehicle. In 1964, Lines Brothers took over

Meccano, which included Dinky Toys. Since they had acquired Dinky, there was no need to continue to make Spot-On toys, which were expensive to produce. Production at the Castlereagh factory in Northern Ireland finally ceased in 1967. One of the last die-cast products made was a TV tie-in, a Batmobile. It was battery operated and featured the small, but powerful Wrenn Maximiser electric motor. They were made in small numbers, so they are quite rare and sought-after.

Model Figures

Representations of military figures date back to Ancient Egyptian times, but the first mass-produced figures were made in Germany and in France in the 18thC. Early figures made in Germany were known as "flats" or *Zinnfiguren* and were made by pouring molten metal through two separately engraved moulds clamped together. Lucotte and Mignot in France are probably the first two recognized toy soldier makers. Figures representing the armies of France were known in the 1760s, while the German manufacturer George Heyde had begun to produce figures by the early 1800s.

HOLLOW-CAST FIGURES

As with most toy production, continental European makers were dominant, but that changed in 1893 with the development of hollow-casting techniques in Britain (see p.14). As the name suggests, this method resulted in hollow figures that were lighter and less costly to make and transport than the solid lead figures of Continental manufacturers. The method, perfected in London by William Britain Junior, created a home grown toy soldier industry that eliminated the need to import figures, as had previously been the case.

• **Post-war** In the years immediately following WWI, military subjects fell out of favour and many firms produced various non-military figures such as the farm, pictured right, c.1930s.

COMPOSITION FIGURES

During the inter-war period, Continental makers introduced the composition figure. Instead of lead, these figures were made from a mixture of kaolin, sawdust, and glue that was moulded, after being heated, around a wire frame.

• **Germany** These figures were mostly made in Germany by the firms of Elastolin and Lineol and featured soldiers of the German and Italian armies and their allies. They also featured leaders such as Hitler, Hess, and Goering. They were given porcelain heads and the limbs were jointed so that they could be made to salute.

PLASTIC FIGURES

By the 1960s, plastic had become the preferred material for manufacture, partly because of advances in plastics technology but also because of concerns about the safety of lead toys. (See p.12 and pp.159–160.)

COLLECTING

Some figures are more easily found in their country of origin. British collectors tend to favour hollow-cast lead figures while solid figures are especially popular in Germany, France, and Italy. Several different manufacturers have produced many different regiments, so the variety for the collector is considerable. There are several reasons why the market for collecting model figures remains strong:

• Toy figures often conjure up fond memories from childhood.
• The subject of military history in particular attracts a vast following, of which the collecting of toy figures is a small but significant part. This widens the pool of collectors and fuels the market.
• Although hollow-cast Britains will form the mainstay of many a collection, they are but one sector of a much wider field that ranges from antique German solids through composition (including the highly collectible Third Reich figures) to sought-after plastic figures from the 1950s onwards.
• This field has been given a boost by the Internet, encouraging a global network of collectors.

Britains

The firm of Britains was founded in 1845 and had manufactured a range of toys. However, it was the development of hollow-cast figures that established the company as a true market leader. The first set of soldiers was of mounted lifeguards and was so successful that other British troops, mounted and on foot, swiftly followed. By 1900, more than 100 sets of figures had been produced and they are keenly collected today.

IDENTIFYING BRITAINS

The success of Britains soon led to copying – many of these copies were made by firms set up by ex-employees of the company. Some of the more successful were Fry, Hanks, Davies, and Mudie. All were eventually prosecuted and in 1900 Britains sought to protect itself in future by re tooling moulds to incorporate the company name, date, and a copyright message. Re-tooling took several years and as a short term measure, printed paper stickers were used on the underside of figures. Many of these stickers have fallen off over the years; look for traces of glue on the base.

• **WWI** International conflict saw the introduction of foreign forces to the range to reflect events.

• **Packaging** This was enhanced by the introduction of good quality red cardboard boxes

• **Post-WWI** Britains continued with military figures, such as the Guards officer and drummer c.1920, left. However, they also catered for a demand for non-military toys with civilian figures including Salvation Army models and footballers (see below). The latter were especially popular and all the major British clubs were represented, as were some (now rare) overseas teams.

"HOME FARM" SERIES

The 1920s saw the "Home Farm" series, featuring large pieces such as a "farm waggon" and driver (below), as well as smaller ones such as a shepherd and sheep. The "village idiot" (see p.155) was inspired by a remark made by Queen Mary at the 1927 British Industries Fair. She said that this was the only thing missing from the farm series, so the figure was designed and put into production. It was issued in beige, pink, green, and blue smocks.

DISNEY & OTHER CHARACTERS

• **Disney** During the 1930s, Britains produced licensed products for Disney. Pluto, Mickey Mouse, and Snow White and the Seven Dwarves were all made and are sought after by Disney as well as Britains enthusiasts.

• **Other Characters** Figures of sci-fi hero Buck Rogers were also made, as were souvenirs for Madame Tussauds waxworks. "Cococubs" (below) were animal figures given away with Cadbury's cocoa.

• **Train accessories** Britains also made station staff and passengers for Bassett-Lowke as well as "00" Gauge figures and accessories for Trix. (See p.154.)

• **Zoo series** This successful range

Key features

When looking at pre-war Britains figures always bear the following in mind:
• foot soldiers were all of a standard size of 2in (54mm) with mounted figures proportionately larger
• early figures are the most desirable and among these the guardsmen, naval figures, and the first khaki troops from the Boer War are particularly sought after
• figures made between 1938–41, after which war stopped production, are also desirable.

included animals, cages, and keepers. The camel from the zoo series pictured above is worth relatively little on its own, but much more when its accompanying sailor boy figure is present – they have usually been separated.
• **WWII** As Britain re-armed in preparation for war, so military subjects became more acceptable again. From 1936, Britains produced a now rare range of contemporary soldiers in battledress with military equipment. Production continued until 1941, when it was stopped for the duration of the war.

POST-WWII PRODUCTION

After the war, production restarted with a limited range and an emphasis on export. The Coronation of 1953 provided a boost and saw the production of one of Britains largest ever sets of some 228 figures, see p.156. Rising material costs soon led to shorter sets and individual "Picture Pack" figures.

PLASTIC FIGURES

It was in 1953 that Britains took over Herald Miniatures, which made plastic figures. By 1960, the use of lead in toys had been banned, but Britains had already developed its plastic "Swoppet" range, see p.160. Knights, cowboys, and infantry were all featured and they had interchangeable parts so that bodies, heads, and equipment could be changed.
• **"Golden Age"** The period 1959–67 saw some of the firm's best plastic civilian and zoo figures made.
• **Collectability** Plastic figures are becoming popular among collectors, but only if they are in excellent condition. Quality began to decline somewhat from the mid-60s onwards however.
• **Limited editions** In 1972, a new range of metal figures was produced with the adult collector in mind and from 1983, limited edition boxed sets were made. These have been successful and have already begun to appreciate in value.

Britains figures have always been popular and continued to be admired throughout the world. They have a particularly strong following in the United States.

Other Companies

While pre-WWII figures by Britains remain the most collectible, interest in the products of other firms is rising. Unlike some other makers, John Hill & Co. did not try to copy Britains, but made their own distinctive range that was less rigid in style than Britains marching figures (see top left p.29).

BMC (Brushfield Manufacturing Company) produced some well-designed figures between 1900–20; it was the distinctiveness of design that allowed other manufacturers to develop their own niche in the market. Different makers became known for particular types of soldiers.

CHARBENS

Founded in 1920, Charbens produced their own, mainly non-military figures as well as making figures for other companies. They closed in 1955.
• **Known for** Their circus series

c.1935 featuring a ringmaster, unicyclists, acrobats, clowns, jugglers, a comic policeman, and boxing midgets is sought after.

TAYLOR & BARRETT

The best known set by Taylor & Barrett (1920–39) was a zoo series that was more imaginative than that of Britains. It included a chimps' tea party, parrots on a stand, a llama, camel, an elephant ride, plus children and zookeepers. The company also made lead vehicles.

PIXYLAND & CO.
Pixyland & Co. (1922–32) is best known for its range of figures based on popular cartoon characters including Tiger Tim and the Bruin Boys from *Rainbow*.

• **Other characters** Pip, Squeak, and Wilfred (above), were based on a comic strip in the *Daily Mirror* newspaper. They also made a figure of Felix the Cat (below), as it was unlicensed it was packaged in boxes marked "Cinema Favourites".

GERMAN FIGURES
• **Elastolin and Lineol** These were the most successful German makers

and both were famous for their composition figures. Their military figures, which included the Nazi leaders, were accompanied by a fine range of tinplate vehicles. Non-military subjects included zoo and farm animals (including a peacock) as well as cowboys and indians.
• **Identifying** There is one obvious difference between the products of these two makers: Elastolin figures have an oval base while Lineol's bases are rectangular.
Lineol's factory was destroyed by the 1945 bombing of Dresden and the firm never re-opened. Elastolin continued after the war, making plastic figures from the 50s. The factory closed in 1984.
• **Heyde of Dresden** Their figures were the most commonly imported figures into Britain before Britains became successful (see p.158). They not only made figures to the now standard 2in (54mm) size, but also to a smaller 1½in (45mm) size using brass moulds. Mounted figures could be removed from their horses; they were secured by a plug that was put into the saddle. Best known are their popular large display groups among which was an oasis set featuring Arabs and camels.

FRENCH FIGURES
• **Lucotte** This French company cast the body and head of their figures separately. The head had a plug on the base to secure it to the body. Weapons and accessories were soldered on later. Figures were slightly larger than the 2in (54mm) standard size. C. B. G. Mignot took over the Lucotte name in 1825 and widened the range considerably to include armies from many historical periods. The "Homme de Corvée" pictured above right was made c.1920 and wears a fatigue duty uniform – he is a common find today.

AMERICAN FIGURES
Barclay and Manoil were two major manufacturers in the United States during the 1920s and 30s. Both produced hollow-cast (or slush cast as they are called in America) toy soldiers and figures to a 2½in (70mm) scale. While Barclay and Manoil covered the same subject matter, they did not copy each other's products but it did mean their figures were compatible with each other. As well as military figures, both made figures representing an idealized view of American farm life. The lady watering flowers in the picture on page 30, is from Manoil's "Happy Farm" series with farm workers and animals. It was issued throughout the 1930s and is an idealized portrayal of an American farming family.
• **Popular subjects** These included figures from the US military and they were sold through stores such as F. W. Woolworth. Barclay sold figures with artillery, anti-aircraft guns, and searchlights.
• **Wild West series** Manoil also made "My Ranch" featuring cowboys and cowgirls at play, instead of traditional fighting scenes.
• **Tommy Toys** This American firm, 1920–25, made nursery rhyme and

Care

• **Storage** It is important to consider environmental factors when storing lead figures. They can disintegrate if stored for long periods in a hot, dry environment. They must also be kept out of direct sunlight, which can cause the paint to fade. The loss of a single soldier can have a large impact on a collection, since collectors look for sets that are complete and in their original, intact boxes.

• **Damage** Condition is paramount for any model figures. Repairs and conversion can reduce value by over half. Repainting can be even more damaging

• **Packaging** The presence of the original box and packaging can add greatly to value so always keep boxes safely.

fairy tale characters such as Humpty Dumpty and Puss in Boots. The firm's Little Miss Muffet figure is especially collectible.

• **Grey Iron** This American company, c.1920–39, as its name suggests, made toy soldiers and figures from cast-iron instead of lead and was the only company to do this. While they were popular, they were not of such good quality as hollow-cast lead figures. They made in 2in (54mm) scale. Grey Iron also produced soldiers and civilians. American toys are rarely found in Europe but is worth looking out for them as their value has risen.

State of the market

Britains items continue in popularity with military items remaining the most collectible.

Top end In spite of the Internet the market for the extremely rare early and expensive sets continues to be a narrow one populated by a small number of wealthy collectors. Recent highlights at auction have seen a non-issued set No. 2020 of Portuguese Infantry MB fetch £4,000 / €5,700 / $6,600. Another rare set No.1903 Indian Army Mountain Battery has achieved £3,000 / €4,300 / $5,000 in auction. Early sets especially in good condition/boxed can reach over £1,000 / €1,400 / $1,650 each, depending on type.

A word of warning though to potential investors and collectors. Some of the highest prices for Britains were reached in the mid-1980s. For example, a Britains set No.1339 Steel Helmeted Gun Team in the original box fetching £6,000 / €8,500 / $10,900. Similarly, set No.1552 Royal Mail van fetched £10,000 / €14,200 / $16,600. These high prices were fuelled by the enthusiasm of a unique concentration of wealthy collectors. It is doubtful today if similar prices could be achieved for such sets.

Middle market Prices for middle-range military sets have remained been stable for many years. This trend has been reinforced by the world-wide market created by the Internet. Occasionally lots offered on eBay, for example, may attain a very high price, but natural caution seems to restrict final sale prices to 60–70 per cent of the top value.

Non-military items Ranges such as farm, gardening, novelty, etc have become more popular recently. which is particularly evident from Internet sales, This trend has been boosted also by the publication of dedicated books on the subject.

• Sold in a recent auction sale was set 163 by Scout Signallers for £500 / €710 / $830, and boxed gardening items frequently fetch high prices on the Internet and in auction sales.

Earlier German manufacturers The products of the earlier German manufacturers (see p.158) such as Heyde, Haffner Heinrichsen, and Noris can be the most valuable of all and have seen a steady rise in their value – the old German figures perhaps reasserting their ascendancy after a century of domination by Britains.

Geographical collecting trends

• Britains are collected wherever their products were sold. Originally principally in territories of the old British Empire but also in the United States (always a large export market for European toys), together with Spain, Portugal, Italy, and South America.

• German solids are collected in the UK, United States, and Germany.

• Composition figures are collected in all these countries and all types of figures are sought-after in the UK. The Internet has strengthened these trends, but also revealed a global collectors' net of all types of figures.

Games

Games are probably as old as humanity itself and board games of a kind date back to ancient civilizations. To command premium prices in the collectors' market, games should come complete with their original boxes and all associated packaging, and accessories including counters and instructions. It is difficult to find early board games in good condition, because the paper or board used to make them has usually deteriorated badly. There are relatively few games' collectors when compared with other fields such as diecast toys for example, but this means that prices are still affordable and there are plenty of opportunities for the new collector to enter the market.

COLLECTING

Games made before 1940 are usually the most desirable, although there are collectors that specialize in those made from the 1840s to the 60s. However, games of any age can be desirable depending on their theme.

• **Post-WWII** These games are usually more complicated and have more counters, dice, cards, and accessories to go with them. For many collectors, this makes them more interesting, but the more pieces there are, the more likely it is that some will have been lost over the years.

• **Themed collections** If a collection is based around a particular subject it adds coherence and value to the collection as a whole. Possible themes include games based on popular cartoon characters, games by a particular company, or from a specific period. Disney is always popular across all collecting categories.

• **The Internet** The web has made it much easier to find old games than it used to be and Internet auction sites can be a good way to find them. Make sure that you study auctions carefully before bidding to get an idea of the sort of prices paid. It is not always essential or wise to buy the first example that comes along. As with buying any collectible, always err on the side of caution if buying "unseen" and make sure your rights are protected.

• **Dealers** Many reputable dealers offer games for sale online and their websites can be very useful. If you are looking for a particular game and cannot find it on their website, always send an email and ask. New stock is likely to be arriving all the time and they can also keep an eye out for what you are looking for. Dealers add the "personal touch".

Bagatelles

Bagatelle was originally a table game with similarities to pool, billiards, or snooker. It became very fashionable during the 19thC and small, bagatelle-style games were made for the home (see p.167). By the early 20thC versions resembling those we know today were being produced. Bagatelle is often regarded as the forerunner of the pinball table and bagatelle toys certainly resemble pinball. Bagatelle toys involve the use of a spring-loaded plunger to fire balls into holes to score points. It can be played as a team or by an individual scoring against themselves. Older bagatelle games made out of wood are beautiful objects in themselves.

LATER BAGATELLES
As colourful, simple, inexpensive games bagatelles have long been marketed as a tie-in with film and TV characters.
• **Manufacturers** In the 1930s, Chad Valley included bagatelles in their range of toys for Disney characters. The firm's Disney range also included the Mickey Mouse Tiddley Winks game pictured on the previous page. Louis Marx and Chad Valley are among the many toy companies that made bagatelles. These games must be in full working order and in a clean, intact box

where applicable to achieve their maximum value.
• **Characters** Later, in the 1960s and 70s, bagatelles featured popular children's characters from programmes such as *Noddy* and the *Magic Roundabout*, as well as characters from *Camberwick Green* and *Rupert the Bear*. This Rupert bagatelle game (right) features all of the main characters. Note that Rupert is depicted as a brown bear; he is a white bear in the cartoons.
• **Subject matter** This can make a big difference to value, as fans will often pay more. This is particularly

true of the character-related toys. (See pp.64–69, 228–225.)

Board Games

The earliest commercially produced board games date from the mid-18thC and were printed from copper or steel plates and coloured by hand. They were mostly race-to-the-finish games of chance involving rewards and forfeits for landing on particular squares (see Cycling game below, c.1890). This is now the familiar snakes &

ladders format but with more ponderous moral and educational themes which may seem amusing from today's perspective (eg "Royal and Most Pleasant Game of Goose", "Overland Route to India"). The advent of lithography in 1839 meant that manufacturers could produce games more cheaply and in quantity.

19THC
Victorian games usually had a moral or educational theme. "A Survey of London", made by William Dart (1755–1819) featured the capital's landmarks while the "Railroad Game", by Wallis (1775–1847), used the steam engine as its central theme.

• **Key features** They have simple rules and are made of paper, cut

into sections, and mounted on canvas. They are mostly rectangular in shape, though there are some round ones.
• **Mass-production** Cheap wood-pulp paper and board made mass production easier and by the 1890s, games were mounted on folded board instead of canvas.
  The turn of the century saw the introduction of many new games, including Ludo and Snakes and Ladders.
• **Makers** As well as those already mentioned, 19thC makers to look out for include Brooks & Co., Thomas Varty, Carrington Bowles, Bowles & Carver, and John Betts, who also produced puzzles. By the late 19thC, most games were made by specialist manufacturers such as

Jaques, Spears, and Waddingtons, all of whom still produce board games today.

• **New subjects** Following the successful development of the airship, air, and even space travel, were becoming new and exciting fields of speculation. The "Trip to Mars" game above dates from c.1900 and is an imaginative interpretation of outer space. It would appeal to both games collectors and space enthusiasts.

• **Inter-war period** Many manufacturers took their inspiration from popular children's characters. An example is the Peter Rabbit game pictured below, which was based on the popular Beatrix Potter characters. Figures were initially of hollow-cast lead and were made by Britains, but they had been replaced by the 1930s with plywood figures covered with printed paper.

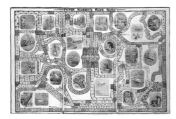

AMERICA

In the United States, Parker Brothers and Milton Bradley were, and still are, among the best-known makers. By the end of the 19thC, board games had become popular on both sides of the Atlantic. Milton Bradley produced more than 400 games and puzzles out of the thousands then available in the United States.

• **Milton Bradley** The company was founded in 1861 to make educational toys and its first board game, the "Checkered Game of Life" in the same year sold 40,000 copies. Board games and toys by Milton Bradley are easy to identify and should have the date and company name displayed on them.

• **Parker Brothers** In 1883, George Parker formed his games company in Salem Massachusetts and was joined by his two brothers four years later to form Parker Brothers. The company was the main competitor to Milton Bradley and rivalry was fierce.

• **Monopoly** Parker Brothers' biggest hit was Monopoly in 1935, a game that has since sold more than 100 million copies worldwide. Its origins date back to an earlier game called "The Landlord Game" credited to Lizzie J. Magie in 1904 but Charles Darrow is credited as the inventor of the game released by Parker Brothers. The company initially turned down Darrow's game as it was considered too complicated. Today, many different versions of the game have been produced, including games based on popular films. Some collectors focus solely on Monopoly, buying versions in various languages and from different periods. Both Parker Brothers and Milton Bradley are now owned by Hasbro.

• **Other games** Not all board games were flat. In "Over the Garden Wall" (below) from the 1880s, players had to land their counters in certain areas within a "walled garden" represented by a printed card box. It was issued by the British firm Spears, but was printed in Bavaria. Bavarian printers were noted for the quality of their colour work. The fountain and rose trees were by Britains (see p.37).

Collecting

• **Damage** Condition is important, but some damage can be overlooked if a game is particularly early and rare, or if it is needed to complete a themed collection.

• **Themes** Interesting subjects such as travel or current events are more desirable than moral and educational games. An example is the airship-inspired "Trip to Mars" game, made c.1900, shown left. Although the identity of the English maker is unknown, its space theme is appealing. If a game's theme is very topical, it is likely to have had a fairly limited shelf life in its day. Themes that are typically of their time are always of interest to collectors. Collectors should always bear the following points in mind when looking for old games:

• **Collectability** The popularity of a game with collectors is often determined by the artwork, therefore the more elaborate and colourful the images, the better.

Collector's Checklist:

• Always check games or puzzles for signs of insect or mildew damage.

• Never glue or tape a board game or puzzle to a backing board – this will dramatically reduce its value.

• Bright light can damage the colours of games and puzzles. If an item is framed for display, it should be in an acid-free environment with UV Plexiglas.

• Do not stack game boxes on top of one another, as those on the bottom can be crushed and damaged. Store them vertically if possible.

• Do not use rubber bands to keep boxes closed. This can result in damage to the box.

GAMES

FANTASY ROLE-PLAYING GAMES
In the 1970s and 80s, a new wave of games known as fantasy role playing games enjoyed a boom. They were mostly based on science fiction or fantasy themes, although there were also more conventional war themes.

• **The best known publisher** In Britain this is Games Workshop, while Flying Buffalo is a well-known American company.

• **Subjects** Some role-playing games are based on popular fantasy works such as *Lord of the Rings* and are of interest because they pre-date the blockbuster film trilogy.

• Although this is a small corner of the games market at the moment, collectors tend to be very enthusiastic. It is always exciting to be part of a new collecting area as there is so much to discover and of course, a new collecting area will be much more accessible in price. The Internet is a good source.

State of the market

Top end Victorian games are highly prized today, particularly those by John Jaques (see pp.162–163). These were often of exceptional quality presented in attractive wooden boxes as well as the usual cardboard ones (e.g. Squails, Gossima, and Minoru see p.163).

Most accessible There is currently a nostalgia-led revival in demand for games of the post-WWII era. The motivation of many of today's buyers is the desire to play the games of their youth with their own children rather than to build a serious archive.

• Look out for Waddingtons' Parker Brothers games (Monopoly, Buccaneer (see p.173), Formula 1, Totopoly (see p.166); Spear's (Scrabble); Chad Valley (Escalado (see p.164), and the earliest themed Disney games from the 1930s, see p.165); Glevum for colourful and quirky games from about 1910–30s (see p.164); Gibson (especially for Dover Patrol and L'Attaque with editions spanning c.1910–80); and Bell (an extensive range of games based on early TV favourites such as *Rawhide, Emergency Ward 10*, etc).

Playing Cards

Playing cards date back to Medieval times, though their precise origin is obscure. Their development is linked with that of the printing press and as technology advanced, so they became cheaper and more available.

Cards from the early 19thC were very different from those of today. The Joker first appeared in American packs in the 1860s and in Britain by the 1880s. It was not until then that most cards had rounded corners.

WADDINGTONS
In Britain, the best-known manufacturer of playing cards was Waddingtons, whose first playing cards were made in the early 1920s. WWI had seen a surge in the popularity of card games, presumably because cards were very portable and popular with soldiers passing the time whilst waiting for action on the front.

• **Most popular** One of Waddingtons most popular early series of cards was called "Beautiful Britain", issued in 1924. It featured scenic views of popular tourist

attractions and resorts and was sponsored by railway companies.

• **Other designs** Waddingtons went on to produce many different designs and in the late 1920s even produced circular cards, which were a big hit in the United States.

The ones pictured here are from the 1930s (see p.179).

While production of most toys and games was halted in Britain during the WWII, it is said that Churchill himself wanted playing cards to be exempted because of their importance for morale. However, the artwork on wartime cards is not always as good as it could be, since the companies had lost key workers to the war effort.

COLLECTING
During the 20thC, playing cards were used as a marketing and

promotional tool for various products. Everything from shipping lines to breweries and tea (see Tetley Tea cards right and p.184) has been advertised on playing cards.

• **Wider appeal** Playing card collecting in itself is an esoteric field, but such cards are also of interest to collectors of advertising memorabilia and of general memorabilia connected with the products advertised.

• **Care** Playing cards come under the heading of ephemera, which generally comprises paper-based collectibles and similar rules must be followed to care for them. Damp conditions and bright sunlight should always be avoided. Gloves should be worn when handling cards whenever possible to avoid damage by grease from the fingers.

Yo-Yos

The yo-yo is often said to have originated in the Philippines as a jungle weapon, but this could well be a myth. Similar toys have appeared in various cultures for at least 2,000 years. The name is believed to be Philippino however, from a local word meaning "come back". They were known in France in the 18thC and in Britain in the 19thC, where they were called "bandalores" but by the early 20thC their popularity was in decline. Pedro Flores, a Philippino, set up a yo-yo making company in California in the 1920s and he was eventually bought out by American entrepreneur Donald Duncan. Duncan encouraged interest in the toy through newspaper competitions and it soon became a worldwide phenomenon.

• **Makers** Look out for makers including Duncan (below), Russell, Cheerio, Goody, and Royal Tops.

• **TV tie-ins** Yo yos have also been associated with TV and film characters and these can be appealing to fans of the characters, shows or films as well as to the dedicated yo-yo collector.

WHISTLING YO-YOS
Manufacturers looked for new ways to enhance this popular toy. One of the most popular was the whistling yo-yo, marketed by Duncan from the 1930s. Made from tinplate, they incorporated holes into the design so that air would be drawn through them in use, making a whistling sound. Pictured right is a Lumar pressed-metal whistling yo-yo c.1950s (see p.185). Whistling yo-yos are interesting, but fairly common.

PROMOTIONAL YO-YOS
Yo-yos have been used as promotional items to market various products, but the best known is Coca Cola. Collecting Coca-Cola yo-yos has become a hobby in itself; the first ones were made in the 30s from Bakelite and are valuable. Bakelite is quite brittle and collectibles made of this should be handled with care. This is another example of "cross-over" appeal.

CARE
Yo-yos were made out of many different materials such as wood, tin, and plastic. Rules for the care of yo-yos will largely depend on the material they were made out of. For example, wooden yo-yos should be checked for signs of rot, while rust is a major enemy of tinplate, so tin yo-yos should be checked for signs of this.

Electronic Games

The microchip revolution of the 1970s and 80s brought a new wave of toys to the market. Although many of these early games look very simple today, they were unlike anything that had been seen before and sold in huge numbers. They are still quite affordable, but they should come in their original box and with instructions.

Educational games were among the early successes, one of the best-known being "Speak and Spell" by Texas Instruments in 1978. A maths version soon followed. Both are collectible; they are not difficult to find, but like many electronic games they are usually lacking their box and instructions which will detract from their value.

• **Japan** Japanese toy firm Tomy made a very successful range of electronic games including a range of six "3-D" games that the user held up and looked through like binoculars. In many ways, they were the descendants of Victorian optical toys.

• **Other manufacturers** Electronic games were also made by many different companies including Atari, Mattel, Entex, Casio, Bandai, Acetronic, and Nintendo. Pictured above is an MB Electronics hand-held Simon game (see p.174)

• **Sporting themes** Sports themes such as football and hockey were made as well as miniature versions of popular arcade hits such as Frogger, Defender, and of course Space Invaders.

COMPUTER GAMES
Old computer games are not necessarily rare because they were produced in such quantities.

Moreover, the games that are rare are not necessarily valuable. Rarity is often an indication that a game was not that popular to begin with and since collectors in this field look for classic games, they are less likely to be interested in such examples.

• **Collecting** Nostalgia is a major factor in the toy collectible market. People tend to return to the toys of their youth and those who grew up in the 1980s were in at the birth of computer gaming. The hand-held electronic games illustrated here and on p.174 are the grandparents

of the Game Boy. In terms of technology, these objects are the equivalent of the penny-farthing. Although they might not have much memory themselves, they are fondly remembered by those who originally played with them, hence their value and appeal today.

• **Electronic games** Collectors are growing in number, but there are still many opportunities for the newcomer to this field. The computer games below date from the 1990s (see p.177). With new collecting fields the Internet is always a good source of items.

Trains

The first European toy trains, made around 1850, were sturdily built but of simple design and not very realistic. The trend towards more sophisticated models only accelerated after the turn of the century. At the Leipzig Toy Fair in 1891 the German maker Märklin introduced standardized gauges and went on to update their products regularly, introducing an ever-increasing range of rolling stock, stations, figures, and accessories. German manufacturers were particularly successful and enjoyed a booming export trade with Britain, where a high standard of living meant that there

were ready buyers for high quality, expensive products. Meanwhile, French makers such as Dessin and Favre made lightweight, tinplate carpet toy trains that were quite detailed, but no more sophisticated than the so-called "dribblers and piddlers" that were made in Britain. Some German makers such as Rock and Graner and Ernst Plank made similar trains. The United States had its own successful toy train industry; makers included Lionel and Ives, who produced trains in the large "Standard" Gauge of 2⅛in (55mm). The cast-iron and wood floor train pictured here is American c.1855 (see p.186).

EARLY 20THC

Trains in the early 20thC were powered by steam, clockwork (see 1920s example below), or early (and dangerous) electric motors. Märklin introduced electric motors in 1898 and by 1900 had several different alternating current designs including four-volt, eight-volt, and the potentially dangerous 110–250 volt. These different voltages were needed to cope with the varied system of AC/DC current at the time. Other makers also introduced electric motors, but clockwork remained the favourite method for powering the less expensive ranges.

- **Offset lithography** The advent of this in 1903, with its use of a drum rather than flat plates for printing, made a major impact on all toymaking. It meant that the technique of using lightweight tabbed lithographed tinplate could augment painted tinplate. It was known as the "Nuremberg style" after the area where it was introduced.
- **Collecting** Many early 20thC trains were made in large gauges, which took a lot of space to set up. They were usually of high quality with additional features such as highly detailed coach interiors and composition figures. Collectors of these early trains are very knowledgeable and demanding, so condition is all-important and damage of any kind can make a huge difference to value. Mechanisms should not have been

replaced and springs should be intact. See p.56 for more on gauges.

INTER-WAR YEARS

This period is very popular with collectors, who often prefer examples from their own countries. WWI disrupted train production and recovery after the war was slow. In Britain, smaller houses were being built, so larger gauge trains were no longer practical. Makers such as Bing and Märklin began to modernize, but they faced increasing competition from British makers such as Hornby.
- **German trains** Germany was still the dominant manufacturer but many British buyers disliked buying German products at this time. Bassett-Lowke, which marketed trains for the German manufacturer Bing, tried to disguise the origin of its products by using the trademark

"BW" for "Bing Werke" on its boxes.

• **Hornby** From 1920 onwards Hornby made a new range of "0" Gauge trains and they continued to improve and develop the range, making them more realistic. By the 1930s, Hornby customers could choose from a range of accessories including figures, signal boxes, and "0" Gauge scale Dinky Toys.

• **"00" Gauge** In 1935 a new company, Trix, which was founded by Stefan Bing, introduced a smaller "00" Gauge. This was instantly popular and Märklin followed suit, as did Hornby with its Hornby-Dublo range. These smaller, more convenient, and more affordable trains would become the most popular type for the next 50 years.

POST-WWII

After WWII, German manufacturers were slow to recover. Their post-war products were initially drab and are not particularly sought after. In 1948 Märklin switched from "00"

to "H0" Gauge, which made their models more realistic. In the 1950s, plastic was introduced to the tenders.

• **The United States** In America, the industry was not so badly affected by the war and major producers Lionel and American Flyer enjoyed post-war success with their feature-packed "0" Gauge ranges. They boasted chimneys that produced steam and stations that could be lit up. However, competition from new companies producing inexpensive "H0" ranges damaged both and American Flyer closed in 1966.

• **Hornby-Dublo** In Britain, the Hornby-Dublo range dominated the post-war market. An important period for collectors is from 1945–53 when Hornby made a wide range of locomotives and accessories. Although the railways were nationalized in 1948, Hornby did not produce trains in the new British Rail livery until 1953. Some of the pre-1953 trains in the livery

of the old railway companies are very collectible today.

• Hornby continued to make "0" Gauge trains, but they were not of the same quality as pre-war trains. By the 1960s, production of the "0" Gauge had been downgraded to a "starter" system.

   Hornby embarked upon an ambitious, but disastrous programme of improvements in 1957. The re-designed locomotives and stock were superbly made but too expensive for the market. In 1964, the company was taken over by Tri-ang, which eventually closed in 1971 and the Triang-Hornby range became Hornby Railways, which continues to this day.

• **Bassett-Lowke** They continued to make trains until 1969.

• **Other collectible British makers** Trix, originally founded in Germany, were based in Britain. The Twin Trix locomotives were especially innovative as two locomotives could be independently operated on the same electric track.

Bassett-Lowke

Wenman Bassett-Lowke was a British entrepreneur who was not interested in making toys himself, but preferred to subcontract design and toymaking. He began selling locomotive and steam engine components by mail order in 1899. In 1900

he met Stefan Bing at the Paris Exhibition and the two joined forces, combining the design skills of Bassett-Lowke's colleague, Henry Greenly, with Bing's manufacturing capabilities. Over the next fifteen years they produced a range of successful locomotives.

• **Availability** Several Bassett-Lowke models are not difficult to find, including the LNWR "Precursor" tank locomotive. It was made for Bassett-Lowke by Bing from 1911 well into the 1920s.

• **Known for** One of the best-known early models is the live steam "Black Prince" locomotive (pictured right) which was available

in three gauges. The one here is the largest in Gauge III, and had many features including a brass boiler, tender with embossed frames and imitation springs, double-acting cylinders, reversing motion, and a water gauge. Although many early Bassett-Lowke models are readily available, their quality makes them desirable to collectors.

• **Standardization** Trains in the liveries of all the British rail companies were produced but, to save money, basic standard parts such as cylinders remained the same in these trains. Bearings and springs were typically visible outside the wheels, not within as was to become common practice.

• **Bing** Bing also provided Bassett-Lowke with numerous finely-

Look out for

• Bing/Greenly models,
these are mostly pre-WWI
• hand-built locomotives –
these are especially
valuable and quality
peaked in the 1950s
• pre-1914 trains, which are
often unmarked
• from around 1925
Winteringham's products
are almost always marked
with the Bassett-Lowke
trademark

detailed accessories including track
signals, buildings, and advertising
signs, often promoting either Bing
or Bassett-Lowke. These accessories often boasted novel features;
a lithographed tinplate station
made for the Gauge "0" trains
came complete with electric lights
• **Carette** Carette also supplied
locomotives to Bassett-Lowke, as
well as a range of lithographed
tinplate Gauge I freight stock; the
quality of the lithography was
extremely high. Carette went out
of business in 1917 and several
companies, including Bassett-
Lowke, bought the tooling for use
in their production. Pre-WWI
Carette parts are therefore often
found on post-war trains, but they
will always carry different
lithography. Bassett-Lowke made
good use of the stock sold off by
Carette; their 1921 Peckett
Southern Tank locomotive is
strikingly similar to Carette's
1907 model.

• **Own models** As larger gauges
became less popular, so the
company developed their own new
models, among the most successful
of which were the live steam 2-6-0
Mogul locomotives (see p.192),
introduced in 1925 in the livery of
all four companies.
• **The Flying Scotsman** The most
admired however of all Bassett-
Lowke trains of the inter-war
period was, however, the Flying
Scotsman, pictured overleaf on
p.50, which was designed by the
managing director of the firm,
Robert Bindon-Blood in 1933. It is
a highly accurate version of the real
train and has an "0" Gauge
locomotive, an electric mechanism,
and pulls a rake of scale-length
coaches designed by Edward
Exley. Its overall appearance is
much finer than that of competing
models and it remained in
production well into the 1950s.
It is still sought after today
by collectors.

TRIX

Bing did not survive the economic
problems of the depression era and
went out of business in 1933.
Bassett-Lowke was forced to look
for other suppliers and turned
briefly to Märklin, who produced
four locomotives for the firm,
including the last "0" Gauge
locomotives to be produced in
Germany for the British market.
After the closure of Bing, Stefan
and Franz Bing, together with
Oppenheimer Erlanger, opened a
new toy company, named Trix.
After the Bing family fled to
England, Bassett-Lowke helped
them to develop a Trix range.
• **Known for** One of the most
celebrated locomotives produced
was a "Princess" Princess Royal
Class locomotive with a diecast
body and tender. Trix modelled the
stock of all of the major railway
companies except for the Great
Western Railway. Southern Railway
stock from this period is especially
sought after and one of the rarest
pieces is the boxed set Southern
Railway EMU (Electric Multiple
Unit).
• **Identifying** All Trix locomotive
bodies and chassis were made of
mazac (see p.12–13). Pre-war
rolling stock is distinguished by
their diecast hook coupling and

bent wire eye (which is often missing).

POST-WWII
Post-WWII the production of unique locomotives, ships, and display models made to order, thrived. Rail production was split between the lithographed tinplate range produced by Winteringham and the high quality hand-built locomotives designed and made by the freelance engineers Victor Hunt and Victor Reader.

• **Collecting** The hand-built locomotives are much sought after today, the lithographed tinplate range less so. The budget end of the market was catered for from 1951 onwards by the "Prince Charles" locomotive, which was produced in a range of liveries. Bassett-Lowke ceased trading in 1969 but has been revived.

Bing

Bing reached the peak of their rivalry with Märklin at the beginning of the 20thC. Since the latter were dominating the top end of the market, Bing decided to concentrate on mass-production. Production methods used folded lithographed tinplate sheets with some hand painting added later. Mechanization and modern production methods enabled them to produce a wide range of trains and other German makers such as Carette, Karl Bub, and Kraus copied Bing's methods. Bing's products varied greatly in price and quality, from lithographed tinplate clockwork "starter" kits to expensive, large, and high-quality Gauge III and IV locomotives. In 1901, Bing began production of the "Black Prince" range for Bassett-Lowke (see p. 49), but continued to make trains under its own name. Bing's flexible production methods made it easy for them to adapt their trains for overseas markets. As well as the important British market, Bing also managed to break into the American market where their trains enjoyed success largely because of their superior quality when compared with toy trains manufactured in the United States.

Key features
- Lighter construction and more realistic modelling than Märklin trains
- Top of the range were hand-painted models, while the cheaper ones were lithographed
- Trains were marked with a Bing maker's plate
- Paint is thinly, but finely applied
- Liveries were crisply lined in red, green, or black

POST-WWI
After WWI, Bing simplified its line, and the top quality trains became less expensive. Quality generally declined during the 1920s.
- **Nationalization** In 1923, Britain's railway companies were merged into four companies, namely Great Western Railway

(GWR), London Midland & Scottish (LMS), London and North Eastern Railway (LNER), and Southern Railway (SR), and makers such as Bing had to adapt their ranges to the new liveries. The locomotive pictured (p.50) demonstrates the transition. The tank locomotive is a continuation of a pre war model, which continued well after WWI.
- **Bing for Bassett-Lowke** Bing had produced a range of coaches for Bassett-Lowke in high quality lithographed tinplate, known as "1921 stock". The events of 1923 made them obsolete therefore modifications would be made at the factory. For example, pieces are found such as a Great Western coach which has been partly factory hand-painted over the original livery on the sides and the roof, but the end sections left untouched. Coaches of this period

in good condition are rare.
- **"Freelance locomotives"** Bing produced their own range of "freelance" locomotives, loosely modelled on contemporary British 4-4-0 locomotives with the same body shell in the different liveries of the railway companies. One of the most valuable in this series is the Southern Railways "King Arthur".
- **Accessories** Bing also produced a range of tinplate accessories including platform lamps and station destination indicators, specifically for the British market.
- **Collecting** Bing produced a wider range of models than Märklin and examples, especially of the less expensive models, are easier to find. They are generally less expensive today than Märklin trains; those made after the 1920s are especially affordable.

Märklin

Märklin trains have the highest status in toy collecting and they are among the most valuable. The early 1900s marked the first "Golden Age" of Märklin trains. Their products became increasingly realistic and were characterized by a distinctive, heavy style with a superb, thickly lacquered finish. Märklin made an unrivalled range of rolling stock and accessories, from ornate station buildings to signals and lamps. Märklin had introduced a standardized system of gauges in 1891 and made a number of Gauge III

locomotives, but from around 1910 there was already a growing demand for smaller, Gauge I (see p.51 top, c.1910) and "0" Gauge models. In that year, the London toy store Gamages stopped accepting Gauge III trains; the store took a large proportion of Märklin's export production. Locomotives were powered by clockwork, live steam, or electricity – the latter two were potentially dangerous. Some early steam models were only briefly in production partly because of this and therefore they can be valuable.

EXPORT MARKETS
Märklin trains were exported to several countries including the United States and Britain. Trains destined for the United States were much the same as those for Germany with only slight modifications, such as the addition of a cowcatcher.

- **Liveries** All the major British rail companies were represented by Märklin, with some companies modelled more frequently.
- **Rarities** A good example of Märklin's production for the British market is pictured p.52 (bottom). The live steam "0" Gauge 0-4-0 tank locomotive, c.1905, is in the

rarely seen dark blue livery of the Great Eastern Railway and is much sought after. Although it has only four wheels, it represents the "Decapod" 10-wheel Great Eastern tank locomotive.

POST-WWI
Early trains of the post-WWI period

still had the feel of the pre-war trains with heavy detailing in the tinplate construction, the lining, and the painted features. The early 1920s paint finish usually has a sticky feel typical of pre-war finishes and tends to craze with age. By the 1930s, paint was thinner and more smoothly applied.

INTER-WAR PRODUCTION

Products of the inter-war years included a range of models for the British market, based on trains from the LNER, LMS, Southern, and GWR companies. They are popular with collectors today, largely because of the quality of the lacquer, which is finely applied and very smooth, but they are hard to find in good condition.
• **Quality** By 1937, Märklin's trains were so detailed that they were more like models than toys. The Swiss-outline Gauge I "Crocodile" locomotive, p.53 top, is a good example. It also shows the specialization of production, as few people could have afforded it at the time.
   A more affordable "H0" Gauge version was produced after WWII

Not all of the firm's trains were of such a high standard; Märklin's version of the "Flying Scotsman" had a German outline cab and grafted-on firebox sides.
• **Collecting** In 1933, Märklin produced a range of six and eight-coupled trains based on contemporary locomotives from around the world. The most popular with collectors today are the black and green versions of the British London and North Eastern Railway "Cock o' the North", which was made 1935–37.
• **Accessories** These were generally plainer at this time, but Märklin did produce large composite buildings.

POST-WAR PRODUCTION

After WWII, Märklin initially continued to make products in the same style as before, but in 1948 the firm changed the scale from "00" to "H0" Gauge, giving a more realistic appearance and rendering their locomotives narrower in relation to their length. In the late 1940s and early 50s, more detailed diecast bodies were introduced and the trains were displayed in strong cardboard boxes with wooden packing pieces.
• **"Triebwagen"** Some of the most sought-after diecast sets of the early 50s include diesel or electric "triebwagen" (express railcar units), such as the ST 800. The bogies were connected to the motor by a series of wormed gears, making them fast and powerful.
• **Plastic** In 1956, plastic was introduced to the tenders and by the late 1960s, metal bodies were used only for special series, such as the Hamo range of locomotives.

COLLECTING

• Collectors are only interested in Märklin pieces in the best condition or particularly rare issues.
• Märklin have always marketed their toys as premium products which were, and still are, expensive to buy new. Therefore they are likely to hold their value.

Key features
• Early trains used a tin loop coupling; from 1904–9 onwards they had a hook and, between 1913 and 1954, they used a sliding drop link
• Pieces from the 1920s are generally less valuable, apart from large Gauge I and "0" Gauge trains
• Post-WWII models have a slightly flatter, less varnished finish
• Dedicated collectors are only interested in pieces in fine condition or which are particularly rare

Hornby

Frank Hornby enjoyed huge success in the toy market with his Meccano construction kits, which had first appeared as "Mechanics Made Easy" in 1901. In June 1920, he entered the model railway market, selling his trains under the slogan "British Toys for British Boys" to capitalize on the patriotic sentiments of the time. The first sets were sturdy, ran on clockwork, and were very toy-like with thin bodies, brass buffers and coupling hooks, and thick-plated wheels and axles. They had no identifying livery. From 1923, more realistic designs were introduced, including a version of the Flying Scotsman, made in 1927. Frank Hornby was not overly concerned with realism however, and this model compresses the 4-6-2 wheel arrangement to fit Hornby's No. II 4-4-0 mechanism. The early models do retain some nice details which are lost later on.

• **Rarities** One of the rarest and most sought-after items made by Hornby during this period is the first issue from the series of Private Owner Vans, which were made until 1941. Produced only between 1923 and 1924, the rare Colman's Mustard van (see p.195) has several typical early features. It has second-type nickel-plated wheels with thin axles and a second-type chassis with pierced axle guards. The supports for the first, thick-axle type were completely solid and were used between 1920 and 1922; the second type was used between 1922 and 1930.
• **Packaging** Hornby products were packed in sturdy, printed cardboard boxes, which were initially plain brown but were later coloured. From 1937, boxes carried date codes and the lettering was changed to a sans serif typeface that was used until the 1950s. Boxes add considerably to value.
• **Snow plough** One of Hornby's most popular products, this was first made in 1924 and became plainer and simpler over the years but the one shown on p.54, made c.1928–30, has several features that were later dropped – a muted colour scheme (after 1933 it was blue and yellow), sliding doors, pierced axle guards, and a lantern.

• **Electric models** Early electric models had a potentially dangerous high voltage mechanism, but later models were safer.
• **Inter-war period** Between the wars when "0" Gauge was most popular, Hornby dominated the toy train market in Britain. Their star locomotive, the "Princess Elizabeth", introduced in 1937 at £5.5.0 with presentation case, is now worth around £2,500 ($4,000) in really nice condition.

HORNBY-DUBLO
In 1938, Hornby launched its successful "Hornby-Dublo" range, to compete with the "00" Gauge

Key features

• Pre-war Hornby-Dublo trains are prone to metal fatigue, which particularly affects the wheels and bogies
• Clockwork trains were made as a cheaper alternative to electric power, but clockwork production stopped in 1941, so they are at a premium today
• Pre-war Hornby-Dublo trains have pale blue boxes with date codes (but a few were issued in 1946 in pre-war boxes)
• Pre-war sets have a horizontal hook and eye coupling made of blued steel
• The post-war coupling is known as a Peco coupling and has vertical bent hooks
• Pre-war sets were only available in landscape format boxes, following the style of Trix. Post-war boxes were made in different shapes
• Of the post-war production, sets in the Southern Railways livery are the most popular with collectors

sets of firms such as Märklin. Of superior quality, they were well designed and had detailed diecast bodies.

• **Technical innovations** These included an efficient permanent magnet mechanism, which enabled the trains to change direction without the need to change the motor polarity and without mechanical switching.

• **Pre-WWII** Hornby-Dublo trains from before WWII are difficult to find and can be easily distinguished from later versions by the features listed on the left.

POST-WWII PRODUCTION

In 1953 Hornby nationalized the liveries of their trains with positive results. The mid-1950s was the

most productive period for Hornby, which produced quality tinplate freight stock, coaches, and locomotives in large numbers.

• **Collectibility** Of this period, Southern Railway trains are the most popular today with collectors.

• **Notable models** From 1957, Hornby began to upgrade and replace their range. Models from this time include the "Dorchester" and "Ludlow Castle" locomotives.

DECLINE

Meccano was taken over by Triang in 1964. Although production of a few plastic accessories continued for a brief period under the name Triang-Hornby, they were not of the same quality as before and the range was discontinued.

COLLECTING

• With many minor livery and casting variations, early post-war Hornby-Dublo trains and accessories are the most interesting to collect.
• It is difficult to find these pieces in pristine condition and these items often suffer from metal fatigue.

Tri-ang

In 1950 a Surrey-based plastic company named Rovex launched a range of inexpensive toys and electric railways. They soon became a rival to makers such as Hornby and Trix. Its products had the advantage that, unlike Hornby's products of the time, its track had no third rail, and they were also keenly priced. In 1951, the firm was absorbed into the Lines Brothers' Tri-ang firm.

TT RANGE
In 1959, the company introduced the TT miniature range of trains to try to develop the market. Of similar appearance to "00" Gauge trains but smaller, the range was never sufficiently developed to satisfy demand and production ceased in 1967. Tri-ang sets did not have the same quality as Hornby-Dublo, but they were less expensive and had many interesting features. If you are collecting the TT range always bear in mind the following:
• **Incomplete sets** These should be avoided as they are far less collectible.
• **Popular products** These included the "Minic Motorway" and locomotives such as the long-running "Princess Elizabeth" and the Pullman car set.
• **Other products** These included wagons that exploded, flying helicopters, battle wagons, and a "00" scale electric slot-car system.

TRI-ANG-HORNBY PERIOD
When Tri-ang took over Hornby in 1964, almost all of the dies, locomotives, and stock were passed to G. & R. Wrenn, which continued to make collectors' versions of Hornby-Dublo until 1993. Among the few items Tri-ang used from Hornby was the tooling for a station kit (see below), but the station's colour was changed from sand to red. These are rare as they were only produced in 1964. It is interesting to note that the box carries a Hornby-Dublo reference number
• **Other collectibles** From the Tri-ang-Hornby period (1964–71) look for Stephenson's Rocket, the Great Western Railway "Lord of the Isles" locomotive, and the Battle of Britain Class "Sir Winston Churchill".

RINGFIELD MOTOR
• One of the finest locomotives made by Tri-ang-Hornby, the "Evening Star" was also one of the last. It used the powerful Ringfield Motor, inherited from Hornby, which was housed inside the tender, allowing for more detailed modelling of the locomotive. The Evening Star was the last steam locomotive to be built by British Rail.

COLLECTING
Tri-ang offers many opportunities for the collector, since their trains are less expensive than most. It is important that they are in good condition and have the original box. Most items from the early period are not particularly collectible as yet, apart from a few pieces of British Rail Southern Region stock.

State of the market

Top end Pre-WWI trains are becoming harder to find – good examples by Bing, Carette, and especially Märklin are currently making good prices. An LNWR black steam tank engine from 1905 in gauge III by Bing for Bassett-Lowke recently sold at auction for £4,400 / €6,250 / $7,300, whilst a Gauge III Märklin 4-4-0 steam locomotive with matching coaches, again from 1905, sold for £22,000 / €31,250 / $36,500.

• Trains by Märklin, in all gauges, have appeal for collectors worldwide and when it comes to prices, they are in a league of their own.

• The market for pre-war Hornby "0" Gauge trains is very strong in Britain and items in top condition are currently making high prices. Often it is the accessory items that are most surprising. Recently an electrically lit boxed Signal Gantry sold for £3,200 / €4,550 /$5,300, and an electrically-lit boxed Water Tower made £2,750./ €3,900 / $4,565.

• The most prolific Bassett-Lowke locomotive of all was the "'Duke of York" which was available free in 1927 by saving BDV cigarette coupons. As something like 100,000 of these models were made, there was certainly plenty of smoking done! This locomotive is worth around £180 / €255 / $300, but the larger Bassett-Lowke locomotives, which were often produced in very small numbers, are a different story and a rare boxed "Arsenal" sold recently at auction for £9,700 /€13,800 /$16,100.

Going up: Hornby-Dublo and Wrenn Railways

• **Hornby-Dublo** Many collectors are wanting "00" gauge trains and prices for three-rail Hornby-Dublo items have surged ahead in the last two years.

• **Wrenn Railways** These models have also increased greatly in value since the demise of the original company in 1992. The more usual Wrenn locomotives such as "Cardiff Castle" are worth around £100 / €142 /$166, whilst some rarer models can make much more, such as an "Exeter" at £900 / €1,278 / $1,495 and a "Silver Jubilee" Tank from 1977 which made a staggering £3,000 / €4,260 / $4,980 at auction.

COLLECTING

• With more collectors seeking toy trains, either through specialist auctions, specialist fairs, or the Internet, the demand is high, but the most important factor affecting the value of a model (as with the majority of collectibles) will probably be its condition. A near perfect item with original box will often be worth twice the price, and perhaps much more, than one in lesser condition, and this price divide is ever widening. For example a Hornby Dublo 'Duchess of Montrose', worth around £50 / €70 / $80 in average condition, sold recently at auction in perfect order with all it's original box packaging for £520 / €740 / $865.

Toy Train Gauges

The gauge of a train is the term used to describe the scale to which the locomotive is made. It is measured from wheel centre to wheel centre. This table shows the different measurements of gauges.

All makers	00/H0 Gauge	⅝in (16.5mm)
All makers	Gauge 0	1⅜in (35mm)
All makers	Gauge I	1⅞in (48mm)
All makers	Gauge II	2⅛in (54mm)
All makers	Standard Gauge	2⅛in (54mm)
Bassett-Lowke	Gauge III	2⅝in (67mm)
Bing		
Carette		
Märklin	Gauge III	3in (75mm)
Schönner	Gauge III	
Bassett-Lowke	Gauge IV	
Bing	Gauge IV	

Sci-Fi

Science fiction as we understand it dates back to the 19thC novels of H. G. Wells and Jules Verne, or even perhaps to Mary Shelley's *Frankenstein*. It was not until the 1920s that Hugo Gernsbach, editor of *Amazing Stories*, coined the term "science fiction". During the 1920s, 30s and 40s, interest in science fiction was fed by so-called "pulp fiction" novels and comics, as well as movie serials such as *Buck Rogers* and *Flash Gordon*. While there are some toys from this pre-war era, science fiction and the toys that went with it did not really take off until after WWII, encouraged by new technology and the dawn of the space age and the race to the moon.

JAPAN

Many space toys of the 50s, such as robots, tinplate spaceships, and ray guns, were made in Japan. This was partly because of favourable trade agreements designed to help that country to rebuild its economy after WWII.

• Well-known Japanese makers to look out for include Yonezawa, Nomura, Horikawa, and Masudaya (see p.208). The latter usually marked their toys with an MT monogram (this stood for "Modern Toys").

• While Japan was the major centre of production, the United States was the most important market. The American company Cragstan often imported Japanese toys and sold them under its own label.

Many science fiction and space-related toys were not made to represent any particular craft or fictional character, but others were. Inspiration came from a multitude of comic strips, TV shows, and films from the British space hero Dan Dare in the 50s (see p.208) to *Thunderbirds* in the 60s to the latest *Star Wars* films. Toys based on characters from sci-fi films and TV series dominate this area of the toy market today. As science fiction became science fact, so toys and models based on real-life craft became popular from the first satellite, the Sputnik, to the craft in which the crew of Apollo 11 first landed on the moon. Sci-fi themes can be found in many different toys.

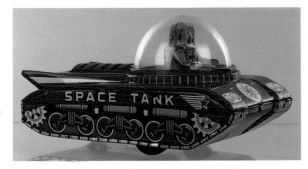

Space Toys

Most space toys of the 1950s and 60s are fantasy creations owing much to science fiction rather than models based on reality; the space age was still in its infancy. Japanese makers dominated the market with tinplate rocket ships, flying saucers, and interplanetary vehicles of all kinds (see pp.208–210). The more elaborate, imaginative and colourful the craft, the more desirable it is to collectors today.

MECHANISMS

The mechanisms of most space toys are not as complex as those found in robots. The "Space Giant" flying saucer by Masudaya (pictured overleaf on p.58) is a battery-powered inter-planetary space craft, possibly heading for Saturn (this planet is depicted on the tail) It moves along the floor using a mystery action device. This is a gyroscopic wheel underneath the toy, which allows it to move for a short distance before automatically changing direction. Many vehicles, battery or friction powered, had a similar movement. The "Space Tank" (above) from the late 1950s

has a similar movement to the Space Giant but is friction-powered.

• **NASA** As the space race developed, space toys responded accordingly. Some toys bore the name of NASA, America's National Aeronautics and Space Administration, although the designs were fantastic and bore no resemblance to contemporary space vehicles.

• **"American Eagle"** As time went by, so space toys became more realistic, some being modelled directly on craft such as the Eagle Lunar Module, which took the crew of Apollo 11 to the moon in 1969. Popularly known as the "American Eagle", the toy's full title is "No.8011 NASA Apollo II American Eagle Lunar Module". The toy (see left) is capable of seven complicated actions: an automatic open and shut hatch, flashing lights, revolving antennae, and even "lunar sound". However the design, technical accuracy, and style of the box means it would originally have appealed more to adults than children as it's more akin to a scientific model. Although these toys may be more realistic, they are not as popular with collectors, who prefer the fantasy of the earlier craft.

Robots

The use of the word "robot" to describe a machine capable of handling human tasks dates back to Karel Capek's 1922 play *Rossum's Universal Robots*. Toy robots are a post-WWII phenomenon, prompted by the booming interest in space and science fiction as the "final frontiers" of space were broken down by advances in technology.

THE FIRST ROBOTS
Early robots of the 1940s are small and have simple clockwork mechanisms. Tinplate was the preferred material for early robots, but clockwork and tinplate gradually gave way to battery power and plastic construction. Some robots were made in both clockwork and battery-powered versions.

• **"Robbie"** One of the most famous robots is Robbie, based on a character from the 1956 film *Forbidden Planet*. Various versions were produced; the one shown here, by Nomura, c.1956, is of tinplate and is battery-powered (the batteries are housed inside the legs). It is in good condition, but the plastic dome is prone to cracking, which lowers the value.

• **Other models** Some robots were designed with a friendly appearance, but others were more aggressive, sporting an array of weapons. These became even more sophisticated, as typified by the "Rotate-O-Matic Super Astronaut" (see opposite page and p.212) made by Horika (founded in 1959). This robot walks, stops, rotates, and opens its chest compartment to reveal a gun that fires.

• **Astronauts** They perform similar actions to robots but they show a human face beneath the helmet. Some models are desirable, but they are generally less popular.

• **Reproductions** Robots are so popular that reproductions of classic designs are being made, often as limited edition collectibles. Look for modern parts in remote control units and differing lithographic print quality. If the feet show evidence of tampering, this could be a sign that a modern limited edition number has been removed.

TRANSFORMERS
These successful plastic toys (see pp.213–214) which converted from robots into vehicles were launched by Hasbro in 1984, and are now becoming increasingly collectible. Although toys were retailed across the world, some objects were only produced for a particular market and as always, enthusiasts look and pay for rarities.

Collecting

• Robots were easily damaged as many were top-heavy and tended to fall over so check them carefully
• Condition is always important, but damaged robots are sometimes bought for spares
• Check for rust on tinplate models
• Check battery compartments for signs of damage from leaking batteries
• Switch on your robots, even if only briefly, every so often to prevent the motor from seizing up
• Keep robots away from dust, which can get into the mechanism

Thunderbirds

Gerry Anderson made numerous puppet series for British television from the 1950s onwards and many of them became major international hits. The biggest of them all was *Thunderbirds*, the story of International Rescue, an organization formed by a philanthropic family that carried out rescue missions using an array of hi-tech craft.

DIECASTS
Many toys based on the vehicles in the show were made, including plastic toys by Lincoln Inc. and Rosenthal.

• **Thunderbird 2** Made by Dinky, this is the most famous toy of all. The workhorse of the show (pictured overleaf p.60) was made in a green diecast version from 1967 (no.101 in the firm's catalogue). A later version (106) was made in 1973 in a metallic blue colour. The 101 version is not only in the correct colour for the actual vehicle, but was also the first and is more desirable. All versions have spring-loaded, extending legs, and a detachable pod with a small Thunderbird 4 craft (a miniature submarine) contained inside.

• **FAB1** Dinky also made FAB1, a diecast version of the pink Rolls-Royce used by International Rescue's London agent Lady Penelope. It has a sliding canopy with a large missile firing from behind a radiator grille, and rear firing harpoons.

• **Packaging** The Dinky *Thunderbirds* toys are well made, but the packaging is not that strong so boxes in good condition add considerably to the value.

• **Thunderbird 5** Rosenthal's *Thunderbirds* toys included a model of the space station Thunderbird 5 (see p.215). This plastic model recalls the tinplate flying saucers of the 50s in its style rather than being a strictly accurate representation. The same firm made a plastic battery powered remote control Thunderbird 1.

• **Other toys** Toys of all of the Thunderbird craft were made, as were puppets and dolls of the main characters, playsuits so that children could dress up as their heroes, and various books and games. Records of the music from the series were also released. (See pp.215–216 and p.250.)

COLLECTING

Thunderbirds has a very loyal following both from original devotees of the progamme, now adults, and new fans who have been captured by the re-runs of this cult show. The range of toys and other collectibles relating to the programme is vast which makes it an ideal collecting area.

Dr. Who

Dr. Who, the story of a mysterious traveller in time and space, first hit British TV screens in November 1963. The show ran for more than 25 years and is now due for a revival. It has been sold to many countries around the world and has a global fan base.

DALEKS

The most desirable of all the collectibles are the toys based on the main villains, the Daleks. Versions have been made by various firms including Mego, Tomy, and Palitoy. Talking versions made by Marx in the 1960s are among the most sought after – generally speaking, the earlier they were made, the better. Palitoy also made a talking Dalek in the 1970s and this is also very collectible. Dalek toys often have a missing weapon or eyepiece; this will affect value.

• **K9** Palitoy also made a toy version of K-9, the Doctor's robotic canine companion. It was designed to speak with the aid of a small disk, like a record, that could be turned over for more phrases.

THE DOCTOR

Of the various actors who played

Packaging

Whatever the toy, boxes are always important for two reasons: firstly, a toy is more likely to be in good condition if it has been kept in its box and secondly, the box can provide important information about the maker. This is useful because it can sometimes be difficult to identify the makers of sci-fi toys of the 50s, as they were not always marked. However, while it is preferable to know something of the manufacturers, toys from unidentified makers can still be collectible, especially if they are interesting or unusual. (See p.15.)

the Doctor, Tom Baker is one of the most popular and action figures of his incarnation of the character are very popular (see right).

• **Tom Baker** A version by Harbert Toys for the Italian market is well known and demonstrates the international popularity of the series. He should come complete with his scarf and hat to achieve

maximum value for collectors.

• **Later figures** In the 80s, Dapol made a series of figures to complement the series. These are collectible but still affordable, today.

• **Other characters** Villains such as the Cybermen were also made, as were figures of his assistants. These figures sometimes have variations, which make them more desirable. For example, the figure of Mel, played by Bonnie Langford, was made with a pink and a blue blouse. The pink version is slightly more valuable. (See p.217.)

• **Rarities** These include an anti-dalek jet immobiliser, made by Lincoln International of Hong Kong in the 1960s.

SCI-FI

Star Trek

There can be few people who have never heard of *Star Trek*, such is its worldwide popularity. The programme was first shown in the 1960s, but was cancelled after just three seasons. A loyal and increasing fan base continued to enjoy the programme through repeat showings and in 1979 the first *Star Trek* film was released. More films, the *Next Generation* TV show and other new shows such as *Voyager, Deep Space Nine,* and *Enterprise* followed, each accompanied by a growing range of toys and merchandise. Fans flock to conventions all around the world.

ACTION FIGURES

Among the most commonly traded items are the action figures, the first of which were made by Mego in 1974 for the now largely forgotten animated series. (See pp.218–219.)

• **Early figures** The first ones can be recognized by the fact that there are five characters on the packaging – the figure of Lt. Uhura was added to make six in the set. Some characters, such as Kirk (below), were produced in large numbers, Iso they are usually worth less than McCoy or Scottie (see p.218).

• **Other characters** More characters were later added to the series and the rarer aliens, such as

the Andorian or Romulan, issued in 1976, are especially valuable.

• **Cheron** There is a potential problem with the figure of Cheron, a half black, half white alien from the classic episode "Let That Be Your Last Battlefield". A type of bacteria thrives on the dyes in the plastic, making the figure appear disfigured. This can affect even those that have never been opened.

• **Limited edition figures** Action figures are still being made and as there have been so many series there are many to choose from. In recent years, there have been attempts to stimulate the market by issuing limited edition figures. These have met with some success as with the figure of Lt. Reginald Barclay, issued by the manufacturer Playmates in an edition of just 3,000. It is worth ten times as much as a more common figure.

• **Packaging** Action figures should ideally be in their original unopened packaging, or "carded" as collectors say. Always check the packaging to

see if it has been opened. If it has, a reputable dealer should adjust the price accordingly. Loose figures can still be worth collecting, but they are not nearly as desirable or valuable. Figures should also come complete with any accessories – this is why carded figures are more desirable, since the accessories are more likely to be with the figure.

• **Diecasts** In the 70s, Dinky issued diecast versions of the *Star Trek* vessels from the original series. The USS Enterprise and a Klingon vessel were made and a gift set offered both. The ships could fire plastic discs, which should be present and they should be in their original boxes.

• **Trade Cards** Many varieties are available. (See pp.250–253.)

Star Wars

Star Wars is credited with having changed the action figure market forever. Figures introduced for the film in 1977 were smaller than had been the norm so that they could fit into the accompanying range of spacecraft. They also came with moulded-on clothing. The collectors market has been fuelled by the movie sequels which have sustained interest and brought new collectors into the fold. Like *Star Trek, Star Wars* is a huge collecting field with lots of opportunities and a global fan base.

but a few had vinyl ones instead and these are much more valuable. It is not difficult to add a vinyl cape to a loose figure, so beware.

VEHICLES
Like the figures, *Star Wars* vehicles were made by Kenner in the United States and by Palitoy in Britain and what is rare in one country might be more common in the other.
• **Variations** There are differences between some of these models, such as Luke Skywalker's Land Speeder. In the original issue of these toys, the bonnet opens on the Kenner version, but not on the Palitoy one. Early Kenner versions can be recognized because they have an "LP" logo (for long play) on the box; this logo was removed in 1979.

AT-AT
The most impressive *Star Wars* toys included Han Solo's ship the Millennium Falcon and the AT-AT (All Terrain Armoured Transport). The battery-operated Millennium Falcon was issued in a variety of packaging and examples are not hard to find, but they are rarely in mint condition. The ship itself remained much the same in spite of the packaging changes and it is important that all the hatches and other gadgets work.
• **Early versions** The AT-AT first appeared in *The Empire Strikes Back*

ACTION FIGURES
• **First series** Figures from the first series are usually the most valuable. The first 12 figures produced bore images of the 12 characters on the back of the card that formed the packaging and these figures are therefore known as "12-backs".
• **Additional characters** The addition of further characters created "20 backs" and so on.
• **Boba Fett** The addition of bounty hunter Boba Fett created the "21 back" and these original figures are desirable. (See pp.221–222.) More desirable still is a 12-inch (30cm) rocket-firing pre-production Boba Fett. It was not put into production after failing safety tests, but some are on the market today.
• **Variations** European editions of *Star Wars* figures may be hard to find in the United States and vice versa, so value can depend on where they are sold. Sometimes, production runs included variations or errors, which make them worth more.
• **Modified figures** Some *Star Wars* figures have been modified to enhance their value. Jawa figures are a good example of this, as they were mostly made with cloth capes,

and the toy version can hold up to a dozen action figures – two in the cockpit and ten inside the body. They were expensive at the time, so they were made in fewer numbers and therefore are rarer today.
• **Early versions** Palitoy made a version to accompany *The Empire*

Strikes Back (1981) where it first appeared (pictured above and see p.222). Hasbro's 1990s version used the same moulds but various modfications were made to differentiate.
• **Mini-rigs** Smaller vehicles, known as "mini-rigs" were also made, including the AST-5 (AST stands for Armoured Sentinel Transport). The AST-5 was first issued in 1983 and was re-released in 1984. The earlier versions show six vehicles on the packaging but the re-release shows only four.

OTHER COLLECTIBLES
There is a vast array of *Star Wars* items (see pp.220–227) including replica models such as the 2002 Hans Solo blaster pictured here.

Alien

Alien was one of the big movie hits of 1979 and has since spawned three sequels. Toys and action figures based on the film were slow to emerge. This is possibly because it was an X-rated (18) film so children could not see it and the collectors' market for adults was still developing. Kenner did plan a line of 3½in (9cm) figures for the film but they were never issued. An 18in (45cm) figure was briefly released and is much in demand today. The first proper figures came out in the 80s, based on the first sequel and on the *Alien* comic books produced by Dark Horse. Between 1992 and 1998, Kenner made more *Alien* figures (see p.227), including a 12 in (30cm) Alien/Corporal Hicks figure (right). This was made in a limited edition of 25,000.

State of the market

• **Going down:** The last couple of years have seen a drop in the value of the original sci-fi collectible great – *Star Wars* – as it has been usurped by its fantasy film competitor – *Lord of the Rings* – as the collectible of the moment. Other sci-fi collectible staples such as *Star Trek* and *Doctor Who* have suffered as well, although *Alien* and *Predator* seem to have weathered the storm.
• The call for Japanese collectibles has dropped off recently, gone are the days of new sci-fi collectibles coming out of the East and instantly fetching a premium, although a lot of the Japanese traffic is being directed straight to the United States.
• Increased availability of collectibles via the Internet has created a larger audience and some of those will become future collectors for older sci-fi collectibles – so hold on to those older, rarer figures, kits, and toys. It also means bargains can sometimes be found. However increased availability also means resultant drop in value

• Collectors should be aware that merchand is from the *Lord of the Rings* trilogy has been mass-produced and therefore is unlikely to become collectible.

• **Going up:** Many collectors are moving away from figures, toys, and kits to autographs and specifically autograph fairs. This may raise authenticity issues in the future and has helped towards the drop in price of other types of collectibles.
• The United States still proves to have the biggest appetite (and wallet) for sci-fi collectibles and easier Internet access has certainly increased the flow back across the Atlantic with the rare kits, figures, and comics all seeming to be in demand.
• There seems to have been an increase in traffic within Europe, with both French and German collectors looking to tap into the market more – this too has been catalysed by the Internet.

Characters

Toys based on distinctive characters, such as those from films, television shows, or comic books represent a large and growing part of the toy market. They are by no means a new phenomenon, since games based on Beatrix Potter creations have been around since the early 20thC, while Disney collectibles have been around since the creation of Mickey Mouse in 1928 and early examples from 1928–38 are highly sought after. Collectors of character toys are very loyal and dedicated and will often try to acquire anything to do with their favourites, however they are still discerning and they are often among the most knowledgeable and demanding of toy collectors. The value and desirability of these toys can fluctuate according to the popularity of the character.

Batman

Batman was originally a comic-book hero, making his debut in DC Comics in 1939. While he was always a popular character in the comics, it was through the tongue-in-cheek TV series in the 1960s that he achieved worldwide popularity. Toys and merchandise of all kinds followed in its wake; rare items include a walking, inflatable Batman by Louis Marx. Playsuits are also collectible since they are rare survivors because of the stress of being worn and played in.

THE BATMOBILE

Mego produced a range of collectible action figures but it is Batman's car, the Batmobile that was perhaps the most popular of Batman toys. It was based on the Lincoln Futura, a concept car that appeared at the Detroit Motor Show in 1955.

• **Japanese versions** In the 60s, the Japanese firm Aoshin made at least three different tinplate versions, with friction or battery power, which did not necessarily resemble the actual vehicle in styling and/or colour. Nevertheless, they are very valuable today.

• **Other versions** Several companies made Batmobiles, including Mego, who made a plastic version of the Batmobile in 1974. While it is collectible, Mego's version is neither as realistic nor as valuable as the Batmobiles made by Corgi, pictured, a few years earlier. The most sought-after Corgi version has red tyres instead of the usual black ones.

In the late 1980s, Batman was revived on the big screen in the first of four outings and a new wave of toys and collectibles followed (see p.250 for Trade Cards). He also returned to the small screen in the early 1990s with an animated series and yet more toys were produced for this new show. Kenner's Robin's dragster is the rarest of toys from this series, since the moulds were destroyed in a factory fire.

James Bond

The adventures of secret agent James Bond, codenamed 007, have thrilled cinema audiences since *Dr. No* hit the screens back in 1962. The longevity of the series has kept alive a popular collectibles market, particularly as the series of films continues to this day always gathering new fans. They have inspired a multitude of related toys.

ASTON MARTIN DB5

Perhaps the best-known of all is the Corgi Aston Martin DB5 (pictured), which was packed with features to emulate those of Bond's car in the film *Goldfinger*. These included a front machine gun, a rear bullet-proof shield, and an operating ejector seat. It became one of the most popular toys ever made, selling nearly three million.

• **Rarities** The rarest version is a revised 1968 model, which is slightly larger and painted silver instead of gold. It has extra features including rotating number plates and telescopic tyre slashers; it is worth three times as much as the gold version.

• **Unlicensed version** This DB5 model, which avoided the use of Bond's name and was labelled "secret agent" to avoid legal problems, was produced by Hong Kong firm Lincoln International in the 1960s. Unlicensed toys based on the character are still collectible.

• **A. C. Gilbert** Many Bond-related items were made by this firm, including a battery powered Aston Martin and a rare James Bond spy watch. In 1965 the firm produced one of the most desirable of all Bond toys, an attaché case containing a gun and various accessories. Other Gilbert products from the 60s include an action figure of Bond (pictured), and another of the villain Oddjob – the latter is the more valuable.

James Bond toys continue to be made, many of them as limited edition collectibles. (See pp.237–238, and p.252 for a range of typical items.) With the Bond films set to continue for the foreseeable future, toys relating to the character are likely to remain in demand.

Masters of the Universe

He-Man and *Masters of the Universe* was created in the early 1980s when the United States repealed a 1969 law that prohibited TV programmes based on toys. Toy giant Mattel and Filmation Associates teamed up to produce the show, which became hugely popular. It established a trend for shows in which the merchandising became the motivating and most profitable factor. A film and a new TV series have sustained interest. However there is a difference in value between vintage and later items.

ACTION FIGURES

The extensive range of accompanying action figures (Skeletor is pictured overleaf) was made to a new size of 5½in (13cm) and set new standards in production.

• **Action features** The figures boasted "action features" (with transforming, moving parts). Many of these features are quite elaborate – the figure of Stonedar, for example, can be folded up into a rock, Mantenna has extending eyes, and Kobra Khan squirts water from his mouth. He-Man, the hero of the series, and Skeletor (overleaf), the arch villain, are the most commonly

comprised Man-at-Arms, Mer-Man, Stratos, Beast Man, Teela, and Zodac. These are known as "eight-back" figures because the eight in the series were illustrated on the back of the packaging.

• **Packaging** Figures in their packaging are worth considerably more than loose examples.

• **Range** More than 70 action figures were produced in all, along with dozens of vehicles and other accessories. (See pp.240–241.)

• **Gift sets** Many of the larger accessories, such as playsets etc. can be hard to find in good condition and fewer of them were made in the first place. Gift sets, featuring more than one character, can also be rare; an example is the gift set featuring Skeletor and Panthor, which is very hard to find.

found as they were made in large numbers.

• **Collectiblity** The most collectible figures are generally those from the first series issued in 1982 which, in addition to He-Man and Skeletor,

• **Variations** There are several variants that make the series more interesting to collect. Among the better known ones are Stratos with blue or red wings, and Rattlor with a neck that is red instead of yellow. Particularly rare variations include Scareglow with a glowing, instead of a green staff, and Beast Man with a green whip.

LATER FIGURES

A new series of figures was released in 2002 to accompany a new *Masters of the Universe* TV series. However, the characters and the figures have been redesigned so the new-look figures cannot be confused with vintage examples. As always doing your research can make a huge difference to spotting bargains.

Muppets

A Muppet is a combination of marionette and puppet (hence the name). They can be fairly simple to operate, but some of the more complex Muppets require more than one operator. Muppets were created by Jim

Henson and their earliest appearances date back to the 50s. In 1969, Muppets starred in the children's show *Sesame Street* and in 1975 Henson was signed up by TV mogul Lew Grade to create 24 new shows. The result was

The Muppet Show, which first aired in 1976 and developed a huge following in over 100 countries, leading to several films and animated spin-offs. All of these have spawned associated toys and collectible merchandise.

• **Manufacturers** Tomy, Palitoy, Corgi, Fisher-Price, and Ideal all have made Muppet-related items.

• **Early puppets** Among the earliest is a series of puppets made by Ideal in the 1960s. These included the character of Rowlf the dog.

• **Fisher Price** They made some of the best muppet dolls and puppets in the late 70s. Note that early examples of Fozzie Bear have a different shaped head than later ones; the character's head was redesigned after the first series.

• **Other collectible Muppets** Include those made by Bendy Toys in the late 70s. They were made in two sizes, 15in (38cm) and 8in (20cm). They are made of rubber, which can crack, and they are rarely found in their original packaging. Kermit is the most common, while the smaller Animal figure is rarest.

• **Corgi** In 1979, Corgi released four cars featuring Kermit, Miss Piggy, Fozzie, and Animal; these are all collectible today. They were re-released in 2002 with new paintwork and packaging.

My Little Pony

My Little Pony is a series of vinyl toy animals that was first introduced by Hasbro in 1983. They are fantasy ponies rather than realistic representations of animals. They have different names and characters and the colour of their bodies and the hair on their manes and tails varies accordingly. They were designed to be collected and are collectible today, but they are still affordable and are readily found at car boot sales and the like. Many different characters and colours have been issued and some were only sold in certain countries, so they are more sought after in countries where they were unavailable. The number of varieties provides scope for collectors. TV series and films accompanied the toys, encouraging sales.

• **Identifying** My Little Ponies are marked, usually on the hoof, with the name of the maker, Hasbro. This helps to distinguish them from other, similar toys that were made by other manufacturers in the wake of the Ponies' success.
• **Date** They also have a date,

which refers to the date of the introduction of the character. It is not necessarily an indication of the year in which the specific toy was made, so that a toy marked 1983 could have been made later.
• **Care** The vinyl from which they were made is fairly durable and not too difficult to clean up if they are dirty or have been defaced with ballpoint pen, or similar. The toys can fade if exposed to strong sunlight and the mane is especially vulnerable. Pink manes in particular have been known to turn white through such exposure.
• **Packaging** Items in their original packaging are always more desirable, but collectors will buy loose examples to fill gaps in their collections. Many collectors like to have ponies on display outside the box.

OTHER HASBRO PRODUCT

Hasbro made another range of ponies for the Cabbage Patch Kids collection and these are not to be confused with My Little Pony. They are slightly larger and have glittery bodies.

The My Little Pony range was withdrawn in the early 1990s, but in 2003 Hasbro launched a new line of these toys.

Noddy

Noddy was created by the celebrated children's author Enid Blyton. The first book based on the character, *Noddy Goes to Toyland*, was published in 1949 with illustrations by the Dutch artist Harmsen van der Beek. It was an instant success and the London *Evening Standard* soon commissioned a cartoon strip; a BBC TV series followed in 1954 and success was assured.

A vast array of toys, games, and other related merchandise quickly followed, produced by many different companies. Among them are Marx (see picture), Wade, Corgi, and Chad Valley; the latter made various items from glove puppets to spinning tops, and even a toy piano. Chad Valley also made bagatelle games, early versions of which are very collectible. Fairylite is another manufacturer whose products are especially desirable.

• **Morestone** From 1954–59, north London-based toy wholesalers Morris & Stone, using the brand name Morestone, produced a range of diecast cars, including a series of Noddy vehicles. These vehicles are popular with collectors, but are rarely found with their boxes.

• **Corgi** Between 1970–72, the diecast toy firm Corgi made a range of cars entitled Corgi Comics. These included vehicles driven by Basil Brush and characters from the *Magic Roundabout* as well as *Noddy*. Noddy's car was made in different versions, some with just Noddy and others with Noddy and Big Ears, Tubby, and Golly. There is a pre-production model featuring Golly with a white face, which is particularly sought after.

• **Characters** Over the years, the characters have been re-invented several times in response to accusations of racism, sexism, and general political incorrectness. The Golly characters were among the first to go and have since become collectible.

• **Wade figures** Ceramic figures made by Wade in the 1950s are also very desirable. This firm is still in business and has in recent years issued Noddy figures as limited edition collectibles.

Smurfs

Smurfs are small blue, troll-like creatures said to be "three apples high" created by the Belgian comic strip artist Pierre Culliford, better known as Peyo, in 1958. They were initially only secondary characters in a comic book, but soon became popular enough to become stars in their own right. Small plastic figures of the Smurfs, made by the Schleich company of Germany, and marked with the company name and country of origin, were first sold at petrol stations in the Netherlands in 1965.

It took time for Smurfs to spread around the world and they reached Britain in 1978. They were used to promote petrol stations as they had on the Continent and even enjoyed success in the pop charts. They reached America soon afterwards and Hanna-Barbera produced a cartoon series based on the characters.

MERCHANDISE

Smurf merchandise ranges from games to lunchboxes but the best-known toys are the Smurf figures themselves. Because so many Smurfs have been made over the years, there are many different variations and this appeals to collectors.

• **Versions** Some Smurfs were only produced in Europe and are eagerly sought by American enthusiasts.

• **Specials** Smurfs issued for special occasions, such as Valentine's Day

Fakes

Some fake Smurfs are on the market and these are recognizable by a rough finish around the seams and the fact that markings are indistinct, or missing.

• There are some unlicensed Smurf figures from Spain, bearing an oval sticker reading "Comics No Toxico". This sticker should not be removed if it is present, since fake Smurfs have become collectible in their own right and they are more desirable with the sticker attached.

• One notorious fake is a copy of the limited edition Good Luck Smurf, issued by Schleich for the collectors' club and showing a Smurf holding an elephant with its trunk raised. They were produced in very small numbers, but numerous fakes have appeared; the real thing was issued with a certificate of authenticity.

or Easter, were produced in smaller numbers than most, so these are among the most collectible.

• **Colours** Unusual colour variations are sought after, but beware. Some enthusiasts have been known to customize their figures with new paintwork; there is nothing wrong with this, provided there is no attempt to pass them off as an unusual factory variation.

Snoopy

Snoopy, an eccentric beagle with Walter Mitty-style fantasies, was created by Charles Schulz for the *Peanuts* cartoon strip in 1950. He soon became established as the most popular character and a wealth of toys and other merchandise followed. The majority of Snoopy toys are very affordable so it is possible to build up a large collection for a minimal outlay. The many makers of Snoopy toys have included Hasbro, Irwin, Kenner, Knickerbocker, and Masudaya; the latter made an appealing Snoopy in a tinplate rocket ship.

• **Licensed toys** Official Snoopy toys have a copyright date, but this refers to the date of the creation of the character or original artwork, not the date of manufacture.
• **Collectibility** Some collectors seek out everything to do with the character, so every Snoopy toy can be said to be collectible.
• **Other characters** Collectors are interested in other *Peanuts* characters and items featuring the lesser characters can sometimes be valuable.

MONEY BOXES OR BANKS
Among the most collectible of Snoopy items are the money boxes or banks. There are many different designs to choose from; among the more common are those that show Snoopy on top of his kennel.
• **Ideal** In 1977 thousands of Snoopy banks made by Ideal were recalled because the lead content in the paint was deemed too high, so they can be hard to find today.
• **Most valuable** The most valuable of the Snoopy banks is a bank with Snoopy as Santa, made by Determined Productions in 1982.
• **Limited editions** Snoopy items have been produced as limited edition collectibles, value generally depends on quality and on the quantity made.

CHARACTERS

Trade Cards

Trade cards date back to the late 19thC. During the 20thC, they became popular as incentives to buy various products. Different sets were made featuring a multitude of topics such as cars, military uniforms, film stars, and sports heroes. Bubble gum became a popular vehicle for giving away cards relating to characters such as Batman, Superman, and the stars from the Gerry Anderson shows. In recent years, trade cards have become very popular as tie-in products to films and TV series from *Buffy the Vampire Slayer* to *Lord of the Rings*. Many popular films are accompanied by sets of trade cards to collect and swap with friends and some have special games that can be played with the cards. It is a vast collecting field.

• **Rarities** Few cards from the 60s have survived unscathed so those that have can command high prices.
• **Chase cards** Card manufacturers often use "chase-" or "bonus-cards" to encourage interest. These extra cards are inserted randomly into a small number of packs. They might be made of a special foil, or they might even feature some relic such as a piece of a character's costume. Their value depends on how many were issued and on the popularity of the character.

Puppets

Puppet shows are a very old form of entertainment. No one knows where or when the first puppets were created, but they are known to have existed in ancient China, Egypt, Greece, and India amongst other places. They were sometimes used as an important part of religious ceremonies. The three best known forms of puppets are: glove puppets operated by the hand of the user, rod puppets, which use sticks to manipulate the character, and marionettes, which are operated by strings. In Europe, puppetry developed as an often subversive form of entertainment. Mr. Punch, one of the best known English puppet characters, developed from Italian street theatre of the 14thC, which was often banned for its political subject matter. In the 19th and 20thC, puppet shows came to be regarded as children's entertainment, but today adults are once again beginning to appreciate this traditional art form.

TV PUPPETS

The advent of television gave puppetry a boost. In Britain, TV made stars out of characters such as Muffin the Mule, Hank and Harry Corbett's creation Sooty, while in the United States, Howdy Doody enjoyed huge popularity. Original puppets based on these 1950s characters are very collectible.

• **Chad Valley** They won the rights to produce puppets based on the Sooty character and produced puppets of Sooty, his friend Sweep and his girlfriend Soo from the 1950s until the 1980s. Sooty remained an important part of children's TV programming in Britain

for decades. Vintage Chad Valley Sooty puppets are very collectible and are quickly snapped up by collectors, even though they are not that hard to come by. (See p.256.)

• **Collectibility** Puppets by Chad Valley, Dean, Steiff, Fisher Price, Pelham Puppets, and Peter Puppet Playthings are all collectible.

STORAGE & CARE

• **Boxes** Puppets – particularly those with strings – are often found with their boxes. As with most toys, valuable information about when and where a puppet was made can be gleaned from the box.

• **Storage** Always store away from

bright sunlight to prevent fading.

• **Before buying** Check for signs of wear and tear and damage.

• **Cleaning** This will depend on the material from which the puppet is made. Some post-war fabrics are washable whereas others, especially those made from natural fibres, can be more problematic.

Pelham

The Pelham Puppets firm was founded in England in 1947 by Bob Pelham and went on to become perhaps the most famous in this field. Pelham Puppets are very collectible and greatly admired today by professional puppeteers who admire their quality; they are very well made and were expensive in their day. In their heyday Pelham Puppets took pride of place in stores from local high streets to Hamley's and even the great New York toy emporium F. A. O. Schwartz. Consequently Pelham Puppets are known and collected on both sides of the Atlantic which maintains their value.

BOXES

Boxes provide an important clue to dating Pelham Puppets.

• **Early puppets** The company

initially used brown cardboard boxes with a Pelham label. Boxes bore a prominent flying pig logo on the label. The earliest of all boxes carry

the trade name "Wonky Toys" which was used only for the first year before the company was renamed Pelham Puppets.

• **1960s** By the sixties the boxes were yellow, solid, and printed with colourful pictures.

• **Later boxes** By the late 1960s and into the 1970s, the boxes were produced with a cellophane window so that the puppet inside was visible. In the 70s, a blue box was introduced for certain special characters and in the 80s a red and yellow striped box was used.

MATERIALS

The materials used to make a puppet can also make a useful rough guide to determining its age.

• **Army surplus** Production costs were originally kept down by utilizing army surplus materials such as sawn-up ammunition cases for bodies, and kit bag toggles for feet.

• **Hands** These were initially made of wood, then lead. Composite hands were introduced in the late 40s and early 50s. Plastic hands were used from the 1970s

SUBJECTS

Pelham's repertoire was extensive (see pp.257–260) and subjects for the puppets include animals such as cats and poodles, fairy tale characters such as witches, wizards, and fairies, and a highly successful range of TV and film characters. The latter ranged from Andy Pandy to Huckleberry Hound, and the stars of the Gerry Anderson shows such as *Thunderbirds* and *Fireball XL5*. Pelham also made puppets of characters such as Charlie Brown and Snoopy, *The Muppets* and *The Wombles*.

• **Disney** In 1953, Pelham acquired the rights to produce puppets based on Disney characters. However, there is an early version of Pinocchio that pre-dates this; it is one of the most scarce and sought after puppets (see right and p.257). Pinocchio also featured in a series of puppets produced in a "collectors' series", which also included characters such as Rupert Bear, Donald Duck, and historical figures such as Henry VIII and his wives. They were numbered and came with a certificate of authenticity.

• **Glove puppets** Pelham is perhaps best known for its marionettes, but also produced glove puppets. These included the

characters from Punch and Judy as well as from Disney, animals, and Hansel and Gretel.

• **Value** Rarity is not necessarily an indication of value, since early Pelham puppets are very desirable. The older the puppet is, the more it is usually worth, even if a later puppet is harder to come by.

The firm went into receivership in 1992 but replicas have been made in recent years. These are signed and dated to avoid confusion with the originals.

State of the market

• **Top end** The advent of TV created new puppet celebrities such as Muffin the Mule, Sooty and Sweep, plus characters from shows such as *The Muppet Show, Magic Roundabout,* and *Thunderbirds* to name but a few. When originals come onto the market they can command huge sums, but versions of many such characters have been produced and form the basis for variously themed collections.

• Pelham "Wonkys" are particularly prized.

• Early Pelham Puppets produced until the mid-1950s were packaged in brown boxes and came with black strings. However, several of the later characters appearing in yellow boxes are just as keenly sought.

• Look out for Pelham puppets designed by Gill Leeper such the *Alice in Wonderland* series and a special range of animal characters produced in 1963.

• **More accessible** Characters such as Tyrolean boys and girls, witches, and clowns, are relatively easy to find due to long production runs.

• It's possible to make interesting collections from single characters such as clowns, since variations in the fabrics used for costumes and the ways the faces were painted are numerous.

• Pelham also produced simpler "Junior Control" ranges and glove puppets, but these are generally less desirable.

• Two other UK manufacturers from this period are Barnsbury Puppets, which were a somewhat lesser quality moulded product but attractive nevertheless, and Picot Puppets, which were slightly smaller with wooden bodies and often have charmingly painted faces and detailed costumes. Although harder to find, the prices fetched by these brands fall short of the ever-popular Pelhams.

Soft Toys

Toy animals have been made in the home from scraps of fur and fabric for many centuries, but the development of a soft toy industry dates only from the 19thC. Steiff is the first documented manufacturer, having applied in 1892 for a patent to make "animals and other figures to serve as playthings". In 1903, Steiff launched its range of bears and their subsequent global success meant that teddy bears would become the most famous of all soft toys. Teddy bears are a separate collecting field in their own right and so they have not been covered here as they have been the subject of numerous books including serious academic research. By contrast, relatively little research has been done into soft toys, which at least means that there are opportunities for amateurs to make real discoveries. Steiff's success prompted other European firms to design their own soft toys, many of them based on popular characters from children's stories or popular characters from film and TV.

MATERIALS

Early soft toys were most commonly made of mohair, velvet, and felt, with excelsior for stuffing. Excelsior is a soft mixture of long, thin wood shavings. Toys stuffed with this material, also known as wood wool, have a hard, crunchy feel and make a crackly sound when squeezed.

• **Eyes** These were typically black boot-button or glass.

INTER-WAR YEARS

Between the wars, toys based on popular characters from stories, comic strips, or films enjoyed success and firms competed to secure licences to produce them.

Disney characters were popular, as was "Bonzo" (below left) a bull terrier based on a Daily Sketch cartoon, and the Beatrix Potter creation Peter Rabbit.

POST-WWII

Post-war shortages prompted manufacturers to use synthetic fabrics and many toys were made fully clothed to cut down on the scarce natural materials used for the bodies. Pre-war firms were joined in the market by newcomers, keen to exploit the market for spin-offs from film, books, and the new medium of television. Makers such as Steiff continued to produce soft toys.

As well as those mentioned on the following pages, other manufacturers worth noting include Farnell (see above), Chad Valley, Knickerbocker, Chiltern Toys, and Schreyer & Co.

Condition

Would be collectors of soft toys should always bear the following in mind:

- Original labels or tags will always add to the value of a soft toy
- Unmarked toys can still be collectible if they are well made and of an unusual design
- Good condition is essential: moth damage, fading, and poor restoration will reduce value
- Beware of replica toys that have been artificially distressed and "aged" to look original. Look for signs of wear where you would expect them to occur on a toy
- Old soft toys tend to have a distinctive smell, so familiarize yourself not only with the appearance but also with the smell of genuine examples
- Pre-1914 toys are rare and a famous maker will fetch premium prices
- Original boxes always add to value
- Steiff fakes are known – beware of crudely made, inaccurately modelled animals

State of the market

Collecting soft toys has increased in popularity over the last decade. Quite apart from the obvious favourite, the teddy bear, many varied and appealing animals are becoming very sought after, but with a little luck, patience and determination some interesting examples can still be found.

- **Top end** Early Steiff animals - dogs, cats, and a surprising variety of wilds animals were made. Some of the early toys were on metal wheels. These can today fetch five-figure sums due to their rarity, but at the beginning of the 1920s wooden wheels replaced metal and it is still possible to find charming examples at relatively affordable prices.
- Many popular cartoon and film characters of the period were made. Early examples of Mickey and Minnie mouse by the English toy manufacturer Deans can still be found, sometimes with their original buttons, which increases their value significantly.
- Always bear in mind condition when collecting: cloth and soft toys are susceptible to moth, wear, and tear, particularly if they have been played with and well-loved.
- **Other collectible areas** These include: clockwork animals and toys by the French company Roullet & Decamps (see p.264); novelty scent bottles and compacts from the 20s made by Schuco, many of these were produced as teddy bears or monkeys with removable heads opening to reveal the scent bottle inside. Most were made in gold mohair plush but some were produced in green, pink, or red and are scarce today.

- A few names to look out for are Deans, Chad Valley, Farnell, and Merrythought, who all produced good quality soft toys either in felt or plush.
- Particular favorites such as Gollys are very collectible; the early examples can fetch hundreds but some from the 1950s turn up at boot fairs and can be bought for relatively little. The two examples below are of a similar date (late 1950s to early 60s) but the one on the left has the original label, which is always a good feature (see p.267).
- As prices for teddy bears become out of reach the appeal of soft toys is ever increasing. They can become a very addictive and create an interesting collection in their own right or as an attractive addition to a doll or teddy collection.

Dean's

Dean's Rag Book Co. was established in London in 1903 by Samuel Dean. The Dean family had been in the publishing business since the 18thC, but rag books were a new departure. They had the advantage that they could simply be washed clean if soiled by sticky young fingers. The rag books were an instant success and the firm soon began to diversify with a range of soft toys. Prices were generally kept low, since part of Samuel Dean's philosophy was to produce affordable toys for children.

Like many other British firms, Dean's tried to fill the gap left by the absence of German products during WWI.
• **Character-based product** After the war, this type of merchandise became more important. In 1923 the firm made a toy based on Dismal Desmond, a comic strip dalmatian created by George Hildebrandt. It was made in a huge range of sizes and poses in velveteen or printed brushed cotton (see p.269). An accompanying character, "Cheerful Desmond" was less successful and is rarer today.
• **Disney** Ten years later, Dean's became the first British company to be granted the license to produce Disney soft toys. Disney characters included Mickey Mouse, Donald Duck, Goofy, and Pluto.

POST-WWII PRODUCTION
The firm turned to war production during WWII, and found it difficult to re-establish itself after the war, due in part to shortages of materials.
• **Post-war range** After the war the immediate range included a Scottie dog which, though he is still appealing to collectors, shows signs of the economy measures still in force. He is less carefully modelled and is of lower quality than pre-war examples.
• **1950s** By this time the company was thriving again and continued to expand its range. A chimpanzee, introduced in 1955, was one of the firm's most popular toys and was produced for the next 30 years.
• Push along toys included dogs, bears, and donkeys.

IDENTIFYING
Identifying the firm's products is not difficult. The company name is printed, usually around the neck or underneath the foot on swing tags or printed labels.

Dean's moved from London to Sussex and in the 70s moved again, to South Wales. By the 80s, cheap imports from the Far East had made it impossible for Dean's to continue in its existing form. The firm was taken over in the late 80s and is still in business, mostly producing quality limited edition bears.

Merrythought

Merrythought was established in 1930 and is among the oldest and most prestigious of Britain's toymakers. The name is derived from the old English word for wishbone and the wishbone was registered as a company trademark when it was set up.
From the early days, the firm's range was extensive and included domestic and wild animals as well as push along animals on wheels. When war broke out in 1939, the Merrythought premises in Shropshire were taken over by the military for map-making but alternative premises were found nearby, where Merrythought's workers produced sleeve badges, helmet linings, and other equipment for the armed forces.

IDENTIFICATION
• **Pre-war** These toys can be recognized by their inset glass eyes, and also by their marking.
• **Button & label** Pre-WWII, Merrythought followed Steiff's example and marked their toys with a button. Embroidered labels were also used
• **Post-war** Printed labels were introduced.

POST-WWII PRODUCTION

After the war, the firm returned to its old factory and production resumed. Post-war products included dogs, cats, clowns, elephants, lions, and rabbits.

• **Unjointed animals** The company made a range of unjointed animals, including bears (which are very collectible), dogs and cats. They used a mohair-Dralon mix on a metal armature that could be twisted into many different poses. In some cases, over enthusiastic twisting has weakened the structure, but it is still possible to find examples in good condition.

• **Disney** Merrythought produced a number of Disney toys under licence. Among them was a range of characters from the film version of A. A. Milne's *Winnie the Pooh*, of which Kanga and Roo is one of the most collectible. Kanga is often found with Roo missing from her pouch – collectors are prepared to pay good prices for a stray Roo that can be reunited with its parent.

The Merrythought factory is still in existence and is still a family concern, producing quality soft toys and teddy bears.

Schuco

Schuco was one of the most innovative of German toy manufacturers and is better known for its tinplate toys (see p.25).

However, from 1910, the firm also made soft toys, many of them derived from tinplate prototypes.

MINIATURES

Schuco enjoyed particular success with its miniature range. Measuring 2 to 4½in (5 to 11.5cm) they had metal-frame jointed bodies covered in mohair and with a tinplate face mask. In the 1920s and 30s, they were made as novelty items containing lipsticks and scent bottles (see p.271), or they served as mascots to clip onto bicycles. Although small, they were well made and are very collectible today.

• **Popular** Bears are especially popular as are monkeys, which were also made as lapel badges or just as novelties in their own right. Green, lavender, pink, red, and blue versions were made and production continued after the war. The brighter the colours, the more desirable they are. Miniatures also included cartoon characters; Felix the Cat, a star of cartoon strips and short films, was immortalized in this way. Whatever the character, it is always identifiable as Schuco by the metal, mohair-covered jointed frame and metal face, even if it is not marked.

• **Other miniatures** These included the collectible "Noah's Ark" range. Elephants and rabbits are especially popular and many other animals from lions to ladybirds were also made. In spite of their small size they are very well made, again with fully jointed metal-frame bodies. Versions produced in synthetic material are less collectible than those in mohair.

POST-WWII PRODUCTION

• **"Tricky" range** Bears and monkeys dominated Schuco's "Tricky" range, introduced shortly after WWII, which also incorporated a Schuco speciality, the "yes/no" mechanism. This was first developed in the 1920s and was copied by other manufacturers. It allowed the owner to make the toy nod or shake its head by moving the tail.

• **Clockwork toys** The "Rolly" range of clockwork toys was also introduced in the post-war era. The range included monkeys, bears, and clowns and a roller-skating rabbit. These toys were expensive to produce and comparatively few were made. Clockwork toys should be in working order, since repairs are expensive and should only be undertaken by a professional.

• **Collectible post-war toys** These include those in the "bigo bello" range. These high quality soft toys were wire-framed and poseable and included Disney characters such as Pluto.

Steiff

Steiff is widely associated with the teddy bear but this firm, which enjoys the highest status in the soft toy world, also made many other animal toys. The firm was ahead of its time in quality control, marking, marketing skills, and its vigorous pursuit of those who infringed its copyright. It is the ambition of most collectors to own a Steiff, but few can now afford Steiff's earliest toys. Production of the inter-war years is more accessible but still expensive, so post-WWII Steiffs are the usual starting point for collectors.

EARLY YEARS

Steiff began not with a bear but with an elephant. Founder Margarete Steiff's first toy was a pincushion in the form of this animal, made as a gift. The success of her home-made toys encouraged the wheelchair-bound seamstress to start the world famous company. The range and diversity of Steiff was always exceptional and others often followed the firm's lead.

• **Skittles** Sets of animal skittles (now very rare) were made from 1892 and were joined by pull-along and ride-on toys.

• **Character-based toys** Steiff was the first to appreciate the potential of character-based toys such as Peter Rabbit and applied for licences to produce toys based on Disney and other characters. Mickey Mouse toys were made by

Steiff between 1931 and 1936 and, like all Steiff toys, can be recognized by the trademark button in the ear (see right).

POST-WWII PRODUCTION

After WWII, Steiff continued to expand and develop its range and this era offers the best opportunities for collectors on a limited budget. Steiff's animal range included many lions and post-war examples are both attractive and affordable.

• **Novelties** Fierce competition led to ever more inventive novelty creations. These are not usually very collectible, but Steiff is an exception. Eric the Bat, with pipe-cleaner legs and vinyl-like wings has become the most collectible and most rare of these unusual animals. He did not sell well when launched, in two sizes, in the early 1960s.

• **Other rarities** Dino the Dinosaur, from the 50s, is another example of a line that did not sell well at the time but is now desirable. The Steiff button should be found on one of his spikes.

Steiff button

• The Steiff button was intended as a guarantee of quality and authenticity and so it is. However, buttons can become detached over the years and they leave holes if lost – such holes have been faked, so beware.

• The version pictured here, with the underscored "F" was in use from 1905 until the 1950s. The yellow label underneath was used from 1934 to 1950.

DATING

Early animals, c.1900, were made in felt and velvet, were unjointed and had black-bead or shoe-button eyes. In the 20s and 30s they were made of mohair with glass eyes. After WWII, animals were manufactured using synthetic fabrics with plastic eyes.

Dolls

Dolls are probably the oldest of all toys, since human figures of one sort or another date back thousands of years. For centuries, dolls were simple wooden or rag affairs, made in the home. In the 16thC and 17thC, wooden dolls carved in the forests of Germany and Austria were sold throughout Europe. In the 18thC, quality wooden dolls were being made in Britain, but by the end of the century, quality had declined. They were superseded by German imports and dolls made from other materials such as wax, papier-mâché (a mixture of glue, paper, ashes, and flour), china, and bisque (unglazed, tinted porcelain). German makers led the market until the 1860s, when the French introduced high-quality bisque fashion dolls and bébé dolls. Other materials such as celluloid and composition came to prominence in the early 20thC, but were superseded in turn by plastic and then vinyl. The later period only is covered here.

The following are some general points to bear in mind when looking at dolls:

- Dolls should be examined as a whole and undressed, to ensure a correct match between head and body – damaged heads and limbs may have been inappropriately replaced.
- Check for original limbs: replacements should be reflected in the price.
- Clothes and hairstyles should reflect the fashions at the time of production.
- Dolls may be marked with the maker's name, country of origin, and the mould number (but wood, papier mâché, china, and parian dolls are rarely marked).

Dolls come in all shapes, sizes, and levels of complexity. The one pictured here is a German woodentop peg doll (see p.275).

Composition

Composition dolls were manufactured in America and Europe in the 19thC and early 20thC as a cheaper alternative to bisque and china. Composition is made from wood or paper pulp, reinforced with other ingredients such as rags, bones, and eggs. In the United States, wood and plastic was also used in the mix. In Europe, composition dolls followed the style of china and bisque dolls, often using the same moulds.

Germany dominated the doll market and its products, in composition and other materials, were exported world-wide. In terms of realism, new heights were reached in the early 20thC by the German maker Marion Kaulitz who produced high quality art dolls modelled on real children and with hand-painted faces. They were in production for only a short period and therefore are highly sought-after and command high prices today.

THE UNITED STATES

- **EFFanBEE** In America, the firm of EFFanBEE (Fleischaker & Baum) produced composition dolls from 1910, claiming that they were indestructible. They specialized in producing dolls with sentimental charm – playing on young girls' emotions, encouraging mother-and-child role play, and home-making. Many dolls were sisters, such as Betty, Alice, and Barbara Lee, and were marketed in the mid 1920s, each sold with EFFanBEE's trademark heart locket. The firm made walking, talking, and sleeping composition dolls in their thousands. American composition dolls are particularly collectible and are often more expensive than those made in Germany and elsewhere.

• **Shirley Temple** As the cinema created new stars, so doll makers were quick to produce their likenesses. One of the best-known examples is the highly collectible Shirley Temple doll, pictured, made by the Ideal Novelty & Toy Company. In their original boxes and with their original clothes, they are very sought after. They were made in 12 sizes and most early dolls were made with jointed composition toddler bodies, brown glass sleep eyes and an open mouth with teeth. They can suffer from crazing on the face and this will affect value if it is very bad. The eyes of some dolls were of

enamelled tin while others had flirty eyes.

• **Collectibility** Affordable composition dolls can still be found fairly easily, many of them in their original clothing. Manufacturers' names to look out for include the English firms of Pedigree (also known for their plastic dolls) and Palitoy. Madame Alexander and the Ideal Toy & Novelty Company, both American, also produced large numbers of composition dolls. Some composition novelty dolls have musical movements, which have a charm of their own. Carefully chosen composition dolls can be a pleasing and interesting addition to a doll collection, especially if they are wearing their original outfits from the period.

Plastic

While composition dolls were relatively inexpensive, they were prone to crazing and flaking, were easily damaged by water, and difficult to clean. Makers on both sides of the Atlantic looked for a more durable yet still inexpensive alternative. Celluloid had

been used as an alternative material for dollmaking in Germany since 1873. Heads and hands made from celluloid were used by many French, German, and American makers. Hard plastic dolls were made after WWII but replaced by vinyl by the 50s.

Hard plastic disease

Plastic dolls are by no means indestructible – they can suffer from what is known as hard plastic disease, a serious problem that disfigures them. Look out for:
• Dry, brittle-looking hands with a grey ting.
• Vinegar odour around the eyes of the doll – if this is evident, then do not buy the doll, because once the disease is established, there is no cure

MATERIALS

There were many problems with celluloid, a mixture of nitro cellulose and powdered camphor: it tends to crack and fade and it is flammable. The advantage to the modern collector is that celluloid dolls are often affordable; examples by Kestner are particularly desirable and celluloid dolls can be recognized by their glossy sheen (see right and p.285).
• **Marks** Most celluloid dolls are marked, sometimes twice if a celluloid firm used another dollmaker's mould. Hard plastic was an inexpensive substitute for

Key features

Madame Alexander dolls can be identified by the following:
• The bodies are jointed at the head, shoulders and hips
• Dolls have a round face with small idealized features
• The hair is wigged
• The eyes are sleeping, slightly round in shape and fringed with eyelashes
• The eyebrows are narrow and set high above the eyes
• The mouth is closed and painted with small pursed lips
• The hands have separately defined fingers
• The clothes are elaborate in design
• The doll is marked on the head or body, on a wrist label, or by tags on the clothes (totally unmarked dolls are uncommon)

both composition and celluloid and was used by doll manufacturers during the late 1940s and early 50s, first in the United States and then in Britain.
• **Post-WWII** After the austerity of the war years, the 1950s marked the beginning of a new age of doll production.

ALEXANDER DOLL COMPANY

Best known of the American manufacturers was the Alexander Doll Company (Madame Alexander). Many of their dolls were walking and talking, wearing the fashions of the day, and with additional clothes and accessories available.
• **Little Women series** Their famous Little Women series, pictured above, based on the characters from Louisa M. Alcott's novel are immensely popular and

very collectible, especially when they are wearing their original dresses, which ideally should be in good condition.

OTHER MANUFACTURERS

• **Britain** English firms such as Pedigree also developed walking and talking dolls and many examples from the 1950s can still be found today.
• **"Rosebud"** Another collectible doll from the 1950s is the Rosebud doll, a trade name for the Northampton doll maker Eric Smith; and the little six-inch thumb-sucking baby is always a favourite with collectors. Rosebud also made black dolls some of which can still be found wearing their original outfits and flowers in their hair (see below). Rosebuds can still be purchased for a comparatively small sum of money which, assuming they are in mint condition, should prove to be a good investment for the future.

VINYL

Hard plastic dolls had a relatively short lifespan; by the mid-1950s they had been virtually replaced by vinyl, which was both soft and durable, if slightly prone to fading. Some dolls of this era are a

combination of the two, having a hard plastic body and vinyl head. Vinyl dolls are not only softer to the touch but they also have rooted hair instead of moulded hair or wigs.

COLLECTING

When collecting any type of doll it is best to buy only the best due to the large numbers that are still around today. Look out for dolls wearing typical 1950s clothes that reflect the style of the time.
• **Documenting your collection** It is important to keep a careful record of your dolls. Written details of size, marks, or mould details, condition, clothes etc. as well as photographic records are all useful for insurance purposes.

Barbie & Sindy

Barbie was the first teenage fashion doll and was the brainchild of Ruth and Elliot Handler, founders of the American toy company Mattel; she was named after their daughter Barbara. Barbies have acquired a massive following with collectors, with rare early examples fetching five-figure sums. Most dolls, however, are worth much less. Sindy was first produced in 1962 in Britain by Pedigree Toys and Dolls in order to compete with Barbie. Although popular she does not have quite the same global status as her rival.

What to look for

Barbie's wardrobe from the "Couture Period", 1959–69, was inspired by the haute couture houses such as Balenciaga, Dior, and Givenchy and garments from this time should have this distinctive label. The rarest outfits include "Gay Parisenne" and "American Stewardess".

Barbie dolls are always marked, usually on the bottom or occasionally on the back of a shoulder. Modern copies from the Far East are found but they are not marked and are of poor quality.

Sindy should always have an identification mark under the hair on the back of the head.

BARBIE

Made from vinyl, Barbie was introduced in 1959. The first doll had holes in her feet for a stand and the second model had a stand that fitted under the arms and therefore lacked holes in the feet. These early versions are particularly collectible, but beware – some dolls have been tampered with. Look out for recently drilled holes in the feet that have not acquired the grime of age. Both dolls had pale flesh and a slightly Oriental appearance with slanting eyes and angular eyebrows. The third version, in 1960, had gently arched eyebrows and the fourth, introduced in the late 60s, had warmer flesh tones.

HAIR

• **Rooted hair** Barbies have rooted hair and early versions were styled with a pony tail.

• **Bouffant bubblecuts** (See left) These were introduced in 1961 and titian hair was introduced in the same year. Titian or brunette Barbies are more valuable than blonde ones.

WARDROBE

• **Quality** Barbie's success owed much to the quality of her wardrobe, though this was not a new development, as 19thC French fashion dolls had the same appeal.
• **Couture period** Dolls dating from the early 60s (see left) had outfits designed by Balenciaga, Dior, and Givenchy.

COLLECTING

More than a billion Barbies have been made and they are still being produced, but adult collectors

favour those made before 1971 Vintage Barbies are subdivided into the "Pony tail era" (1959–66) and the "Mod era" (1967–72).

• **Marks** Genuine Barbies are marked on the right buttock, or occasionally on the shoulder, (see previous page), but the date could be the copyright date rather than the date of manufacture. Collectible Barbies are marked "Japan", where the early dolls were made.

BARBIE'S FRIENDS

Barbie's boyfriend, Ken, arrived in 1963 (see left) but she also had other friends including Stacey, supposedly a British model, who was introduced in 1967 (see p.293).

OTHER COLLECTIBLES

The passion for Barbie dolls and associated merchandise cannot be underestimated. Everything from dolls' houses, elaborate accesesories, to licensed toys (see pp.290–295) were produced and are collected today. The Mattel Barbie tote bag and record above are an example of this.

SINDY

Sindy was designed by Dennis E. Arkinstall and was first produced by Pedigree Toys and Dolls in 1962. Sindy was intended to compete with Barbie, but she was modelled on an adolescent girl rather than a

sophisticated woman. A more grown-up version was, however, introduced in 1971.

• **Dating** Until 1966 Sindy had plain eyes with straight limbs. Bendable limbs were introduced later and in 1968, realistic eyelashes were added. In 1971 the first "walking" Sindy was produced with moving head, shoulders, elbows, waist, hips, and knees.

WARDROBE

Like Barbie, clothes were an important ingredient in Sindy's success and Pedigree issued a new outfit every six months. Rare Sindy dolls include a black version, pictured, made in 1977, of which only 250 were ever produced (see below).

SINDY'S FRIENDS

Just as Barbie had friends, so too did Sindy. In 1967 a French girl called Mitzi was introduced and

the following year she had another friend, Vicki. More friends followed and she also acquired a boyfriend, Paul, and a little sister, Patch. They were short-lived, however, and had been discontinued by 1973.

ACCESSORIES

Like Barbie, a vast range of accessories were produced for Sindy in the early 70s including a fully-equipped kitchen, bedroom, fillable bath, and a grand piano. She also had a chestnut pony called Peanuts and a battery-operated scooter (see p.282). Many of these items are highly collectible.

COLLECTING

Barbies and Sindies were made by the million and it is only rare models and those in mint condition which are really collectible.

• **Packaging** Dolls without the original box are worth half as much as those with the box or less, even if they are in perfect condition and have never been played with.

• **Condition** Condition is crucial. The Sindy c.1975, pictured here, has been much-loved and carried everywhere by her hair. Her thinning hair reduces her value to very little.

DOLLS

G.I. Joe & Action Man

American toy firm Hasbro first introduced the concept of a doll that boys could play with in the form of G.I. Joe, whose features were based on photographs of decorated American war veterans. It was the first doll designed specifically for boys and, like Barbie, his appeal lay in the number of outfits available. The first British dolls of this type were produced in 1966 and were initially named Action Soldier. By the 1970s it was estimated that there was one Action Man for every boy in Britain. They were made under the name of Palitoy by Cascelloid of Leicester; the name honours the firm's founder, Mr A. E. Pallet, who began making small toys in 1919.

G.I. JOE

• **G.I. Joe** The original, jointed plastic action figure was first produced in 1964; manufacture ceased in 1984 due to lack of demand but he was reintroduced again in 1993.

• **Marks** The toy and the box are marked as follows:
Hassenfeld Brothers (1923–68)
Hasbro Industries, Inc (1968–85)
Hasbro, Inc (1986–Present)

• **Action figures** The Hasbro figures came in a variety of guises including a military policeman, action sailor, and an explorer.

• **Accessories** Like Barbie and Sindy a vast array of accessories were produced for G.I. Joe (see p.239)

ACTION MAN

The British version of G.I. Joe, Action Man, measures 11in (28cms) high and is marked in relief on the back "Made in England by Palitoy under licence from Hasbro" with the copyright date 1964. His body is a light flesh-colour and he has a scar on his cheek.

• **Dating** Early dolls have static hands and painted hair. In the 70s, realistic hair was introduced along with gripping hands. These features were followed by "eagle eyes" that moved from side to side when operated by a gadget on the back of the head.

COLLECTIBILITY

Early Action Man dolls are very desirable because of the superior quality, not only of the dolls themselves, but also of clothes and accessories. In the early years, uniforms were made from a thick twill material with insignia either stitched to the material or produced as metal or plastic badges and buttons. Later uniforms were of a much thinner cotton, insignia were printed and badges and buttons were more likely to be plastic than metal. (See p.296 for a range of items.)

SUBJECTS

Action Man appeared in many guises, as a skydiver (see above and p.296), a footballer, Superman (see left), and even an astronaut. The footballer is particularly popular, followed by the Red Devil skydiver, and Superman. Whatever version you may find, it will always be worth at least twice as much if it is in the original box.

• **Collecting trends** It is difficult to predict for media-based toys. Characters from series such as *Thunderbirds* or *Captain Scarlett* will have additional appeal to collectors of TV series merchandise.

Dolls' Prams

It seems likely that some form of vehicle for transporting a baby has been around for a long time, but the pram (an abbreviation from perambulator) as we know it dates from the 19thC. In this era, fresh air was considered a potential cure for most ills and even babies were thought to benefit from its health-giving properties. Consequently, small hand-propelled carriages were developed, designed to allow mothers or nannies to give this benefit to infants. Naturally, this innovation soon found its way into the toy world and dolls' prams reflected the real thing in terms of style and features. They are popular with doll and teddy bear collectors for display purposes.

EARLY PRAMS

These were made of wood or wicker, although Germany supplied many tinplate examples, frequently with a cloth hood. Later prams were usually of steel. Many early prams faced the direction of travel, but models in which the infant faced the nurse finally became the norm.

• **Early toy prams** Like the real thing, these had iron-framed wooden wheels, but later Victorian models had wheels with solid rubber tyres for extra comfort. By the late 19thC/early 20thC, prams were becoming ever more sophisticated with sunshades, rain hoods, rubberized covers, and later, braking systems.

MODERN PRAMS

It was in Britain that the modern pram developed and British prams are particularly admired for their quality.

• **Tri-ang** One of the most prominent British makers of the 20thC was Tri-ang, who offered many different models. In their 1937–38 catalogue, no fewer than 18 different designs were offered, as well as a range of pushchairs. After WWII, the range was streamlined somewhat, but continued to offer dolls' prams that matched the quality and features available on full sized versions.

• **Silver Cross** The most prestigious and collectible of all prams are those of the British company Silver Cross, founded in 1877, who count royalty among the customers for their full-sized versions. Twin prams by this firm are particularly rare.

• **Collectibility** Collecting prams is a very specialist niche. When buying prams, check for signs of rust on steel examples, mildew on cloth hoods, and signs of cracking on leather hoods. Inspect rubber tyres for signs of decay. Specialist restorers of prams do exist, but restoration can be an expensive option.

Dolls' Houses

The earliest known doll's house was commissioned in 1558 by Albrecht V, Duke of Bavaria, for his daughter. These toys were the preserve of the wealthy and would remain so for a long time. They were not exclusively for children however, and in the 18thC and 19thC were enjoyed by children and adults alike.

EARLY DOLLS' HOUSES

The earliest existing dolls' houses are German and Dutch "cabinet" houses, built like an elaborate piece of furniture and with detailed interiors populated by wax dolls. They are almost all in museums and very rarely come onto the market.

• **Baby houses** English houses of the 18thC are often known as "baby houses", since dolls were often called babies at the time.

They were of simpler construction than German or Dutch examples and were intended as supervised playthings for children of the wealthy. Dolls' houses were prized possessions and were often handed down through the generations.

19THC

In the 19thC, dolls' houses were made in larger numbers and were affordable further down the social scale. Their small, cluttered room settings reflect the changing styles of architecture and eclectic mixture of contemporary furnishing styles.
• **Mass-production** Most British houses were individually crafted until mass-production and chromolithography transformed

the market from the 1860s onwards. London-based wholesalers began to distribute houses made in Germany and Britain. They were usually simple wooden designs that opened to reveal four empty rooms that could be decorated to suit. Later models became more elaborate, with brick-printed paper and imitation stucco surrounds; some were expensive.

LINES BROTHERS

From the mid-1920s, Lines Brothers introduced a range of houses in modern styles under the Tri-ang name and these are eagerly sought by collectors. Particular favourites include the "Stockbroker Tudor" houses, representing the suburban

dream of aspirational Britons.
• **Dinky** From 1930, Dinky made its "Dolly Varden" range for girls, which included hollow metal dolls' houses and small-scale furniture.
• **Other makers** The English Toy Co. made flat-packed cardboard houses, which are rare survivors today, while other makers included Chad Valley, who made tinplate houses, and Tudor Toys, who made imitation Tudor houses.

UNITED STATES

Pennsylvania, Philadelphia, and Connecticut were the main centres of American production, although houses were also imported from Britain.
• **19thC** Houses of this period reflect Dutch and English as well as American architectural styles.
• **American makers** These include the Bliss Manufacturing Co. of Pawtucket, Rhode Island, who specialized in houses covered in lithographed paper. Bliss houses are all carefully marked, although the signature may be printed on doors, under gables or hidden on floors.

Dolls' House Furniture

Dolls' house furniture was made in various materials and styles. The most sought after is that decorated with inlay or made from blonde woods such as yellow cherry. The finest furniture has features like those of the real thing, with opening and closing drawers and metal handles. Antique dolls' house furniture can fetch huge sums.

• **Metal furniture** This was made in Britain, Germany, and the United States.
• **German manufacturers** Notable German makers include Rock & Graner and Märklin. Gilt metal furniture and accessories are particularly sought after. Germany was also known for its intricately-carved ivory furniture.

• **Other items** Other household accessories were produced; food is particularly rare and sought after.
• **Collecting** Antique dolls' houses and furniture command serious money at specialist auctions therefore there may be more opportunities to enter the market by collecting later models that are not quite so sought-after.

POST-WAR

By the 1950s, dolls' houses were smaller, but they were crammed with furniture, consumer durables, and domestic appliances. These desirable accessories were made by manufacturers such as Tiny Toy, Dol-Toi, Pit-a-Pat, Elgin, Britains in London, and Meccano in Liverpool.

what to pay

Wood

A fruitwood boat, with two figures, both heads rise when wheels rotate, Chinese, late 19thC, 9in (23cm) long.
£630–700 / €890–990
$1,000–1,150 ⊞ CRN

A Curly Skittles game, c1900, in a box, 10 x 20in (25.5 x 51cm).
£50–60 / €70–85
$85–100 ⊞ J&J

▶ **A push-along merry-go-round toy,** early 20thC, handle 24in (61cm) long.
£45–50
€65–75
$75–85
⊞ CHAC

A child's painted wooden wheelbarrow, early 20thC, 37in (94cm) long.
£135–150 / €190–210
$220–250 ⊞ JUN

▶ **A wooden pond yacht,** 'Claughton', painted and varnished, with lined decking, heavily-weighted keel, mast and rigging, early 20thC, 27½in (70cm) long.
£220–260
€310–370
$370–430
⚒ AH

A wooden horse racing game, with six counters, early 20thC, 4in (10cm) diam.
£35–40 / €50–55
$55–65 ⊞ RUSS

A Dover Toys Mr Jolly articulated wooden toy, 1910, 12in (30.5cm) high, with original box.
£55–65 / €80–90
$90–100 ⊞ J&J

◀ **A pine ram's horn sledge,** German, c1920, 30in (76cm) long.
£60–70
€85–95
$100–110
⊞ HRQ

A Bassett-Lowke steam-powered destroyer, *Vivacious*, with wooden hull, minor damage, 1934, 39in (99cm) long, with original box and a postcard showing the *Vivacious* at sea.
£1,400–1,650 / €2,000–2,350
$2,300–2,750 ➚ Bon(C)

A Gamages wooden pond yacht, with painted hull, c1930, 38in (96.5cm) high.
£310–350 / €440–500
$510–580 ⊞ PEZ

▶ **A steam-powered model ocean liner,** with wooden hull and tinplate upper decks, 1950s, 24in (61cm) long.
£100–120 / €145–170
$170–200 ➚ Bon(C)

◀ **A set of painted pine skittles,** 1950, 15in (38cm) high.
£90–100 / €130–145
$150–165 ⊞ MLL

A balsa wood model of a 1930s Swordfish biplane, 1980s, 59in (150cm) wide.
£400–450 / €570–640
$660–750 ⊞ CYA

◀ **A large scale wooden model of Seattle tug** *Shelley Foss,* with twin screws and accommodation for electric motor, deck detail includes six figures, 1980s, 37in (94cm) long, on a stand.
£280–330 / €400–480
$470–560 ➚ AH

Building Blocks

◄ A set of child's educational blocks, printed with animals, c1880, each block 4 x 2in (10 x 5cm).
£270–300 €380–420 $450–500 ⊞ YC

A wooden architectural game, c1880, in original box, 20in (51cm) wide.
£130–145 / €185–210 $210–240 ⊞ MLL

A set of Anchor building blocks, German, c1890, in original box, 9 x 14in (23 x 35.5cm).
£135–150 / €190–210 $220–250 ⊞ YC

A set of pine French Architecture building blocks, 1910, in a pine box, 12in (30.5cm) wide.
£30–35 / €45–50 $50–55 ⚒ G(L)

A Walt Disney's Mickey Mouse Picture Cubes, West German, c1955, in original box, 7in (18cm) wide.
£14–18 / €20–25 $25–30 ⊞ DAC

Noah's Arks

A painted wood Noah's Ark, containing eight figures, 110 pairs and 36 single animals, German, c1840, 22¾in (58cm) long.
£12,000–14,400 / €17,000–20,400 $20,000–24,000 ⚒ S

A painted pine Noah's Ark, containing painted pine and composition figures and animals, losses and damage, Swiss, c1850, 18½in (47cm) long.
£600–720 / €850–1,000 $1,000–1,200 ⚒ BR

A painted wood Noah's Ark, containing four figures and over 100 pairs of animals and birds, sliding side panel replaced, German, c1890, 25in (63.5cm) wide.
£1,500–1,800 / €2,150–2,550
$2,500–3,000 ♫ Bon(C)

A painted wood Noah's Ark, containing eight figures and 70 pairs of animals, minor damage, c1890, 14in (36cm) long, with original inventory in three languages.
£1,300–1,550 / €1,850–2,200
$2,150–2,550 ♫ Bon(C)

A painted wood Noah's Ark, containing five figures and approximately 65 animals, slight damage, German, c1890, 28in (71cm) long.
£1,400–1,650 / €2,000–2,400
$2,300–2,750 ♫ VEC

A hand-painted Noah's Ark, with stylized tile-hung roof and four sash windows to each side, containing hand-painted animals and figures, German, c1900, 18in (45.5cm) long.
£1,600–1,900 / €2,300–2,700
$2,650–3,150 ♫ G(B)

Puzzles

A Feltham & Co The Chequers Puzzle, c1890, 6in (15cm) square.
£45–50 / €60–70
$75–85 ⊞ J&J

▶ A wooden jigsaw puzzle, c1900, 9 x 11in (23 x 28cm).
£20–25 / €30–35
$35–40 ⊞ J&J

Jigsaw puzzles

The jigsaw puzzle was invented in 1760 by London map maker John Spilsbury, who applied a map to a mahogany board, and cut round the countries using a hand-held saw. The work was laborious and puzzles were expensive, costing as much as a guinea each.

In the 1870s came the invention of the power scroll saw, known as the jigsaw, from which the jigsaw puzzle gained its now familiar name. Thanks to improved technology, puzzles could be made more quickly and affordable. Designs became more complex, subjects more entertaining, and for the first time jigsaws were popular with adults.

► **A Bystander jigsaw puzzle,** by Capt Bruce Bairnsfather, entitled 'Now where does this blinkin' bit go?', 1918, 8½in (21.5cm) high.
£85–95
€**120–135**
$140–155
⊞ **HUX**

A Zig Zag Puzzles wooden jigsaw puzzle, Boyhood of Raleigh, 1910, 5 x 7in (12.5 x 18cm).
£30–35 / €**45–50**
$50–55 ⊞ **J&J**

A jigsaw puzzle, depicting the *Aquitania*, 1920, 14 x 21in (35.5 x 53.5cm).
£75–85 / €**105–120**
$125–140 ⊞ **COB**

◄ **A Lawson Gro-Quik Fertilizer advertising jigsaw puzzle,** c1920, 9 x 7in (23 x 18cm).
£35–40
€**50–55**
$60–70 ⊞ **J&J**

A jigsaw puzzle, c1920, 7 x 6in (18 x 15cm).
£11–15 / €**16–21**
$18–24 ⊞ **J&J**

◄ **A wooden picture blocks puzzle,** 1920s, 18 x 17in (45.5 x 43cm).
£25–30 / €**35–45**
$40–50 ⊞ **J&J**

A Father Tuck's Picture-Building Puzzle,
c1920, 10 x 9in (25.5 x 23cm).
£50–55 / €70–80
$80–90 ⊞ J&J

A Puzzle Drive with Anchor Stone Puzzles, 1920s,
3¾in (9.5cm) square.
£20–25 / €30–35
$35–40 ⊞ HUX

◀ A Gibbs
Dentifrice
advertising
jigsaw puzzle,
No. 4, Defeat of
the Giant Decay,
c1930, 4 x 5in
(10 x 12.5cm).
£20–25
€30–35
$35–40 ⊞ J&J

A Victory jigsaw puzzle, depicting a coaching
scene, 1930, 11 x 16in (28 x 40.5cm).
£50–60 / €75–85
$85–100 ⊞ RGa

A GWR jigsaw puzzle, 'Locomotives Old and New', c1934,
9½ x 19½in (24 x 49.5cm).
£105–120 / €150–165
$175–195 ⚲ RAR

◀ A Hayter &
Co Picture Book
Box of Victory
jigsaw puzzles,
A Tale of Toyland,
c1930, 11 x 9in
(28 x 23cm).
£20–25
€30–35
$35–40 ⊞ J&J

A Victory wooden jigsaw puzzle, depicting
pilots and their Bristol Bulldogs, c1935,
6¾ x 8¾in (17 x 22cm).
£30–35 / €45–50
$50–55 ⊞ HUX

A **Waddington's jigsaw puzzle,** Last of the Mohicans, 1930s, 11 x 9in (28 x 23cm).
£11–15 / €16–21
$18–24 ⊞ J&J

A **Victory wooden jigsaw puzzle,** depicting the Cunard White Star liner *Queen Mary*, 1936, 8 x 10in (20.5 x 25.5cm).
£40–45 / €55–65
$65–75 ⊞ COB

◀ A **Victory jigsaw puzzle,** depicting the Cunard White Star liner *Mauretania*, 1939, 9 x 11in (23 x 28cm).
£40–45
€55–65
$65–75 ⊞ J&J

A **Moko Toy Muffin the Mule jigsaw puzzle,** early 1950s, 10 x 8in (25.5 x 20.5cm).
£310–350 / €440–490
$510–570 ⊞ MTMC

A **Tower Press Junior Jigsaw puzzle,** c1950, 7 x 6in (18 x 15cm).
£11–15 / €16–21
$18–24 ⊞ J&J

▶ A **Skipper frame-tray puzzle,** from the Barbie series, c1965, 14 x 11in (35.5 x 28cm).
£60–70 / €85–100
$100–120 ⊞ T&D

A **plywood 56-piece jigsaw puzzle,** 1950s, in original box, 8 x 6in (20.5 x 15cm).
£4–8 / €6–11
$7–14 ⊞ J&J

A James Bond jigsaw puzzle, *Thunderball*, 1966, 11 x 7in (28 x 18cm).
£45–50 / €60–70
$75–85 ⊞ TOY

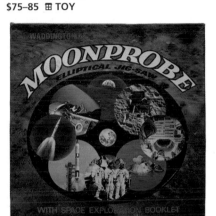

A Victory plywood jigsaw puzzle, 1960s–70s, 9in (23cm) wide.
£20–25 / €30–35
$35–40 ⊞ HYP

A Waddington's jigsaw puzzle, Moonprobe, with space exploration booklet, 1969, 13in (33cm) square.
£15–20 / €20–25
$30–35 ⊞ RTT

A Blue Peter jigsaw puzzle, 1971, 9½ x 11½in (24 x 29cm).
£1–5 / €2–7
$3–8 ⊞ CMF

◄ A Playboy Playmate centrefold puzzle, 1960–70, 6in (15cm) high.
£20–25 / €30–35
$35–40 ⊞ PB

A Dr Who jigsaw puzzle, 1979, in original box 8¼in (21cm) wide.
£8–12 / €12–16
$13–18 ⊞ UNI

► A Hope Hestair Products jigsaw puzzle, *The Muppet show*, 1997, 6 x 10in (15 x 25.5cm).
£1–5 / €2–7
$3–8 ⊞ J&J

Rocking Horses

An F. H. Ayres pine rocking horse, on a carriage springs base, late 1800s, 49in (124.5cm) high.
£5,400–6,000 / €7,700–8,500
$8,900–9,900 ⊞ STE

A Victorian rocking horse, on a traditional rocker base, restored, 80in (203cm) long.
£1,400–1,650 / €2,000–2,400
$2,300–2,750 ≯ JM

A painted wood rocking horse, with glass eyes, on a wooden trestle rocker, late 19thC, 37in (94cm) high.
£370–440 / €530–630
$610–730 ≯ RTo

A painted wood rocking horse, with glass eyes and leather saddle, on a wooden trestle rocker, late 19thC, 38¼in (97cm) high.
£300–360 / €430–510
$500–600 ≯ RTo

A carved and painted wood rocking horse, on a trestle rocker, restored, late 19thC, 51in (129.5cm) high.
£540–600 / €770–850
$900–990 ≯ L

A Victorian carved and painted wood rocking horse, later painted and restored, new rocker, 36¼in (92cm) high.
£620–740 / €880–1,050
$1,050–1,250 ≯ SWO

A rocking horse, with later paint, French, c1890, 38in (96.5cm) long.
£270–300 / €380–420
$450–500 ⊞ YT

A carved and painted wood rocking horse, with horsehair mane and tail, original leather bridle and saddle, on a trestle rocker, marked for Henry's, Winchester, c1880, 44in (122cm) high.
£700–840 / €990–1,150
$1,150–1,350 ⚒ B(Ch)

An F. H. Ayres painted rocking horse, on a trestle rocker, restored by Stevenson Bros, c1890, 39½in (100.5cm) high.
£1,100–1,300 / €1,550–1,850
$1,800–2,150 ⚒ BR

▶ A late Victorian wooden rocking horse, on a bow rocker, 29in (74cm) high.
£670–750
€950–1,050
$1,100–1,250
⊞ WL

A G. & J. Lines wooden rocking horse, some restoration, 1875–1925, 24in (106.5cm) long.
£1,600–1,800 / €2,250–2,500
$2,650–2,950 ⊞ CRU

An F. H. Ayres rocking horse, with swivel head, on a trestle rocker, fully restored, c1900, 39in (99cm) high.
£2,500–3,000 / €3,550–4,250
$4,150–4,950 ↗ SWO

A carved and painted wood rocking horse, c1900, 51¼in (130cm) long.
£350–420 / €500–600
$580–690 ↗ SWO

An F. H. Ayres ponyskin covered rocking horse, with horsehair mane and tail, original leather bridle, saddle and metal stirrups, on a trestle rocker, minor losses, c1900, 53in (134.5cm) high.
£600–720 / €850–1,050
$1,000–1,200 ↗ B(Ch)

A wooden rocking horse, on a trestle rocker, early 20thC, 46in (117cm) high.
£580–650 / €820–910
$960–1,100 ⊞ KA

A G. & J. Lines rocking horse, on a trestle rocker, refurbished, c1900, 36in (91.5cm) high.
£2,650–2,950 / €3,750–4,200
$4,400–4,950 ⊞ RGa

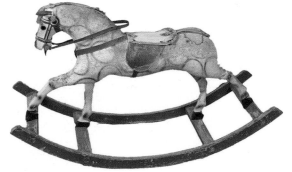

A rocking horse, with padded body and wooden base, possibly eastern European, early 20thC, 34¼in (87cm) long.
£220–260 / €310–370
$360–430 ↗ SWO

A rocking horse, with hair mane and leather saddle, on a pine rocker, restored, early 20thC, 48in (122cm) long.
£800–960 / €1,150–1,350
$1,300–1,550 ↗ EH

A painted rocking horse, c1910, 48¾in (124cm) high.
£730–870 / €1,050–1,250
$1,200–1,400 S(O)

A carved wood rocking horse, probably by G. & J. Lines, 1920s, 36in (91.5cm) high.
£380–420 / €540–600
$630–700 GAZE

A wooden rocking horse, by J. Collinson & Sons, with cowhair mane and tail, stud eyes, corduroy saddle and imitation leather trimming and tack, mid-20thC, 39½in (100cm) high.
£270–320 / €380–450
$450–530 DN

A wooden rocking horse, probably by J. Collinson & Sons, with saddle, bridle and stirrups, on a pine trestle rocker, probably repainted, c1950, 46in (117cm) high.
£400–480 / €570–680
$660–790 PF

A Leeway carved and painted wood rocking horse, on a pine trestle rocker, with imitation leather tack, glass eyes, 1950s, 41¼in (105cm) high.
£250–300 / €350–420
$410–490 SWO

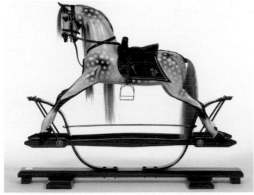

A Stevenson Bros Golden Jubilee rocking horse, limited edition of 50, 2002, 48in (122cm) high.
£5,000–6,000 / €7,100–8,500
$8,300–9,300 STE

A Stevenson Bros painted wood rocking zebra, No. 27, limited edition of 100, 2003, 38in (96.5cm) high.
£4,600–5,000 / €6,500–7,800
$7,600–9,100 STE

Cast Iron

A J. & E. Stevens monkey and coconut money bank, trapdoor to base missing, American, late 19thC, 8½in (21.5cm) high.
£800–960 / €1,150–1,350
$1,350–1,600 🏺 Bon(C)

A J. & E. Stevens cast-iron money bank, American, 1879, 10in (25.5cm) long.
£310–350 / €450–500
$520–580 ⊞ HAL

A John Harper cast-iron County money bank, 1892, 5in (12.5cm) wide.
£105–120 / €150–165
$170–190 ⊞ HAL

A John Harper cast-iron money bank, 1892, 9in (23cm) high.
£1,600–1,800
€2,250–2,450
$2,650–3,000 ⊞ HAL

A J. & E. Stevens cast-iron Paddy and the Pig mechanical money bank, American, 1892, 8in (20.5cm) high.
£630–700 / €900–1,000
$1,050–1,200 ⊞ HAL

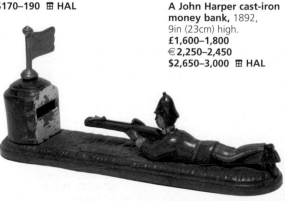

▶ **A John Harper cast-iron Wimbledon money bank,** 1892, 12in (30.5cm) high.
£1,600–1,800 / €2,250–2,550
$2,650–3,000 ⊞ HAL

▶ **A Sydenham & McOustra cast-iron bear and beehive money bank,** c1908, 7in (18cm) high.
£90–100
€ **130–145**
$150–165
⊞ **HAL**

A Kenton cast-iron cabriolet, minor replacement, American, c1905, 15½in (39.5cm) long.
£3,300–3,950 / € 4,700–5,600
$5,500–6,500 ⋊ **S(NY)**

A Dent cast-iron oversized fire pumper, c1911, 25in (63cm) long.
£5,000–6,000 / € 7,100–8,500
$8,300–10,000 ⋊ **S(NY)**

◀ **A cast-iron money box,** in the form of a Golly, c1910, 6½in (16.5cm) high.
£360–400
€ **510–570**
$600–660 ⊞ **MFB**

▶ **A cast-iron mechanical money box,** the dog performs a trick, American, c1930, 9in (23cm) wide.
£360–400
€ **510–570**
$600–660
⊞ **HAL**

◀ **A Dent cast-iron Mack dump truck,** American, c1923, 15in (38cm) long.
£8,000–9,500
€ **11,350–13,600**
$13,300–16,000
⋊ **S(NY)**

Tinplate

A pull-along tinplate train on a track, the train navigates the track as the toy is pulled along, German, c1900, 8in (20.5cm) long.
£270–300 / €380–420
$450–500 ⊞ YC

A Stollwerk child's printed tinplate gramophone, playing chocolate records, c1903, 11in (28cm) high, with original boxes.
£1,800–2,000 / €2,550–2,850
$3,000–3,300 ⊞ HHO

A Märklin tinplate battleship, with single-screw clockwork mechanism, deck details include eight gun turrets, twin funnels, working capstan and lifeboat davits, 1905–10, 28½in (72.5cm) long.
£2,300–2,750 / €3,250–3,900
$3,800–4,550 ⋏ G(L)

◀ **A tinplate money box,** German, c1905, 3in (7.5cm) high.
£80–90 / €115–130
$130–145 ⊞ HAL

A wood and tinplate model car, coachbuilt, 1910–20, 18in (45.5cm) long.
£90–100 / €125–140
$150–165 ⊞ MRW

A J. Roullot aeroplane donkey cart, the wooden wagon drawn by a tinplate donkey, propelled by a pull-string mechanism, by releasing a latch on the wagon the cart is converted into a monoplane, c1911, 22in (56cm) long.
£3,700–4,400 / €5,250–6,300
$6,150–7,350 ⋏ S(NY)

A Burnett tinplate clockwork General bus, c1912, 9in (23cm) long.
£720–800 / €1,000–1,100
$1,200–1,350 ⊞ HAL

◀ A tinplate wizard money box, c1912, 6in (15cm) high.
£105–120 / €150–165
$175–195 ⊞ HAL

▶ A Bing tinplate raceabout roadster, 1915, 5½in (14cm) long.
£140–165 / €200–240
$230–270 🔨 DuM

◀ A tinplate mechanical clown bank, German, c1920, 5in (12.5cm) high.
£720–800
€1,000–1,100
$1,200–1,350
⊞ HAL

A tinplate penny toy-style military horse-drawn communications limber, comprising a two-horse team with two French soldiers and a separate limber, with camouflage finish, German, 1920, 17½in (44.5cm) long.
£100–120 / €140–165
$170–200 🔨 VEC

A Whitanco tinplate clockwork bus, c1920,
14in (35.5cm) long.
£720–800 / €1,000–1,100
$1,200–1,350 ⊞ HAL

A DRP Junior tinplate typewriter, with tin cover,
German, 1920s, 8in (20.5cm) wide.
£60–70 / €85–95
$100–110 ⊞ JUN

**A Victor Bonnet & Cie tinplate clockwork side-
tipping wagon,** with liveried driver, French, c1920,
8in (20.5cm) long.
£220–260 / €310–360
$370–430 ⚒ G(L)

▶ **A Louis
Marx & Co
tinplate
clockwork
Coo-Coo car,**
c1920, 7½in
(19cm) long.
£100–120
€140–165
$165–195
⚒ DuM

A tinplate saluting sailor money box,
German, c1920, 7in (18cm) high.
£450–500 / €640–710
$750–830 ⊞ HAL

**A Meier tinplate
penny toy
trotter,** 1920s,
5in (12.5cm) long.
£400–450
€570–630
$660–730 ⊞ RGa

▶ **A tinplate
penny toy
rocking horse,**
1920s, 4in
(10cm) long.
£260–290
€370–410
$430–480 ⊞ RGa

A metal pedal **Pursuit Plane**, 'Juvenile Delinquents', with wooden propeller and rubber tyres, restored, c1920
£2,000–2,400 / €2,850–3,400
$3,350–4,000 ⚒ S(Cg)

A **tinplate penny toy**, 1920s, 3in (7.5cm) high.
£80–90 / €115–130
$130–145 ⊞ CBB

▶ A **Meier tinplate penny toy open landau**, with horse and driver, 1920s, 4in (10cm) long.
£270–310 / €380–420
$450–500 ⊞ RGa

A **Bing Pigmyphone toy gramophone**, 1920s, 6in (15cm) high.
£70–80 / €100–110
$115–130 ⊞ JUN

▶ A **tinplate bucket with lid**, c1925, 7in (18cm) high.
£35–40 / €50–55
$60–70 ⊞ HUX

A **metal fort**, on a wooden base, 1920–50, 18in (45.5cm) wide.
£50–55 / €70–80
$80–90 ⊞ UNI

Two Bing Pigmyphone tinplate gramophones, c1925, 6in (15cm) square.
£105–120 / €150–165
$175–195 each ⊞ HHO

A Jouets tinplate clockwork Citroën car, 1930s, 12in (30.5cm) long.
£150–180 / €210–250
$250–300 ⚒ Bon(C)

A tinplate clicker, 1930s, 3in (7.5cm) high.
£15–20 / €20–30
$30–35 ⊞ MRW

A tinplate bucket, decorated with a beach scene, 1930s, 7in (18cm) high.
£35–40 / €50–55
$60–70 ⊞ HUX

A tinplate cowboy clicker, 1930s, 2½in (6.5cm) long.
£25–30 / €35–40
$40–45 ⊞ HUX

A tinplate biplane, c1930, 18in (45.5cm) wide.
£200–240 / €290–340
$330–390 ⚒ VEC

A tinplate clockwork Mercedes German Army staff car, probably by Hausser, with driver and three passengers, 1930s, 9in (23cm) long.
£900–1,050 / €1,300–1,550
$1,500–1,800 ✗ AH

A Ubilda tinplate Tower Bridge building kit, with approximately 92 screw-together parts, 1930s, 16in (40.5cm) wide, with original box.
£230–260 / €330–370
$380–420 ✗ BKS

A tinplate clockwork military vehicle, Japanese, 1930s, 4in (10cm) long.
£40–45 / €55–65
$65–75 ⊞ CBB

A Casio tinplate sewing machine, 1930s, 7in (18cm) wide.
£45–50 / €60–70
$75–85 ⊞ PC

A tinplate clockwork German Army troop carrier, probably by Hausser, with four-tracked driving wheels, driver and eight passengers, German, 1930s, 8¾in (22cm) long.
£520–620 / €740–880
$850–1,000 ✗ AH

A tinplate Microphone dancer, American, c1935, 12in (30.5cm) high.
£310–350 / €440–500
$510–580 ⊞ AUTO

A tinplate ship, SS *Normandie*, c1935, 22in (56cm) long.
£310–350 / €440–500
$510–580 ⊞ HUX

A Märklin tinplate clockwork liner,
German, mid-1930s, 16in (40.5cm) long.
£2,000–2,400 / €2,850–3,400
$3,350–4,000 ⚒ WAL

◀ **A Bing tinplate clockwork U-boat,**
with detachable flag, German, 1930s,
13½in (34.5cm) wide.
£470–560 / €670–790
$780–930 ⚒ WAL

A Kingsbury fire engine, American, 1930s, 32in (81.5cm) long.
£220–260 / €310–370
$360–430 ⚒ VEC

A tinplate bucket, decorated with anthropo-
morphic dogs playing on a beach, c1940,
5½in (14cm) high.
£30–35 / €45–50
$50–55 ⊞ HUX

A Hubley cast-metal racing car, with moveable cylinders, 1938,
8in (20.5cm) long.
£290–340 / €410–480
$480–570 ⚒ BAu

▶ **A tinplate peacock
whistle,** 1940s–50s,
1½in (4cm) high.
£8–12 / €11–16
$13–18 ⊞ RUSS

▶ **A tinplate
clockwork
musician,**
Japanese,
c1950, 10in
(25.5cm) high.
£500–550
€700–770
$810–900
⊞ SMAM

A tinplate clockwork racing car, French, 1950s.
£220–250 / €310–350
$360–400 ⊞ JUN

A tinplate battery-operated bulldozer,
Japanese, c1950, 10in (25.5cm) long.
£200–220 / €280–310
$330–370 ⊞ GTM

**A Louis Marx & Co tinplate clockwork police
motorcycle,** with siren, 1950s, 7in (18cm) long.
£160–180 / €230–260
$260–290 ↗ RAR

A tinplate battery-operated Mercedes racing car, German,
1950s, 10in (25.5cm) long.
£180–200 / €250–280
$300–330 ⊞ GTM

▶ **A Brimtoy Pocketoy
tinplate clockwork
steamroller,** No. 9/501,
1950s, 4in (10cm) long,
with original box.
£55–65 / €80–90
$90–105 ⊞ GTM

**A Cragstan painted tinplate wind-
up monkey baseball player,** 1950s,
7½in (19cm) high, with original box.
£460–550 / €650–780
$760–910 ↗ BAu

A tinplate clockwork swan, Japanese, 1950s, 7in (18cm) long.
£115–130 / €165–185
$190–210 ⊞ CBB

A Wells tinplate coach, 1950s,
7in (18cm) long.
£55–65 / €80–90
$90–105 ⊞ JUN

**A Tomiyama tinplate battery-operated
Firebird Race Car,** 1950s, 15in (38cm) long.
£400–450 / €560–640
$660–750 ⊁ RAR

A GAMA tinplate tractor, No. 178, c1955,
8in (20.5cm) long.
£310–350 / €440–500
$510–570 ⊞ KOLN

A tinplate clockwork motorcycle, German, c1950s,
7in (18cm) long.
£200–220 / €280–310
$330–370 ⊞ CBB

An Alice in Wonderland tinplate paint box, 1955–60,
15in 938cm) wide.
£25–30 / €35–40
$40–45 ⊞ HUX

A Wyatt Earp tinplate paint box, c1950s, 9in (23cm) wide.
£20–25 / €30–35
$35–40 ⊞ HAL

◄ **A Roadmaster tinplate battery-operated car,** late 1950s,
8in (20.5cm) long, with original box.
£65–75 / €90–100
$105–120 ⊞ RTT

A tinplate car, late 1950s, 4½in (11.5cm) long.
**£20–25 / €30–35
$35–40 ⊞ RTT**

TINPLATE

A tinplate clockwork clown,
Japanese, late 1950s, 9in (23cm) high.
**£260–290 / €370–410
$430–480 ⊞ CBB**

**A tinplate battery-operated
Mercedes Benz SL,** Japanese,
c1960, 9in (23cm) long.
**£60–70 / €85–95
$100–110 ⊞ JUN**

**A Yone tinplate battery-operated
Jumbo the Bubble Blowing
Elephant,** Japanese, 1950s–60s,
7in (18cm) high, with original box.
**£135–150 / €190–210
$220–250 ⊞ HAL**

◄ **An SSS Toys tinplate friction-
driven Cadillac and caravan,**
with picnic table, car fits inside
base of caravan, Japanese, 1960,
caravan 9in (23cm) long.
**£160–190 / €230–270
$270–320 ⚒ VEC**

**A Louis Marx & Co tinplate and plastic
battery-operated Nutty Mad Indian with
War Whoop,** No. J-9619, 1950s–60s,
14in (35.5cm) high, with original box.
**£105–120 / €150–165
$175–195 ⚒ MED**

A tinplate battery-operated Super Flying Police Helicopter,
Japanese, 1960s, 14in (35.5cm) long.
**£110–125 / €155–175
$180–200 ⊞ RTT**

A Bandai tinplate battery-operated Ferrari Gear Shift car, Japanese, c1960, 11in (28cm) long, with original box.
£160–180 / €230–260
$270–300 ⊞ HAL

A tinplate battery-operated Sonicon Bus, Japanese, 1960s, 13in (33cm) long.
£50–60 / €70–80
$85–95 ⊞ HAL

A TN tinplate battery-operated Super Eagle machine gun, Japanese, c1960s, 24in (61cm) long.
£60–70 / €85–95
$100–110 ⊞ HAL

◄ **A tinplate clockwork Winki,** 1960s, 7in (18cm) high.
£55–65 / €80–90
$90–100 ⊞ UD

► **A Taiyo tinplate US Army tank,** Japanese, 1960s, 11in (28cm) long.
£80–90 / €115–130
$135–150 ⊞ JUN

A Tomy tinplate battery-operated Combat GI, Japanese, 1960s, 10in (25.5cm) wide, with original box.
£180–200 / €260–290
$300–330 ⊞ GTM

A tinplate clockwork fire engine, German, 1960s, 4in (10cm) long.
£15–20 / €20–25
$30–35 ⊞ RTT

Two tinplate clockwork motorcycles and riders, Russian, 1965–75, 8in (20.5cm) long, with original box.
£60–70 / €85–95
$100–120 ↗ BLH

A Bandai tinplate Saab, Japanese, c1965, 7in (18cm) long.
£135–155 / €190–210
$220–250 ⊞ CBB

◀ **An Alps tinplate battery-operated Mambo Jolly Drumming Elephant,** 1960s, 10in (25.5cm) high, with original box.
£180–200
€260–290
$300–330 ⊞ UNI

A tinplate bucket and spade, 1960s, 8in (20.5cm) high.
£35–40 / €50–55
$60–65 ⊞ JUN

A Tomiyama tinplate Man Blowing Bubbles, Japanese, 1960s, 10in (25.5cm) high.
£45–50 / €60–70
$75–85 ↗ RAR

A tinplate Volkswagen Beetle, 1970s, 12in (30.5cm) long.
£55–65 / €80–90
$90–100 ⊞ GTM

Chad Valley

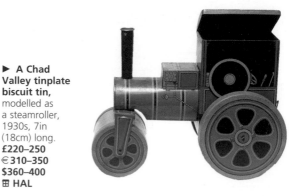

▶ **A Chad Valley tinplate biscuit tin,** modelled as a steamroller, 1930s, 7in (18cm) long.
£220–250
€310–350
$360–400
⊞ HAL

A Chad Valley tinplate pull-along biscuit tin, modelled as a lion cage, 1930s, 7in (18cm) long.
£220–250 / €310–350
$370–410 ⊞ HAL

▶ **A Chad Valley tinplate clockwork racing car,** c1935, 11½in (29cm) long.
£195–220 / €280–310
$320–360 ⊞ HUX

Distler

▶ **A Distler tinplate clockwork fire engine,** with extending ladder, four seated firemen and Balloon Cord tyres, German, 1920s, 11½in (19cm) long.
£230–270 / €330–390
$380–450 ➹ Bon(C)

A Distler Toonerville tinplate trolley, with animated character, German, 1920s, 5in (12.5cm) high.
£420–500 / €600–720
$700–840 ➹ BAu

▶ **A Distler tinplate battery-operated Porsche 7500 electromatic car,** German, 1950s, 10in (25.5cm) long.
£310–350 / €440–490
$510–570 ⊞ HAL

Günthermann

A Günthermann tinplate car, with clockwork motor and electric lights, German, c1930, 14in (35.5cm) long.
£540–600 / €770–850
$900–990 ⊞ GTM

A Günthermann tinplate clockwork model of a General double-decker bus, German, c1910, 10in (25.5cm) long.
£1,100–1,300 / €1,550–1,850
$1,850–2,150 ↗ BWe

▶ A Günthermann Kaye Don's Silver Bullet, tail-fin resoldered, German, c1930, 22in (56cm) long, with box.
£750–900 / €1,050–1,250
$1,250–1,500 ↗ S(S)

Lehmann

A Lehmann Oh My tinplate clockwork dancing figure, German, pre-WWI, 11in (28cm) high.
£580–650 / €820–910
$960–1,100 ⊞ HAL

▶ A Lehmann clockwork EPL679 ITO sedan car, with Lehmann tinplate flag to bonnet, German, 1920s, 7in (18cm) long.
£650–780
€920–1,100
$1,100–1,300
↗ Bon(C)

A Lehmann tinplate clockwork WWI van, German, c1918, 7in (18cm) long.
£310–350 / €440–490
$510–570 ⊞ HAL

A Lehmann tinplate wind-up delivery truck, German, c1920, 5in (12.5cm) long.
£450–500 / €640–710
$750–830 ⊞ HOB

TINPLATE

Meccano

A Meccano non-constructor two-seater sports car, 1930s, 8¼in (21cm) long, with original box.
£490–550 / € 700–770
$810–900 ✗ RAR

A Hornby Meccano copy of a shop display windmill, fully-lit, mounted on a wooden base, c1933, 30in (76cm) high.
£140–165 / € 200–240
$230–260 ✗ VEC

A Meccano Motor Car Constructor, 1930s, 14in (30.5cm) long, with original box.
£375–425 / € 530–590
$620–690 ⊞ JUN

A Meccano Motor Car Constructor, 1930s, 12in (30.5cm) long, with original box.
£810–900 / € 1,150–1,300
$1,350–1,500 ⊞ HAL

◄ A Meccano Elektron Electrical Experiments kit, 1935–36, in original box, 15in (38cm) wide.
£200–230
€ 290–330
$330–380 ✗ RAR

► A Meccano model traction engine, shop display, 1950s, 13in (33cm) long.
£400–450
€ 570–630
$660–730 ⊞ JUN

Mettoy

► **A Mettoy tinplate clockwork tractor,** 1950, 6in (15cm) long.
£65–75
€90–100
$105–120 ⊞ JUN

A Mettoy tinplate Rolls-Royce, rusted, 1930s, 14in (35.5cm) long.
£50–60 / €70–80
$85–95 ⊞ DRJ
In good condition this toy could be worth as much as £600 / €850 / $1,000.

► **A Mettoy tinplate Indianapolis car,** 1950s, 13in (33cm) long.
£280–320 / €400–440
$460–510 ⊞ JUN

Schuco

► **A Schuco tinplate car,** damaged, German, 1930s, 5in (12.5cm) long.
£45–50
€65–75
$75–85 ⊞ RTT

A Schuco tinplate clockwork clown drummer boy, wearing felt clothes, German, 1910–20, 4in (10cm) high.
£90–100 / €125–140
$150–165 ⊞ A&J

A Schuco tinplate clockwork Mercedes racing car, No.1050, with spare parts, German, c1930s, 6in (15cm) long.
£75–90 / €105–125
$125–150 ⚒ G(B)

◀ **A Schuco tinplate clockwork Examico 4001 car,** German, 1940s, 6in (15cm) long.
£135–150 / €190–210
$220–250 ⊞ HAL

A Schuco tinplate battery-operated dump truck, No. 6077, German, 1950s, 10in (25.5cm) long.
£380–450 / €540–640
$630–750 ⚒ TQA

◀ **A Schuco tinplate Motodrill,** No. 1006, German, 1950s, 5in (12.5cm) long.
£170–200 / €240–280
$280–330 ⚒ TQA

Tipp & Co

◀ **A Tipp & Co tinplate racing car,** with electric light, driver missing, German, 1920–30, 12in (30.5cm) long.
£450–500
€640–710
$750–830
⊞ HAL

A Tipp & Co tinplate fire engine, with working bell under, manually-controlled front wheels and tin tyres, German, 1927, 10in (25.5cm) long.
£160–180 / €230–260
$270–300 ⚒ BKS

A Tipp & Co tinplate clockwork saloon car, with battery-operated lights and tinplate garage, German, 1930s, garage 12½in (32cm) long.
£240–280 / €340–400
$400–480 ⚒ FHF

A Tipp & Co tinplate clockwork Royal Mail van, German, 1930s, 9in (23cm) long.
£430–480 / €610–680
$710–790 ⊞ CBB

Tonka

A Tonka trencher, No. 534, 1960s, 24½in (62cm) extended.
£17–21 / €22–25
$25–28 ✎ TQA

▶ **A Tonka car carrier truck,** No. 840, 1963, 28in (71cm) long.
£30–35 / €45–50
$50–60 ✎ TQA

A Tonka jeep and horse trailer, 1960s, 9½in (24cm) long.
£70–80 / €100–120
$115–135 ✎ TQA

A Tonka pick-up truck, No. 302, 1963, 13in (33cm) long.
£45–50 / €65–75
$75–90 ✎ TQA

A Tonka jeep pumper, No. 425, 1963, 10¾in (27.5cm) long.
£120–140 / €170–200
$200–240 ✎ TQA

A Tonka Dragline crane, No. 514, 1963, 20in (51cm) long.
£60–70 / €85–100
$100–120 ✎ TQA

A Tonka bottom dump truck, 1963, 25in (63.5cm) long.
£50–60 / €70–80
$85–100 TQA

A Tonka wrecker truck, No. 518, 1963,
14in (35.5cm) long.
£40–45 / €55–65
$65–75 TQA

A Tonka cement mixer truck, No. 620, 1963,
14in (35.5cm) long.
£160–190 / €230–270
$260–310 TQA

▶ **A Tonka ramp hoist
truck,** No. 640, 1963,
19¼in (49cm) long.
£210–250 / €300–360
$350–420 TQA

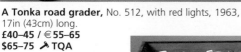

A Tonka road grader, No. 512, with red lights, 1963,
17in (43cm) long.
£40–45 / €55–65
$65–75 TQA

A Tonka dump truck and sand loader, No. 616,
1963, 24in (61cm) long.
£110–130 / €155–185
$180–210 TQA

▶ **A Tonka Airlines
luggage service,**
No. 420, 1963,
16½in (42cm) long.
£42–50 / €60–70
$70–80 TQA

Tri-ang

A Tri-ang Minic tinplate clockwork car, 1930s, 5in (12.5cm) long.
£155–175 / €220–250
$260–290 ⊞ CBB

A Tri-ang tinplate Gyro cycle, 1930s,
8in (20.5cm) long, with original box,
operating leaflets and oil bottle.
£185–210 / €260–290
$310–350 ➤ BKS

▶ **A Tri-ang Minic tinplate 50 ME
Rolls-Royce Sedanca,** with electric
lighting, c1936, 5¼in (13.5cm) long.
£310–350 / €440–500
$510–570 ➤ RAR

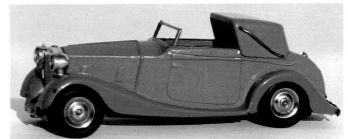

A Tri-ang tinplate wheelbarrow,
c1930, 22in (56cm) long.
£15–20 / €20–25
$25–30 ⊞ GAZE

▶ **A Tri-ang
Minic tinplate
police car,**
c1948, 5in
(12.5cm) long.
£60–70
€85–95
$100–110
⊞ HAL

A Tri-ang Minic tinplate racing car, 1950s,
6in (15cm) long.
£70–80 / €100–110
$115–130 ⊞ CBB

A Tri-ang Minic tinplate steamroller, 1960,
5½in (14cm) long.
£55–65 / €80–90
$90–100 ⊞ GTM

TINPLATE

Diecast

A Tootsie Toy Ambulance, American, c1920, 4in (10cm) long.
£45–50 / €60–70
$75–85 ⊞ MRW

A Chad Valley diecast clockwork Wee Kin cable layer,
1949–53, 4½in (11.5cm) long, with original box.
£80–90 / €115–130
$130–145 ⊞ GTM

A Shackleton David Brown Trackmaster 30 tractor, 1950s,
11in (28cm) long, with original box.
£800–960 / €1,150–1,350
$1,350–1,600 ⚒ VEC
This model is extremely difficult to find and only 50 are
believed to have been produced.

A Jo Hill Co land speed record car, c1929,
5½in (14cm) long.
£180–200 / €250–280
$300–330 ⊞ CBB

A Britains Napier Bluebird record car,
c1937, 4in (10cm) long, with original box.
£180–210 / €250–300
$300–350 ⚒ IM

A Shackleton Foden flat truck, 1949–58,
11in (28cm) long.
£1,100–1,300 / €1,550–1,850
$1,800–2,150 ⚒ VEC
British company Shackleton Toys (est 1948)
produced a range of high-quality, large-
scale diecast Foden FG lorries. Sturdily
made and including a clockwork motor,
Shackleton toys were more expensive
than Dinky. Low sales, combined with a
shortage of materials during the period
of the Korean War, caused the company
to close in 1952, and thanks to this short
production run, Shackleton toys are very
collectible today. This truck would
normally sell for £500–600 / €710–850 /
$830–1,000. However there must have
been more than one eager bidder for it
to have fetched such a high price.

A plastic and metal flareside pick-up truck, American, 1950s, 8in (20.5cm) long.
£35–40 / €50–55
$60–65 ⊞ RTT

A Chad Valley Fordson Dexta tractor, 1950s, with box.
£320–360 / €450–510
$530–600 ⚒ AH

A Crescent Toys D-type Jaguar, No. 1292, 1957–60, 4in (10cm) long, with box.
£115–130 / €165–185
$190–210 ⊞ CBB

A Techno B17 Flying Fortress, Danish, 1950s, 6in (15cm) wide.
£45–50 / €60–70
$75–85 ⊞ HAL

A Denzil Skinner Nuffield tractor, 1950–60, 7in (18cm) long, with original box.
£360–400 / €510–570
$600–660 ⚒ RAR

A Crescent Kansas Kid 100-shot revolver, unused, 1960s, 12in (30.5cm) long, boxed.
£60–70 / €85–95
$100–110 ⊞ HAL

DIECAST

A Politoys Fiat 850 Coupé, No. 517, Italian, 1960s, 4in (10cm) long, with original box.
£50–55 / €70–80
$85–95 ⊞ HAL

A Solido Fiat 850 Abarth, French, 1960s, 4in (10cm) long, with original box.
£50–55 / €70–80
$80–90 ⊞ HAL

◄ **A Lone Star diecast metal Scout Repeater Cap Pistol,** 1960s, 7in (18cm) long.
£30–35 / €45–50
$50–60 ⊞ HAL

► **A Wrenn formula 152 electric model motor racing set,** c1961, in box, 17½in (44.5cm) wide.
£90–100 / €125–140
$150–165 ⊞ PrB

► **A Solido Porsche GT Le Mans,** French, 1960s, 4in (10cm) long, with box.
£50–60 / €75–85
$90–100 ⊞ HAL

A Solido tank, 'Patton' M-47, French, 1960s, 6in (15cm) long, with box.
£45–50 / €60–70
$75–85 ⊞ CBB

► **A Solido Lotus F1,** French, 1960s, 4in (10cm) long, with original box.
£40–45
€55–65
$65–75 ⊞ HAL

A Politoys Alfa Romeo Giulia Canguro, No. 529, Italian, 1960s, 4in (10cm) long, with box.
£50–55 / €70–80
$80–90 ⊞ HAL

A Politoys Fiat 1500 Coupé Siata, No. 502, Italian, 1960s, 4in (10cm) long, with original box.
£45–50 / €60–70
$75–85 ⊞ HAL

A Mercury Fiat 2300S Coupé, No. 23, Italian, 1960s, 4in (10cm) long, with original box.
£45–50 / €60–70
$75–85 ⊞ HAL

A Moscovich 412 car, Russian, 1960s, 5in (12.5cm) long, boxed.
£15–19 / €23–27
$27–32 ⊞ CBB

A Mercury Ferrari Dino, No. 48, Italian, 1960s, 4in (10cm) long, with original box.
£45–50 / €60–70
$75–85 ⊞ HAL

A Britains Fordson Super Major Diesel Tractor, No. 9525, 1960s, 4in (10cm) long, with original box.
£200–240 / €280–340
$330–390 ⤢ RAR

DIECAST

A friction-drive scale model Mercedes-Benz 219 Sedan,
The Automobiles of the World series, No. 732, Japanese, 1960s, 8in (20.5cm) long, with box.
£130–145 / €185–210
$210–240 ⊞ GTM

A Fiat Campagnola, 1970s, 6in (15cm) long.
£15–19 / €23–27
$27–32 ⊞ CBB

A Hornby Minic Ships diecast Naval Harbour Set, 1:1200 scale, 1972, in original box, 12 x 11in (30.5 x 28cm).
£50–60 / €70–85
$85–100 ⊞ COB

A C.K.O. friction-drive Mercedes-Benz Muldenkipper, No. 428, early 1970s, 7in (18cm) long, with box.
£28–32 / €40–45
$47–53 ⊞ CBB

▶ **A Britains Kettenkrad half-track motorcycle,** No. 9780, 1974, in box, 6in (15cm) long.
£50–55
€70–80
$80–90 ⊞ CBB

A Britains US Jeep, No. 9786, 1974, in unopened box, 6in (15cm) long.
£40–45 / €55–65
$65–75 ⊞ CBB

▶ **A Lone Star London bus and fire engine,** 1980, in unopened box, 9½in (24cm) long.
£30–35 / €45–50
$50–60 ⊞ CBB

Corgi

A Corgi Toys Smiths Karrier Bantam mobile shop, No. 413, late 1950s, 4in (10cm) long, with box.
£85–100 / €120–140
$140–165 ⊞ HAL

A Corgi Toys Karrier Bantam two-ton lorry, No. 455, late 1950s, 4in (10cm) wide.
£65–75 / €95–105
$110–125 ⊞ HAL

A Corgi Toys Major Chipperfield's Circus crane truck, No. 1121, 1960–62, 8in (20.5cm) long, with box.
£115–130 / €165–185
$190–210 ⊞ CBB
In mint boxed condition this truck could be worth £150–200 / €210–280 / $250–330.

A Corgi Toys AFS fire service tender, No. 405, 1956–60, 4in (10cm) long, with box.
£100–110 / €140–155
$165–180 ⊞ HAL

A Corgi Toys Major Midland Motorway Express coach, No. 1120, 1961–62, 5½in (14cm) long, with box.
£80–90 / €115–125
$135–150 ⊞ CBB

A Corgi Toys Bristol Bloodhound guided missile, with launching pad, loading trolley and Land Rover, gift set No. 4, 1959–62, in box, 11in (28cm) wide.
£175–195 / €250–280
$290–320 ⊞ GTM

DIECAST

A quantity of Corgi Toys cars, 1950s–60s, 4in (10cm) long.
£6–10 / €8–14
$10–16 each ⊞ HAL

A Corgi Toys Ford 5000 Super
Major tractor, No. 67, 1960,
4in (10cm) high, with original box.
£70–80 / €100–115
$115–130 ⊞ HAL

A Corgi Toys VW Beetle, in East Africa Safari trim, c1960, 6in (15cm) long,
with original box.
£110–120 / €155–170
$180–200 ⊞ GTM

A Corgi Toys Massey-Ferguson
combine harvester, 1960,
7in (18cm) long, with original box.
£125–150 / €175–210
$210–250 ⊞ HAL

A Marlin Rambler Fastback, 1961, 5in (12.5cm) long.
£320–380 / €450–540
$530–640 ⚒ VEC

A Corgi Toys Chipperfield's circus horse
transporter, No. 1130, 1962–70,
10in (25.5cm) long, with box.
£115–130 / €165–185
$190–210 ⚒ RAR
In mint boxed condition this transporter
could be worth £150–175 / €210–250 /
$250–290.

A Corgi Toys Chipperfield's circus animal cage, No. 1123,
1961–62, 4in (10cm) long, with original box.
£35–40 / €50–60
$60–70 ⊞ WI
In mint boxed condition this animal transporter could
be worth £70–90 / €100–130 / $115–150.

A Corgi Toys Bristol Bloodhound guided missile,
No. 1109, 1960s, 9in (23cm) long, with original box.
£110–120 / €155–170
$180–200 HAL

A Corgi Toys ERF 44G drop-side lorry, No. 456,
early 1960s, 5in (12.5cm) long, with box.
£60–70 / €80–100
$100–115 HAL

A Corgi Toys Mercedes-Benz 220 SE Coupé, No. 230, 1960s,
4in (10cm) long, with box
£45–50 / €60–70 / $75–85 HAL
**In mint boxed condition this car could be worth £60–70 /
€85–100 / $100–115.**

◀ **A Corgi Toys VW
mobile camera van,**
No. 479, 1960s, boxed,
4in (10cm) wide.
£90–100 / €125–140
$150–165 HAL

A Corgi Toys Plymouth station wagon,
No. 219, 1960s, 4in (10cm) long, with
original box.
£65–75 / €90–105
$110–125 HAL

◀ **A Corgi Toys Oldsmobile Tornado,**
No. 264, 1960s, 4in (10cm) long, with
original box.
£30–35 / €40–50
$50–60 HAL

DIECAST

A Corgi Toys BMC Mini Countryman, No. 485,
1965–69, 3in (7.5cm) long, with box.
£45–50 / €60–70
$75–85 ⊞ DAC
In mint boxed condition this car could be worth
£100–150 / €140–210 / $165–250.

A Corgi Toys Chevrolet Impala, No. 248, 1960s,
5in (12.5cm) long, with box.
£55–65 / €80–90
$90–105 ⊞ HAL

◄ **A Corgi
Toys Neville
cement tipper
body,** No. 460,
4in (10cm) long,
with box.
£45–50
€60–70
$75–85 ⊞ HAL

A Corgi Toys Lotus Elan, No. 318, 1960s,
4in (10cm) long, with box.
£65–75 / €90–105
$110–125 ⊞ HAL

◄ **A Corgi
Toys E-type
Jaguar,**
No. 312, 1960s,
4in (10cm) long,
with original box.
£70–80
€100–115
$115–130
⊞ HAL

A Corgi Toys Machinery Carrier gift set, No. 27,
1960s, in original box, 11in (28cm) long.
£125–140 / €175–200
$200–230 ⊞ HAL

◄ **A Corgi Toys Chipperfield's Circus gift set,**
No. 23, 1962–66, in original box.
£380–450 / €540–640
$630–750 ⚒ WAL

A Corgi Toys Simon Snorkel fire engine, No. 1127, 1960s, in original box, 11in (28cm) long.
£50–60 / €75–85
$85–100 ⊞ HAL

A Corgi Toys Ford Consul Classic, No. 234, 1960s, 5in (12.5cm) long, with original box.
£40–45 / €55–65
$65–75 ⊞ HAL

A Corgi Toys Fiat 2100, No. 232, 1960s, 4in (10cm) long, with original box.
£25–30 / €35–40
$45–50 ⊞ HAL
In mint boxed condition this car could be worth £40–50 / €55–70 / $65–85.

A Corgi Toys Citroën Safari Olympic Winter Sports, No. 475, 1964, 5in (12.5cm) long, with box.
£50–60 / €75–85
$85–100 ⊞ HAL
In mint boxed condition this car could be worth £80–120 / €115–170 / $130–200.

◀ A Corgi Toys E-type Jaguar, No. 307, 1960s, 4in (10cm) long, with original box.
£60–70
€85–100
$100–115 ⊞ HAL

▶ A Corgi Toys Euclid TC12 tractor with dozer blade, No. 1102, 1960s, 7in (18cm) long, with original box.
£85–100
€120–140
$140–165 ⊞ HAL

DIECAST

A **Corgi Toys Superior ambulance,** No. 437, 1965, 5in (12.5cm) long, with original box.
£70–80 / € 100–115
$115–130 ⊞ WI

A **Corgi Toys Hillman Hunter rally car,** No. 302, with kangaroo, late 1960s, 7in (18cm) long, with box.
£110–120 / € 155–170
$180–200 ⊞ HAL

▶ A **Corgi Toys Mobilgas tanker,** No. 1140, late 1965–67, 8in (20.5cm) long, with box.
£290–320
€ 410–450
$480–530
⊞ UCO

A **Corgi Toys Rallye Monte-Carlo gift set,** No. 38, comprising Citroën DS19, Rover 2000 and Mini Cooper-S, 1965–67, in original box, 10in (25.5cm) high.
£400–480 / € 570–680
$660–790 ⚲ VEC
The popular series of Rally Cars was produced by Corgi from 1964–70. Inspired by real life races, Corgi chronicled all the major rallies until the Hillman Hunter World Cup Rally of 1970. This Monte Carlo Rally set includes a rare group of vehicles.

A **Corgi Toys Chipperfield's Menagerie,** 1960s–70s, in original box, 10in (25.5cm) long.
£270–300 / € 380–430
$450–500 ⊞ HAL

A **Corgi Toys Monte Carlo Hillman Imp rally car,** No. 340, 1967, 4in (10cm) long, with box.
£115–130 / € 165–185
$195–220 ⊞ HAL

A Corgi Toys Ford Cortina GXL, No. 313, with Graham Hill figure, 1970, 5in (12.5cm) long, with box.
£50–60 / €75–85
$85–100 ⊞ HAL

A Corgi Toys Chevrolet Astro 1 experimental car, No. 347, 1970s, 4in (10cm) long, with box.
£30–35 / €45–50
$50–60 ⊞ HAL

◀ A Corgi Toys Rolls-Royce Silver Shadow, No. 273, with golden jacks take-off wheels, 1960s–70s, 5in (12.5cm) long, with box.
£50–60 / €75–85
$85–100 ⊞ HAL

A Corgi Toys Land Rover, No. 438, box worn, 1960s–70s, 4in (10cm) long.
£50–60 / €75–85
$85–100 ⊞ HAL

A Corgi Toys Bond Bug, No. 389, 1970, 3in (7.5cm) long, with box.
£80–90 / €115–130
$135–150 ⊞ HAL
This lime green version is much rarer than the usual orange car.

A Corgi Toys space shuttle, No. 1364, 1981–82, in box, 7in (18cm) wide.
£50–55 / €70–80
$80–90 ⊞ GTM

DIECAST

Dinky

A Dinky Toys Aeroplanes set, No. 60, comprising six various aircraft, 1930s, in a presentation display box, 10in (25.5cm) square.
£1,100–1,200 / € 1,550–1,700
$1,850–2,000 ⚒ WAL

A Dinky Toys Imperial Airways airliner, 1930s, 4in (10cm) long.
£120–135 / € 170–190
$200–220 ⊞ CBB

▶ **A Dinky Toys Junkers JU90 airliner,** No. 62N, 1930s, 4¾in (12cm) wide, with original box.
£270–320
€ 380–450
$450–530
⚒ VEC

A Dinky Toys Hall's Distemper No. 13 lead advertising figural group, 1930s, 5¼in (13.5cm) high, with original box.
£160–175 / € 230–250
$260–290 ⚒ RAR

A Dinky Toys 25 Series Esso petrol tanker, 1930s, 4in (10cm) long.
£220–240 / € 310–340
$360–400 ⊞ CBB

A Dinky Toys trade pack of six caravans, in various colours, 1930s, in box, 7 x 4in (18 x 10cm).
£900–1,050 / € 1,300–1,500
$1,500–1,750 ⚒ WAL

▶ **A Dinky Toys tinplate petrol filling station,** No. 48, 1930s, with original box.
£350–420 / € 500–600
$580–700 ⚒ WAL

A Dinky Toys trade pack of six Motor buses, early 1930s, with original box.
£1,800–2,100 / €2,550–3,000
$3,000–3,500 ✗ WAL

A Dinky Toys Short Shetland Flying Boat, No. 701, 1947–49, 7in (18cm) long.
£250–280 / €350–400
$410–460 ⊞ CBB

A Dinky Toys RAF Aeroplanes gift set, No. 61, 1937–41, in original box, 7½in (19cm) wide.
£300–360 / €430–510
$500–600 ✗ Bon(C)

A Dinky Toys postal set, No. 12, 1937–41.
£700–840 / €1,000–1,200
$1,150–1,350 ✗ WAL

A Dinky Toys 25 Series petrol tanker, 1930s–40s, 4in (10cm) long.
£270–300 / €380–430
$450–500 ⊞ MRW

A Dinky Toys Oldsmobile 6 Sedan, American, 1947–50, 4in (10cm) long.
£90–100 / €125–140
$145–165 ⊞ CBB

◄ **A Dinky Supertoys Foden 14-ton tanker,** No. 504, first type, late 1940s, 8in (20.5cm) long, with box.
£180–200 / €250–280
$300–330 ⊞ HAL

DIECAST

A Dinky Toys Chrysler Royal Sedan, No. 39f, late 1940s, 4in (10cm) long.
£110–130 / €155–185
$180–210 ⚲ WAL

A Dinky Toys Buick Viceroy Saloon, No. 39d, American, late 1940s, 4in (10cm) long.
£140–155 / €200–220
$230–260 ⊞ CBB

A Dinky Supertoys dumper truck, No. 562, 1948–54, 4in (10cm) long, with original box.
£35–40 / €50–60
$60–70 ⊞ DAC

A Dinky Toys Lincoln Zephyr, No. 39c, late 1940s, 4in (10cm) long.
£135–150 / €190–210
$220–250 ⊞ CBB

A Dinky Supertoys Leyland Octopus wagon, No. 934, c1950, 7in (18cm) long, with original box.
£160–180 / €230–260
$270–300 ⊞ HAL

A Dinky Supertoys Guy 4-ton lorry, No. 511 1st type, 1947, 5½in (14cm) long, with box.
£130–145 / €185–200
$210–240 ⊞ CBB

▶ **A Dinky Toys Jaguar XK120 Coupé,** No. 157, c1950, 4in (10cm) long, with original box.
£80–90 / €115–125
$130–150 ⊞ HAL

A **Dinky Toys Kodak Bedford van,** No. 480, 1950, 3in (7.5cm) long, with box.
£75–85 / €105–120
$125–140 ⊞ HAL

A **Dinky Supertoys recovery tractor,** No. 661, 1950s, 5in (12.5cm) long, with box.
£80–90 / €115–130
$135–150 ⊞ HAL

A **Dinky Toys Foden flat truck,** No. 505, first type, with chains, c1952, 8in (20.5cm) long, with original lift-off box.
£11,700–14,000 / €16,700–20,000
$19,500–23,500 ⤤ VEC
This truck must have been highly sought after by a number of bidders for it to have fetched such a high price, as it would normally sell for £2,500–3,000 / €3,550–4,250 / $4,150–5,000.

A **Dinky Toys Rolls-Royce,** No. 150, 1950s, 6in (15cm) long, with box.
£55–65 / €85–95
$95–110 ⊞ HAL

A **Dinky Toys Slumberland Guy van,** No. 514, 1950–52, 6in (15cm) long.
£150–180 / €210–250
$250–300 ⤤ BLH

A **Dinky Toys racing cars gift set,** No. 4, comprising a 23g Cooper-Bristol, 23f Alfa Romeo, 23h Ferrari, 23j HMW and a 23n Maserati, 1953–54, in box, 12in (30.5cm) long.
£800–950 / €1,150–1,350
$1,350–1,600 ⤤ Bon(C)

DIECAST

A Dinky Toys Guy flat truck, No. 512, 1950s,
6in (15cm) long, with original box.
£220–250 / €310–350
$360–410 ⊞ UCO

A Dinky Toys Nestlé's Austin van, No. 471, 1950s,
3in (7.5cm) long, with original box.
£65–75 / €95–105
$110–125 ⊞ HAL

A Dinky Toys Bentley Coupé, No. 194, 1950s,
4in (10cm) long, with box.
£155–170 / €220–240
$260–280 ⊞ HAL

A Dinky Toys Plymouth estate car, No. 344, 1950s,
4in (10cm) long, with box.
£50–60 / €75–85
$85–100 ⊞ HAL

A Dinky Supertoys Coles mobile crane, No. 971,
1950s, 7in (18cm) long, with original box.
£50–55 / €70–80
$85–95 ⊞ HAL

A Dinky Supertoys Pompiers fire engine, No. 32D,
French, 1950s, 7in (18cm) long, with original box.
£160–180 / €230–260
$260–300 ⊞ HAL

A **Dinky Toys Ford Sedan,** No. 675 made in the UK for the US market, 1950s, 4in (10cm) long.
£200–240 / €290–340
$330–390 ⊞ HAL

A **Dinky Supertoys Blaw Knox bulldozer,** No. 561, 1950s, 5in (12.5cm) long, with original box.
£35–40 / €50–60
$60–70 ⊞ HAL

A **Dinky Toys Ford Fordor Sedan,** lowline example, No. 170, 1950s, 4in (10cm) long, with box.
£200–220 / €280–310
$320–360 ⊞ HAL
This model has a rare colour combination.

A **Dinky Toys Royal Mail van,** No. 260, 1955–61, 3in (7.5cm) long, with original box.
£100–110 / €140–155
$165–185 ⊞ UCO

A **Dinky Toys Talbot-Lago racing car,** No. 230, 1950s, 4in (10cm) long, with original box.
£50–55 / €70–80
$80–90 ⊞ HAL
In mint boxed condition this truck could be worth **£80–100 / €115–140 / $130–165.**

A **Dinky Toys Maserati racing car,** No. 231, 1950s, 4in (10cm) long, with box.
£50–60 / €75–85
$85–100 ⊞ HAL
In mint boxed condition this truck could be worth **£80–100 / €115–140 / $130–165.**

DIECAST

A Dinky Toys elevator loader, No. 564, 1950s, 9in (23cm) long, with original box.
£45–50 / €60–70
$75–85 ⊞ HAL

A Dinky Toys Leyland Comet cement wagon, No. 933, 1950s, 6in (15cm) long, with original box.
£105–120 / €150–170
$180–200 ⊞ HAL

A Dinky Toys Austin Raleigh Cycles van, No. 472, 1956–60, 3½in (9cm) long, with original box.
£155–175 / €220–250
$250–290 ⊞ UCO

A Dinky Supertoys Coles 20-ton lorry-mounted crane, No. 972, 1950s, 10in (25.5cm) long, with original box.
£70–80 / €100–115
$120–135 ⊞ HAL

A Dinky Supertoys tank transporter with tank gift set, No. 698, 1950s, 13in (33cm) long, with original box.
£200–220 / €280–310
$330–370 ⊞ HAL

A Dinky Toys Trojan Cydrax 15cwt van, No. 454, 1950s, 4in (10cm) long, with original box.
£155–170 / €220–240
$260–280 ⊞ HAL

▶ **A Dinky Toys Foden flat truck,** No. 905, with chains, in green, 1950s, 8in (20.5cm) long, with box.
£180–200 / €250–280
$290–320 ⊞ HAL
The maroon flat truck is more expensive at £220–250 / €310–350 / $360–410.

A Dinky Supertoys 10-ton army truck, No. 622, 1950s, 6in (15cm) long, with box.
£70–80 / €100–115
$120–135 ⊞ HAL

▶ **A Dinky Toys Big Bedford lorry,** No. 922, 1954–56, 5½in (14cm) long, with box.
£135–150 / €190–210
$220–250 ⊞ UCO

A Dinky Toys Big Bedford van, No. 923, 1955–58, 6in (15cm) long, with box.
£310–350 / €440–500
$510–580 ⊞ GTM

A Dinky Toys Guy Warrior flat truck, No. 432, 1956, 10in (25.5cm) long, with box.
£240–290 / €340–410
$400–480 ⋗ VEC

A Dinky Toys 15-pounder field gun set, No. 697, 1950s, 10in (25.5cm) long, with box.
£90–100 / €125–140
$150–165 ⊞ HAL

DIECAST

◀ **A Dinky Toys Guy van,** No. 917, 1954–56, 6in (15cm) long, with box.
£340–380 / €480–540
$560–630 ⊞ **CBB**

A Dinky Toys Rover 75 Saloon, No. 156, 1954–56, 4in (10cm) long, with original box.
£150–180 / €210–250
$250–300 ⚲ **Bon(C)**

A Dinky Toys MG Midget sports car, No. 108, 1955–59, 3½in (9cm) long, with original box.
£100–120 / €140–165
$165–195 ⚲ **Bon(C)**

A Dinky Toys police box, No. 42a, 1954–60, 3in (7.5cm) high.
£30–35 / €45–50
$50–60 ⊞ **UCO**

A Dinky Toys Foden flat truck, No. 902, 1957–59, 7in (18cm) long, with original box.
£150–180 / €210–250
$250–300 ⚲ **WAL**

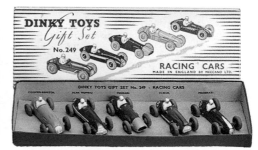

A Dinky Toys racing cars gift set, No. 249, comprising five cars, minor damage, 1955–58, in original display box, 12in (30.5cm) wide.
£630–750 / €890–1,050
$1,050–1,250 ⚲ **WAL**

A Dinky Supertoys Golden Shred Guy van, No. 919, with second-type cab and Supertoy wheels, some corrosion marks, 1957–58, 5¼in (13.5cm) long, with original box.
£200–220 / €290–340
$330–390 ✗ VEC

A Dinky Supertoys tractor and semi-trailer, No. 36B, French, 1959, 12in (30.5cm) long, with box and inner packaging.
£110–130 / €155–185
$185–220 ✗ VEC

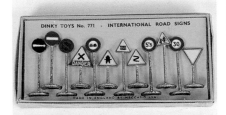

A Dinky Toys international road signs set, No. 771, 1953–65, in original box, 7in (18cm) wide.
£85–95 / €120–135
$140–155 ⊞ DAC

A Dinky Toys Post Office services gift set, No. 299, 1959, in original box, 10in (25.5cm) long.
£180–200 / €250–280
$300–330 ✗ RAR
In mint boxed condition this truck could be worth £370–450 / €520–640 / $610–750.

A Dinky Supertoys BBC TV roving eye vehicle, No. 968, 1959–64, 3¾in (9.5cm) long, with original box.
£80–95 / €115–135
$135–160 ✗ Bon(C)

A Dinky Toys Ford Consul Corsair, No. 130, 1960, 5in (12.5cm) long, with original box.
£50–55 / €70–80
$80–90 ⊞ HAL

DIECAST

A Dinky Toys Bristol Britannia airliner, No. 998, with Canadian Pacific decals, one propeller missing, 1959–64, 5½in (14cm) wide, with original box.
£110–130 / €155–185
$180–210 ⚲ WAL

► **A Dinky Supertoys snow plough,** No. 958, some wear, 1961–66, 7in (18cm) long, with original box.
£100–120 €140–170 $165–200 ⚲ WAL

A Dinky Supertoys BBC TV mobile control room, No. 969, minor wear and chips, 1964, 7in (18cm) long, with original box.
£100–120 / €140–170
$165–200 ⚲ WAL

A Dinky Supertoys missile servicing van, No. 667, 1960–64, 9in (23cm) long, with box.
£150–165 / €210–230
$250–270 ⊞ GTM

► **A Dinky Supertoys Albion lorry mounted cement mixer,** No. 960, with revolving drum, minor chips to bumper, 1960–68, 4½in (11.5cm) long, with box.
£60–70 / €85–100
$100–120 ⚲ WAL

A Dinky Toys motorway police car, No. 269, 1962–66, 4in (10cm) long, with box.
£110–120 / €155–170
$180–200 ⊞ UCO

► A Dinky Toys Ford Anglia, No. 155, early 1960s, 3in (7.5cm) long, with original box.
£50–55 / €70–80
$80–90 ⊞ HAL

A Dinky Supertoys Autobus Parisien ou Urbain,
No. 889, made in the UK for the French market,
early 1960s, 9in (23cm) long, with original box.
£180–200 / €250–280
$300–330 ⊞ UCO

A Dinky Toys AA patrol service Mini van,
No. 274, 1964–73, 3in (7.5cm) long, with box.
£135–150 / €190–210
$220–250 ⊞ UCO

A Dinky Supertoys Leyland Octopus Wagon,
No. 934, 1963, 10in (25.5cm) long, with box.
£2,800–3,300 / €4,000–4,600
$4,600–5,500 🔨 VEC

A Dinky Toys Jaguar Mk X, No. 142, with opening
boot and trunk, 1960s, 4in (10cm) long, with box.
£50–55 / €70–80
$80–90 ⊞ HAL

A Dinky Toys RAC patrol Mini van, No. 273,
1965–70, 3in (7.5cm) long, with box.
£135–150 / €190–210
$220–250 ⊞ UCO

A Dinky Toys Camion Amphibie Militaire DUKW,
No. 825, French, 1968, 7in (18cm) long, with box.
£130–145 / €185–200
$210–240 ⊞ GTM

DIECAST

◀ **A Dinky Toys Sinpar 4 x 4 Gendarmerie Militaire,** No. 815, French, 1968–72, 2½in (6.5cm) long.
£160–175 / €230–250
$260–290 ⊞ GTM

▶ **A Dinky Toys Alfa Romeo O.S.I. Scarabeo,** No. 217, 1970, 3¾in (9.5cm) long, with original box.
£40–45 / €55–65
$65–75 ⊞ OTS

A Dinky Toys Ford Escort, No. 168, early 1970s, 4in (10cm) long, with box.
£50–55 / €70–80
$80–90 ⊞ HAL

A Dinky Toys Ford Capri, No. 2162, 1:25 scale, 1973–76, in unopened packaging, 6¾in (17cm) wide.
£90–100 / €130–140
$150–165 ⊞ CBB

▶ **A Dinky Toys Chieftain tank,** No. 683, late 1970s, in unopened packaging, 10in (25.5cm) long.
£50–55 / €70–80
$80–90 ⊞ CBB

A Dinky Toys Ford Capri, No. 165, 1970s, 4in (10cm) long, with box.
£50–55 / €70–80
$80–90 ⊞ HAL

▶ **A Dinky Toys London taxi,** No. 234, 1978, in unopened box, 5in (12.5cm) long.
£18–24 / €25–33
$30–40 ⊞ CBB

Matchbox

Four Matchbox cars, c1950, 2in (5cm) long, with original boxes.
£15–20 / €20–25
$25–30 each ⊞ HAL

A Matchbox steamroller, No. 1,
early 1950s, 21in (53.5cm) long,
with box.
£30–35 / €45–50
$50–55 ⊞ HAL

A Matchbox Ferret scout car, No. 61,
1950s, 2½in (6.5cm) long, with box.
£13–17 / €18–24
$21–27 ⊞ HAL

A Matchbox Ford Prefect, No. 30,
1950s, 2½in (6.5cm) long, with box.
£25–30 / €35–40
$40–50 ⊞ HAL

A Matchbox cement mixer, No. 3,
1950s, 2½in (6.5cm) long, with box.
£20–25 / €30–35
$35–40 ⊞ HAL

A Matchbox Rolls-Royce Silver Cloud, No. 44, 1950s,
2½in (6.5cm) long, with box.
£25–30 / €35–40
$40–50 ⊞ HAL

A Matchbox milk float, No. 7, 1954,
2in (5cm) long, with original box.
£35–40 / €50–60
$60–70 ⊞ GTM

DIECAST

A Matchbox Austin A50, No. 36, 1950s,
2½in (6.5cm) long, with box.
£25–30 / €35–40
$40–50 ⊞ HAL

A Matchbox Dennis Fire Escape, No. 9, 1955,
2in (5cm) long, with original box.
£40–45 / €55–65
$65–75 ⊞ GTM

A Matchbox Diamond T
prime mover, No. 15, 1955,
2in (5cm) long, with box.
£35–40 / €50–60
$60–70 ⊞ GTM

A Matchbox caterpillar bulldozer,
No. 18, second type, mid-1950s,
2in (5cm) long, with original box.
£20–25 / €30–35
$35–40 ⊞ HAL

A Matchbox Models of Yesteryear
B–type London bus, No. 2, 1956,
3¼in (8.5cm) long, with box.
£40–45 / €55–65
$65–75 ⊞ CBB

A Matchbox Models of Yesteryear Y-11 Aveling
& Porter steamroller, late 1950s, 3¼in (8.5cm) long,
with box.
£40–45 / €55–65
$65–75 ⊞ CBB

A Matchbox Foden cement mixer, No. 26, 1956,
2in (5cm) long, with box.
£950–1,100 / €1,350–1,550
$1,600–1,800 ⋏ VEC
This model has a rare colour to the cement drum.

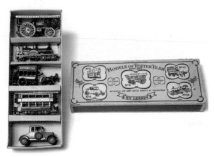

A Matchbox Models of Yesteryear gift set,
No. G7, comprising five vehicles, 1960, in box,
10in (25.5cm) long.
£200–220 / €280–310
$330–370 ⊞ GTM

A Matchbox King-size Hatra tractor shovel K-3, c1960,
6in (15cm) long, with original box.
£40–45 / €55–65
$65–75 ⊞ HAL

**A Matchbox King-size Foden dumper
truck K-5,** c1960, 5in (12.5cm) long,
with original box.
£35–40 / €50–60
$60–70 ⊞ HAL

◄ **A Matchbox
commercial vehicle set
G–1,** comprising No. 5
double-decker bus, No. 11
Esso road tanker, No. 21
long-distance coach, No.
25 Bedford 12cwt van,
No. 35 Marshall horse
box, No. 40 Bedford 7-ton
tipper, No. 47 Trojan
Brooke Bond Tea and
No. 60 Morris J2 pick up,
1962–63, with box.
£300–360 / €430–510
$500–600 ⚹ WAL

A Matchbox sugar tanker, No. 10, series A, 1960s,
3in (7.5cm) long, with original box.
£25–30 / €35–40
$40–50 ⊞ HAL
**In mint boxed condition this tanker could be worth
£80–120 / €115–170 / $135–200.**

A Matchbox VW Camper, No. 34, series B, 1960s,
3in (7.5cm) long, with original box.
£20–25 / €30–35
$35–40 ⊞ HAL

DIECAST

A Matchbox Major M1 BP tanker, 1960s, 4in (10cm) long, with box.
£35–40 / €50–60
$60–70 ⊞ HAL

A Matchbox excavator, No. 58, series B, 1960s, 3in (7.5cm) long, with original box.
£15–20 / €20–25
$25–30 ⊞ HAL

◄ **A Matchbox Models of Yesteryear London Transport tram,** early 1960s, 3in (7.5cm) long, with box.
£50–60 / €75–85
$85–100 ⊞ HAL

► **A Matchbox Snow-Trac,** No. 35B, 1964, 2½in (6.5cm) long, with box.
£20–25
€30–35
$35–40 ⊞ GTM

A Matchbox BRM racing car, No. 52B, 1965, 2½in (6.5cm) long, with box.
£15–20 / €20–25
$25–30 ⊞ GTM

Lesney

The Lesney company was founded in 1947 by two ex-servicemen and marketed through a distribution company called Moko. Moko toys were big and full of charm, but were not very successful at the time and few were sold – hence their rarity and value now.

In 1956 the company introduced Models of Yesteryear, a series that is still in production today. These soon began to be collected by adults, which means that they are more likely to be found boxed and in good condition than the Matchbox miniatures, which were aimed at children and known as the 1-75 series after the numbers applied to each model and which appears on the box. The toys were small, cheap enough for children to buy with their pocket money and were a huge success. The most prized Matchbox models often date from the 1950s and early '60s when the quality of manufacture was extremely high.

Schuco

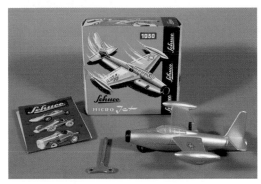

A **Schuco 1030 Micro Jet,** German, 1950s, in original
box, 5½in (14cm) square.
£45–50 / €60–70
$75–85 ✗ TQA

A **Schuco 1031 Micro Jet,** German, 1950s, in original
box, 5in (12.5cm) square.
£40–48 / €55–65
$65–75 ✗ TQA

A **Schuco Ford Custom 300,** No. 1045, German,
1950s, 4¾in (12cm) long, with box.
£85–100 / €120–140
$140–165 ✗ TQA

A **Schuco Grand Prix racer,** No. 1070, German, 1950s,
6¼in (16cm) long, with box.
£50–60 / €75–85
$85–100 ✗ TQA

A **Schuco Mercedes 220S,** No. 1038, German, 1950s,
5in (12.5cm) long, with box.
£55–65 / €80–90
$95–110 ✗ TQA

A **Schuco Ford Custom Roadster Micro Racer,**
No. 1036, German, 1950s, 4in (10cm) long, with box.
£70–80 / €100–115
$115–135 ✗ TQA

▶ A **Schuco Porsche
Formel II Micro Racer,**
No. 1037, German, 1950s,
4in (10cm) long, with box.
£45–50 / €60–70
$75–85 ✗ TQA

DIECAST

A Schuco Elektro Amphibio, No. 5560, German, 1950s, 10in (25.5cm) long, with box.
£120–140 / €170–200
$200–240 ⚡ TQA

► A Schuco Varianto Elektro, No. 3112u, late 1950s, 5in (12.5cm) long, with box.
£60–70
€85–100
$100–115
⊞ CBB

► A Schuco wind-up remote-control Mercedes, No. 1088, German, 1950s, 8½in (21.5cm) long, with box.
£250–300 / €350–420
$420–500 ⚡ TQA

A Schuco battery-operated dumper truck, No. 6077, German, 1950s, 10in (25.5cm) long, with box.
£380–450 / €540–640
$630–750 ⚡ TQA

A Schuco Jaguar E-type Micro Racer, No. 1047/1, German, 1960s, 4in (10cm) long, with box.
£75–90 / €105–125
$125–150 ⚡ TQA

A Schuco battery-operated Mercedes 190 SL, No. 5503, German, 1950s, 8in (20.5cm) long, with box.
£165–195 / €230–270
$270–320 ⚡ TQA

A Schuco Studio 1050 race car, German, 1960s, 5½in (14cm) long, with box.
£60–70 / €85–100
$100–120 ⚡ TQA

Tri-ang

◄ **A Tri-ang Spot-On Arkitex Construction Kit,** c1950, in original box, 17in (43cm) wide.
£15–20 / €20–25 $25–30 ⚲ GAZE

► **A Tri-ang electric Austin Healey 100/6,** 1:20 scale, 1950s, 9in (23cm) long, with original box.
£160–180 / €230–260 $270–300 ⊞ UCO

◄ **A Tri-ang double-decker bus,** c1950, 7in (18cm) long, with box.
£220–250 / €310–350 $360–410 ⊞ CBB
This harlequin box is scarce.

A Tri-ang Spot-On ERF 68g dropside lorry, No. 109/3, 1960, 8½in (21.5cm) long, with original box.
£175–195 / €250–280 $280–310 ⊞ GTM

◄ **A Tri-ang Spot-On crane,** No. 117, early 1960s, 12in (30.5cm) long, with box.
£135–150 / €190–210 $220–250 ⊞ HAL

A Tri-ang Spot-On Mulliner coach, No. 156, early 1960s, 11in (28cm) long.
£145–160 / €200–230 $240–270 ⊞ HAL

DIECAST

A Tri-ang Spot-On Bull Nose Morris, No. 266, 1960s, 5in (12.5cm) long, with original box.
£30–35 / €45–50
$50–55 ⊞ HAL

▶ **A Tri-ang Spot-On ERF 68g flatbed lorry,** No. 109/2, 1960s, 8in (20.5cm) long, with original box.
£200–220 / €280–310
$330–370 ⊞ HAL

A Tri-ang Spot-On gift set, No. 702, comprising Ford Zephyr 6, Morris 1100 with canoe, Austin 1800 and a dinghy and trailer, 1963, with original window box.
£230–270 / €330–380
$380–450 ⚒ VEC

A Tri-ang Spot-On United Dairies milk float, No. 122, 1960s, 6in (15cm) long, with original unopened box.
£100–110 / €140–155
$165–185 ⊞ HAL

A Tri-ang Spot-On sports cars gift set, with four cars, No. 4A, 1960s, in original box, 8 x 7in (20.5 x 18cm).
£450–500 / €640–710
$750–830 ⊞ HAL

▶ **A Tri-ang Spot-On Hillman Minx De-Luxe,** 1960s, No. 287, 6in (15cm) long, in original unopened box.
£100–110 / €140–155
$165–185 ⊞ HAL

Model Figures

Britains

A Britains set of Germanic 16th Lancers, comprising nine figures including officer and trumpeter, with moveable arms and twistable pennons, losses, 1893, in associated box.
£2,000–2,400 / €2,850–3,400
$3,300–3,950 ⚒ B(Ch)

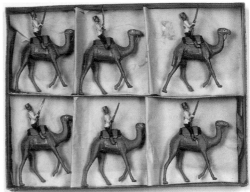

A Britains set of Egyptian Camel Corps, No. 48, with wire tails and removable riders, 1899, in original box.
£550–650 / €780–920
$910–1,050 ⚒ B(Ch)

◀ **A Britains set of 21st Lancers,** No. 94, comprising four mounted Lancers and a mounted officer, minor damage, 1901, in original box.
£400–480 / €570–670
$660–790 ⚒ VEC

A Britains Middlesex Regiment set, No. 76, comprising eight figures, 1903.
£180–210 / €260–300
$300–350 ⚒ B(Ch)

A Britains Royal Sussex Regiment set, No. 36, minor wear and chipping, early 20thC, in Whisstock box, 14½in (37cm) wide.
£150–180 / €210–250
$250–300 ⚒ WAL

A Britains US Infantry set, comprising ten marching infantrymen, 1906.
£250–300 / €360–430
$410–490 ⚒ VEC

MODEL FIGURES

▶ **A Britains French Army Chasseurs à Cheval set,** No. 139, minor wear and chipping, early 20thC, in Whisstock box, 15in (38cm) long.
£180–210 / €260–310
$300–360 ⚒ WAL

◀ **Three Britains American mounted soldiers,** from set No. 149, 1907–16.
£550–650 / €780–920
$910–1,050 ⚒ VEC

A Britains Mountain Artillery set, No. 28, comprising six gunners, a mounted officer, four mules and dismantled R. A. gun, 1910.
£160–190 / €230–270
$260–310 ⚒ VEC

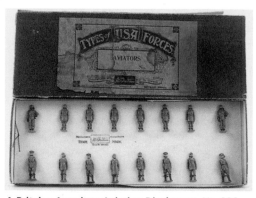

A Britains painted lead figure of a farmer, cane missing, 1920s–30s, 2¼in (5.5cm) high.
£1–5 / €2–7
$4–10 ⊞ HAL
With its cane, the price range of this figure would be £7–8 / €10–11 / $11–13.

A Britains American Aviation Display set, No. 336, comprising 16 figures of aviators and marching privates, 1929, in original box.
£600–720 / €850–1,000
$1,000–1,200 ⚒ VEC

A Britains painted lead figure of a lady railway passenger, 1920s–30s, 2¼in (5.5cm) high.
£20–25
€30–35
$35–40 ⊞ HAL

▶ **A Britains painted lead figure of a milkmaid,** 1920s–30s, 1in (2.5cm) high.
£3–7 / €4–9
$5–11 ⊞ HAL

A Britains Royal Horse Artillery set, No. 318, comprising artillerymen mounted on standing horses, a mounted officer and fumed metal limber and gun, standing artillery men missing, 1930.
£850–1,000 / € 1,200–1,400
$1,400–1,650 ⚮ B(Ch)
This is a rare set, because boys wanted the horse cantering or trotting – standing still was considered dull.

A Britains set of King's African Rifles, No. 225, comprising eight marching figures with fixed bayonets, 1926–41, boxed, 15in (38cm) long.
£90–105 / € 125–150
$150–180 ⚮ G(L)

◀ **A Britains painted lead figure of a shepherd,** 1920s–30s, 2¼in (5.5cm) high.
£8–12 / € 11–16
$13–18 ⊞ HAL

A Britains painted lead figure of a village idiot, 1930s, 2¼in (5.5cm) high.
£190–220 / € 270–310
$310–350 ⚮ RAR

A Britains Austro-Hungarian Infantry of the Line set, No. 177, comprising seven marching troopers and an officer with a sword, later version without equipment, 1930s, 2½in (6.5cm) high.
£220–260 / € 310–370
$370–430 ⚮ G(L)

MODEL FIGURES

A Britains set of Royal Navy Bluejackets and Whitejackets, No. 254, comprising nine figures including Petty Officer, some retouching to paint, 1935.
£100–120 / €140–165
$165–195 ⚒ B(Ch)

▶ **A Britains mushroom,** from the Garden Set, 1939, 2½in (6.5cm) high.
£135–150
€190–210
$220–250
⊞ RUSS
This mushroom is a rare piece.

A Britains Coronation coach, No. 953, 1953, in original box, 8 x 18in (20.5 x 45.5cm).
£290–330 / €410–460
$480–530 ⊞ HAL

A Britains gnome, partly painted, c1939, 5½in (14cm) high.
£60–70 / €85–90
$100–115 ⊞ RUSS

▶ **A Britains set of eight lead soldiers,** No. 2035, 1949–59, 2in (5cm) high, with original box.
£160–180 / €230–260
$270–300 ⊞ UCO

A Britains set of African Zulu Warriors, No. 147, 1950s, in original box, 14¾in (37.5cm) wide.
£115–130 / €165–185
$190–210 ⚒ RAR

A Britains set of 12 lead soldiers, No. 2108, Drums and Fifes of the Welsh Guard, 1956, 2¼in (5.5cm) high, with original box.
£560–670 / €800–950
$930–1,100 ⚒ VEC

A Britains Togoland Warriors set, 1954–59, 2in (5cm) high, with original box.
£160–180 / €230–260
$270–300 ⊞ UCO

A Britains 10th Duke of Cambridge's Own Bengal Lancers set, No. 46, minor wear, 1950s, in original box, 15in (38cm) wide.
£140–165 / €200–240
$230–270 ✗ WAL

A Britains set of Royal Welch Fusiliers, No. 2124, with officer and goat mascot, 1958, with original box.
£140–165 / €200–240
$230–270 ✗ B(Ch)

A Britains Naval Landing Party set, No. 79, comprising eight naval ratings and gun, some wear, 1950s, in original box, 12in (30.5cm) wide.
£230–270 / €330–390
$380–450 ✗ WAL

▶ **A painted lead figure of Andy Pandy,** 1950s, 3in (7.5cm) high.
£50–60 / €70–80
$85–100 ⊞ RUSS

A Britains State Coach set, No. 1470, 1950s, in original box, 10in (25.5cm) long.
£140–165 / €200–240
$230–270 ✗ WAL

◀ **A Britains Model Farm set,** No. 152F, comprising ten pieces, slight damage, 1950s, in original box.
£110–130 / €155–185 $180–210 ➹ WAL

Britains figures

Britains success in making toy solider figures led to many smaller companies, such as Fry, Hanks and Davies that were run by ex-Britains employees, producing exact reproductions of Britains' early issues. All were eventually prosecuted and figures are extremely rare and now very sought after.

▶ **Two Britains Eyes Right sets,** Scots Guards Band and Royal Marines Band, c1970, in original boxes, 4 x 14in (10 x 35.5cm).
£70–80 €100–115 $115–130 ⊞ GTM

German Figures

◀ **A Heyde Serbian Cavalry set,** German, c1900, 2in (5cm) high, with original box.
£490–550 €700–780 $810–910 ⊞ SAND

A Heyde set of Red Indians, incomplete, German, c1900, 2in (5cm) high, with original box.
£310–350 / €440–500 $510–580 ⊞ SAND

◀ **A Heyde set of Greek evzones,** German, c1900, 2in (5cm) high, boxed.
£400–450 €570–640 $660–750 ⊞ SAND

A Heyde Greek Cavalry set, German, c1900, 2in (5cm) high, boxed.
£450–500 / €640–710 $750–830 ⊞ SAND

▶ **A Heyde set of Prussian hussars,** German, c1900, 2¾in (7cm) high.
£450–500 €640–710 $750–830 ⊞ SAND

Later Figures

▶ **A cast-metal horse and cowboy,** 1950s, 3½in (9cm) long.
£22–26
€30–35
$38–42 ⊞ **CBB**

An elastolin lucky camel money box, German, c1920, 4in (10cm) high.
£60–70 / €85–95
$100–115 ⊞ **HAL**
Elastolin figures were made by the German toy figure company Hausser between 1920 and 1941. Elastolin is a compound made of kaolin, sawdust and glue.

A Cherilea Toys plastic military figure, 1950–60, 3in (7.5cm) high.
£1–5 / €2–7
$3–8 ⊞ **HAL**

A Kellogg's plastic give-away figure of a Native American, by Crescent Toys, 1960s, 2½in (6.5cm) high.
£1–5 / €2–7
$3–8 ⊞ **HAL**

MODEL FIGURES

A Britains plastic figure of a Native American, from the Detail Range, on a metal base, 1970s–80s, 2¼in (6.5cm) high.
£1–5 / €2–7
$3–8 ⊞ HAL

A Britains plastic Swoppet figure of a War of the Roses Knight, with removable parts, 1960s, 3in (7.5cm) high.
£11–15 / €16–21
$19–24 ⊞ HAL

A Tinpo toys plastic figure of a knight, 1960–80, 3in (7.5cm) high.
£1–5 / €2–7
$3–8 ⊞ HAL

A Britains plastic figure of a French Foreign Legionnaire, from the Detail Range, on a metal base, 1970s–80s, 2½in (6.5cm) high.
£1–5 / €2–7
$3–8 ⊞ HAL

A set of Labayen figures of Napoleon and his Generals, comprising seven pieces, 1970, 2¼in (5.5cm) high.
£510–610 / €720–860
$850–1,000 ➴ P(Ba)

Four Lone Star diecast metal Metallions, modelled as famous cowboys and Indians, 1970s, 2in (5cm) high.
£5–9 / €7–11
$8–14 ⊞ HAL

Games

◀ **A selection of 'onion skin' glass marbles,** c1850, largest ½in (12mm) diam.
£50–60
€75–85
$85–90 each
⊞ MRW

A satin walnut counter box, decorated with transfer scenes of the life and times of Napoleon, containing four lift-out boxes, each with a sliding cover and containing ivory counters, c1850, 9in (23cm) wide.
£280–330 / €400–470
$460–550 ⚒ TMA

◀ **A Victorian mahogany, rosewood and satinwood-inlaid games box,** 18½in (47cm) wide.
£130–155 / €185–220
$210–250 ⚒ SWO

▶ **A Bussey's table croquet set,** lid loose, one ball and one peg missing, c1860, in maker's original box, with internal instructions.
£20–25 / €30–35
$35–40 ⚒ MUL

Three miniature bone dice, 1850–70, 4mm square.
£11–15 / €16–21
$19–24 ⊞ MRW

A wooden table game, 'Squails', c1870, 12in (30.5cm) wide.
£60–70 / €85–95
$100–110 ⊞ J&J

A Victorian leather dice shaker, 4½in (11.5cm) high.
£11–15 / €16–21
$19–24 ⊞ HO

A set of ceramic spongeware carpet balls, Scottish, c1880, 3in (7.5cm) diam.
£50–60 / €70–85
$85–100 ⊞ TWr

A J. Jaques table game, 'Squails', c1870, in a mahogany case, 9 x 5in (23 x 12.5cm).
£135–150 / €190–210
$220–250 ⊞ HUM

▶ **A hand-made glass marble,** with basket-weave incisions, c1880, 1in (2.5cm) diam.
£25–30 / €40–45
$45–50 ⊞ MRW

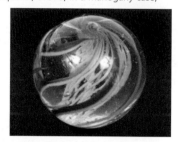

A J. Jaques and Hamley Bros table game, 'Ping Pong or Grossima', c1900, in original box, 9 x 32in (23 x 81.5cm).
£90–100 / €130–145
$150–165 ⊞ J&J

A magic set, French, c1880, in a box, 10in (25.5cm) wide.
£540–600 / €770–850
$900–990 ⊞ AUTO

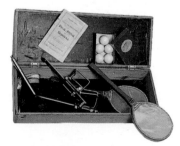

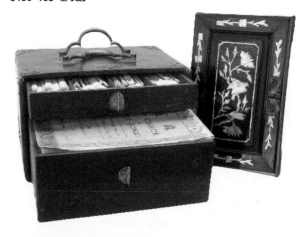

A J. Jaques Ping Pong table tennis set, with vellum-covered bats, brass uprights, original net, balls and rules, c1901, in original box, 21in (53.5cm) wide.
£180–200 / €260–290
$300–330 ⊞ STK

◀ **A Mah Jong set,** in a fitted wood case, the sliding front inlaid with mother-of-pearl, Chinese, early 20thC, 8¼in (21cm) wide.
£170–200 / €240–280
$280–330 🪚 L&E

A British Domino set, c1910, in a tin, 7in (18cm) wide.
£35–40 / €50–60
$60–70 ⊞ TOP

A ball bearing puzzle, depicting a mounted soldier, German, c1910, 2½in (5cm) diam.
£8–12 / €11–16
$13–19 ⊞ HUX

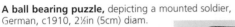

◄ A Chad Valley Cocoa-nut Pitch ball game, c1910, in a box, 13in (33cm) wide.
£60–70 / €85–100
$100–115 ⊞ J&J

A Spilli-Wobble game, c1910, in original box, 12in (30.5cm) wide.
£30–35 / €40–50
$50–60 ⊞ J&J

◄ A J. Jaques horse-racing game, Minoru, c1910, 15in (38cm) wide.
£70–80
€100–115
$115–130
🔨 GAZE

► A Wembley Exhibition Electrical Mah Jong set, 1924, 5 x 7in (12.5 x 18cm).
£35–40
€50–60
$60–70 ⊞ COB

A Bing The Witch's Cauldron game, German, c1920, 8 x 4in (20.5 x 10cm).
£40–45 / €55–65
$65–75 ⊞ J&J

GAMES

A Durable Toy and Novelty Corp Radio Questionnaire game, American, 1928, 9in (23cm) square.
£15–20 / €20–25
$25–30 ⊞ J&J

A Toys & All Fair Games Blinky Blinx Tiddledy Winks game, American, 1928, 9 x 10in (23 x 25.5cm).
£20–25 / €30–35
$35–40 ⊞ J&J

A Parker Bros Humpty Dumpty game, American, 1920s, in original box, 7 x 13in (18 x 33cm).
£50–55 / €70–80
$80–90 ⊞ J&J

A Spear's Games Comical Tivoli Game, 1920s, 11 x 8in (28 x 20.5cm).
£90–100 / €130–145
$150–165 ⊞ J&J

▶ **A Chad Valley Escalado horse-racing game,** c1930, 8 x 11in (20.5 x 28cm).
£180–200 / €260–290
$300–330 ⊞ RGa

◀ **A Roberts & Co Glevum Bounce Ball game,** c1930, 8in (20.5cm) wide.
£11–15 / €16–21
$19–24 ⊞ J&J

▶ **A Kiddi-Golf game,** possibly by Glevum, comprising a wood and metal nine-hole crazy golf course, c1930, in a cardboard box, 13 x 10½in (33 x 26.5cm).
£195–220 / €280–310
$320–360 ⊞ ARo

A Cardora Derby Dog Race Game, with six hollow-cast painted lead dogs, c1930, 18 x 11in (45.5 x 28cm).
£105–120 / €150–165
$175–195 ⊞ ARo

A Chad Valley Stumpy Joe Quoits game, c1930, in original box, 8in (20.5cm) square.
£15–20 / €20–25
$25–30 ⊞ J&J

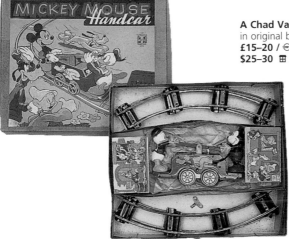

A Wells Mickey Mouse handcar set, No. 99, comprising a four-wheel clockwork-powered handcar, with Mickey Mouse and Donald Duck composition figures, with track, 1930s, in a box, 12in (30.5cm) wide.
£400–480 / €570–680
$660–790 ✦ WAL

A tinplate cat and mouse game, German, 1930s, 1½in (4cm) diam.
£20–25 / €30–35
$35–40 ⊞ LBe

A Chad Valley Mickey Mouse Ring Quoits game, 1930s, 13½in (34.5cm) square.
£70–80 / €100–110
$115–130 ⊞ ARo

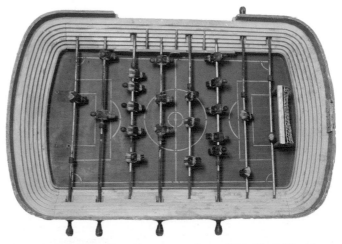

A wooden football table, with terracotta players, 1940, 38in (96.5cm) long.
£125–140 / €180–200
$200–230 ⊞ TRA

GAMES

A Chad Valley set of Muffin The Mule Picture Cubes, with six sheets showing the scenes to be created on the six sides of the cubes, c1949, 6in (15cm) square.
£270–300 / €380–420
$450–500 ⊞ MTMC

A Reno Series Table Tennis set, 1950, 11 x 14in (28 x 35.5cm).
£15–20 / €20–25
$25–30 ⊞ JUN

▶ **A game of 'Toupe Royale',** the gilt-brass gallery with leaf finials enclosing a playing surface with five figures of a Jester and four other attendants, within an outer gallery, on turned legs, 1950s, 35in (89cm) high.
£1,950–2,200
€2,770–3,150
$3,250–3,650 ⊞ CAG

A Table Golf game, comprising a baize golf course, four metal golfers, nine metal hole markers, metal balls and bunkers, 1940s, in a cardboard box, 10 x 8½in (25.5 x 21.5cm).
£195–220 / €280–310
$320–360 ⊞ ARo

▶ **A Merit Grand Prix game,** 1950s, 20 x 16in (51 x 40.5cm).
£20–25
€30–35
$35–40 ⊞ GTM

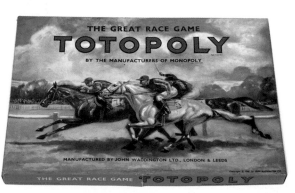

A Spear's Games Bali card game, 1950s, 6 x 3in (15 x 7.5cm).
£5–9 / €7–11
$8–14 ⊞ RTT

A Waddington's The Great Race Totopoly, 1960s version of 1949 game, 14 x 20in (35.5 x 51cm).
£110–125 / €160–180
$180–200 ⊞ RGa

A Beetle Drive game, 1960s, 7in (18cm) square.
£6–10 / €8–14
$10–16 ⊞ RTT

► A Standard Toy Craft Supercar Road Race Game, American, 1960s, 15 x 11in (38 x 28cm).
£180–200
€260–290
$300–330
⊞ HAL

An Ariel Odds-on Greyhound Race Game, c1970, 17in (43cm) square.
£35–40 / €50–60
$60–70 ⊞ ARo

◄ A Marx Speedmarx Over and Under Auto Racing Set, 1960s, in original box, 19in (48.5cm) wide.
£11–15 / €16–21
$19–24 ➤ GAZE

An Ideal Rubik's Revenge cube, 1980s, 3½in (9cm) high, with original packaging.
£15–20 / €20–25
$25–30 ⊞ CWo

Bagatelles

A mahogany folding bagatelle board, with numbered arched bridge and nine balls, 19thC, 37in (94cm) wide.
£170–200 / €240–280
$280–330 ➤ BWL

A Chad Valley wooden Bruin Boys bagatelle game, with printed paper pop-up figures, 1920s, in original box, 21in (53cm) long.
£40–45 / €55–65
$65–75 ⊞ CDC

► A pinball machine, with Bakelite bumpers, c1940, 40in (101.5cm) long.
£135–150 / €190–210
$220–250 ➤ AMc

GAMES

A Riders of the Range bagatelle game, based on the characters in *Eagle* comic, 1950s, 12in (30.5cm) high.
£20–25 / €30–35
$35–40   J&J

A *Magic Roundabout* bagatelle game, 1967, 7in (18cm) diam.
£16–18 / €22–25
$25–28   CMF

A plastic *Batman and Robin* bagatelle pinball game, 1960s, 22in (56cm) high.
£40–45 / €55–65
$65–75   HarC

A plastic Superman bagatelle pinball game, c1970, 22in (56cm) high.
£40–45 / €55–65
$65–75   HarC

▶ **A plastic Noddy bagatelle pinball game,** Spanish, c1970, 17in (43cm) high, with original packaging.
£25–30 / €35–40
$40–50   HarC

A plastic *Space 1999* bagatelle pinball game, c1970, 22in (56cm) high.
£25–30 / €35–40
$40–50   HarC

A Lido plastic Popeye bagatelle pinball game, American, c1970, 13in (33cm) high.
£30–35 / €45–50
$50–60   HarC

▶ **A plastic Yogi Bear bagatelle pinball game,** American, c1970, 7in (18cm) diam, unopened.
£15–20 / € 20–25
$25–30 ⊞ HarC

A Walt Disney plastic bagatelle pinball game, c1980, 17in (43cm) high.
£15–20 / € 20–25
$25–30 ⊞ HarC

A plastic Paddington Bear bagatelle pinball game, c1970, 16in (40.5cm) high.
£25–30 / € 35–40
$40–50 ⊞ HarC

▶ **A plastic TinTin bagatelle pinball game,** Spanish, c1980, 10in (25.5cm) diam.
£15–20 / € 20–25
$25–30 ⊞ HarC

A Walt Disney plastic bagatelle pinball game, c1990, 15in (38cm) high.
£11–15 / € 16–21
$19–24 ⊞ HarC

Board Games

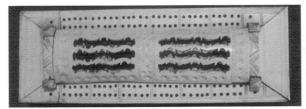

A bone cribbage board, made by Napoleonic prisoners-of-war, modelled as a casket, the domed hinged lid carved with scrolled bars, enclosing a figure of a mean wearing military uniform, flanked by pierced scorers, the shaped apron on square legs, French, early 19thC, 9in (23cm) long.
£800–950 / € 1,150–1,350
$1,350–1,600 ⚶ PF

A mahogany solitaire board, with spiral marbles, 19thC, 14in (35.5cm) diam.
£800–960 / € 1,150–1,400
$1,350–1,600 ⚶ G(B)

GAMES

► **A marquetry games board,** inlaid with bone and brass, the interior marked with two panels for backgammon, German, 19thC, 21¾ x 19in (55.5 x 48.5cm).
£2,000–2,400
€2,850–3,400
$3,300–3,950 ⚒ P

An arbutus games box, with marquetry-inlaid banding, the interior fitted for backgammon, Irish, 19thC, 18in (45.5cm) square.
£500–600 / €710–850
$830–990 ⚒ WW

◄ **A walnut games compendium,** label for Stephenson, c1850, 12½in (32cm) wide.
£1,350–1,600
€1,900–2,250
$2,250–2,700
⚒ B(Ed)

A painted Parcheesi game board, American, New England, 1870–80, 27½in (70cm) square.
£4,250–5,100 / €6,000–7,250
$7,000–8,450 ⚒ SK(B)

A Box Top Familiar Objects board game, c1890, 11 x 11½in (28 x 29cm).
£15–20 / €20–25
$25–30 ⊞ RUSS

◄ **A Jeu du Cheval Blanc board game,** French, c1900, 9 x 12in (23 x 30.5cm).
£95–110 / €135–150
$160–180 ⊞ RGa
This is similar to the English board game of Ball and Hammer.

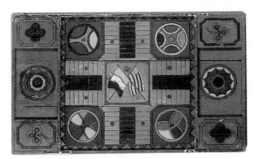

An incised and painted board game, possibly Canadian, early 20thC, 19in (48.5cm) wide.
£4,200–5,000 / €6,000–7,100
$7,000–8,300 ⚒ SK(B)

A Snakes and Ladders board game, box missing, c1910, 10 x 20in (25.5 x 40.5cm).
£20–25 / €30–35
$35–40 ⊞ J&J

◄ **A Jeu de l'Oie board game,** French, c1910, 16 x 20in (40.5 x 51cm).
£20–25 / €30–35
$35–40 ⊞ J&J

► **A Burnett tin Lucky Race board game,** c1910, 12in (30.5cm) high.
£50–60 / €75–85
$85–100 ⊞ J&J

A Spear's Games Playing for the Cup board game, c1930, 7 x 10in (18 x 25.5cm).
£40–45 / €55–65
$65–75 ⊞ J&J

The Bonzo Chase game, 1920s–30s, 10 x 7in (25.5 x 18cm).
£85–95 / €120–135
$140–155 ⊞ HYP

► **A Hiking board game,** with lead figures, c1930, 9 x 10in (23 x 25.5cm).
£40–45
€55–65
$65–75 ⊞ J&J

GAMES

A Spear's Games Ludo game, 1930s, 11in (28cm) wide.
£55–65 / €80–95
$90–105 ⊞ HYP

A H. P. Gibson & Sons Dover Patrol or Naval Tactics game,
instructions missing, 1930s, 8 x 15in (20.5 x 38cm).
£25–30 / €35–40
$40–50 ⊞ J&J

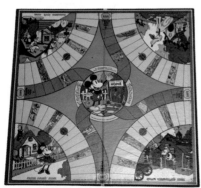

► A Chad
Valley Walt
Disney's
Mickey Mouse
game board,
c1940, 17in
(43cm) square.
£25–30
€35–40
$40–50 ⊞ J&J

A Chad Valley Grand National Steeplechase
board game, 1930s, 15 x 40in (38 x 101.5cm).
£80–90 / €115–130
$135–150 ⊞ RGa

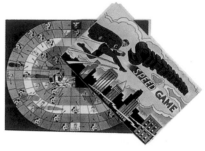

A Milton Bradley Co Superman Speed
Game, with four painted wooden pieces and
wooden die, American, early 1940s, in original
box, 16 x 9in (40.5 x 23cm).
£700–840 / €1,000–1,200
$1,150–1,400 ⚒ CBP

A Chad Valley Walt Disney's Pinocchio
board game, c1950, 14in (35.5cm) square.
£15–20 / €20–25
$25–30 ⊞ J&J

◄ A Chad Valley Wig Wam game, 1950,
19 x 15in (48.5 x 38cm).
£11–15 / €16–21
$19–24 ⊞ J&J

◀ An Ilex
Speedway
board game,
c1950,
9 x 12in
(23 x 30.5cm).
£30–35
€45–50
$50–60 ⊞ J&J

A Waddington's Buccaneer game, 1950s,
in original box, 24in (61cm) wide.
£15–20 / €20–25
$25–30 ⊞ ARo

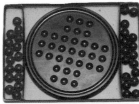

A Chad Valley Tug of War board game, 1950s, 5 x 19in (12.5 x 48.5cm).
£20–25 / €30–35
$35–40 ⊞ J&J

An Ilex Solitaire set, c1950, in a
box, 7 x 10in (18 x 25.5cm).
£15–20 / €20–25
$25–30 ⊞ J&J

▶ A TT Race board
game, incomplete, 1950s,
10in (25.5cm) square.
£6–10 / €8–14
$10–16 ⊞ RTT

◀ A Touring
England board
game, 1950s,
14½ x 10in
(37 x 25.5cm).
£15–20
€20–25
$25–30 ⊞ RTT

A Chad Valley Race to Toy Town game, 1950s, 7 x 12in
(18 x 30.5cm).
£15–20 / €20–25
$25–30 ⊞ J&J

GAMES

A Bell Toys *Double Your Money* quiz game, 1950s, 14in (35.5cm) square.
£15–20 / €20–25
$25–30 ⊞ **J&J**

A Bell Toys Bruce Forsyth *I'm in Charge* board game, 1960s, 14in (35.5cm) square.
£15–20 / €20–25
$25–30 ⊞ **J&J**

A Denys Fisher War of the Daleks board game, with eight plastic Dalek mascots and a moving track, 1970s, 14 x 18in (35.5 x 45.5cm).
£70–80 / €100–110
$115–130 ⊞ **ARo**

Computer & Electronic

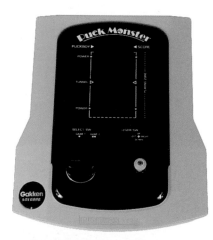

A Gakken hand-held Puck Monster computer game, 1970s, 9in (23cm) high.
£15–20 / €20–25
$25–30 ⊞ **CGX**

◀ **An MB Electronics Super Simon game,** 1970s, 12in (30.5cm) wide.
£15–20
€20–25
$25–30 ⊞ **CGX**

An MB Electronics hand-held Simon game, first model, one of only 30, 1970s, 10¾in (27.5cm) diam, boxed.
£25–30 / €35–40
$40–50 ⊞ **CGX**

◀ **An Onko electronic hand-held Super Space Jack game,** 1970s, 10in (25.5cm) high.
£25–30 / €35–40
$40–50 ⊞ **CGX**

Condition

Condition, as always, is important. Check for signs of corrosion around the battery compartment. Applied decals on the game should be intact with no signs of lifting, bubbling or fading. The game should be in working order; controls can stick and sound is usually the first thing to go. Games that do not work can be bought very cheaply and with the necessary expertise they can be repaired and restored.

**A Mattel Electronics Intellivision
television entertainment centre,**
late 1970s, 13½in (34.5cm) wide.
**£105–120 / €150–165
$175–195** ⊞ CGX

A Grandstand Video Sports Centre
game, c1978, 10in (25.5cm) wide.
**£45–50 / €65–75
$75–85** ⊞ CGX

A Cosmic Scramble computer
game, c1980, 8½in (21.5cm) high.
**£25–30 / €35–40
$40–50** ⊞ CGX

**A Tomy Caveman computer
game,** c1980, 8½in (21.5cm) high.
**£11–15 / €16–21
$19–24** ⊞ CGX

A Sinclair ZX Spectrum personal computer, 48 RAM, 1981, in original
box, 8 x 14in (20.5 x 35.5cm).
**£140–160 / €200–220
$230–260** ⊞ OW

**A Nintendo Mickey and Donald Game
& Watch Multi Screen electronic game,**
1982, in original box, 4 x 6in (10 x 15cm).
**£80–90 / €115–130
$130–145** ⊞ OW

▶ **An Action Leisure Ground Grandstand
Cave Man electronic game,** 1982, in original
box, 7 x 9in (18 x 23cm).
**£35–40 / €50–60
$60–70** ⊞ OW

GAMES

Two Nintendo Game & Watch Multi Screen electronic games, Donkey Kong and Donkey Kong II, 1982, in original boxes, 4 x 7in (10 x 18cm).
£45–50 / €65–75
$75–85 each ⊞ OW

A Super Color-screen hand-held electronic game, Tarzan, Pirates of the Caribbean, 1982, in original box, 4 x 7in (10 x 18cm).
£115–130 / €165–185
$190–210 ⊞ OW

A Nintendo Game & Watch Panorama Screen electronic game, Popeye, 1983, in original box, 5 x 7in (23.5 x 18cm).
£115–130 / €165–185
$190–210 ⊞ OW

A Nintendo Game & Watch pocket-size Multi Screen electronic game, Mario Brothers, 1983, 5in (12.5cm) square, with original box.
£45–50 / €65–75
$75–85 ⊞ OW

Three Tomy Tomytronic 3-D electronic games, Planet Zeon, Thundering Turbo, Sky Attack, 1983, in original boxes, 8 x 7in (20.5 x 18cm).
£35–40 / €50–60
$60–70 ⊞ OW

▶ **A Tomy Tomytronic 3-D stereo electronic game,** Skyfighters, 1984, 6 x 8in (15 x 20.5cm).
£15–20 / €20–25
$25–30 ⊞ OW

A **Sega Game Gear game cartridge,** Sonic the Hedgehog, c1988, 3in (7.5cm) high.
**£3–7 / €4–8
$5–9 ⊞ MEx**

A **Mosaic Bookware computer game and diary,** The Adrian Mole Secret Diary Kit, 1986, 8½ x 6in (21.5 x 15cm).
**£1–5 / €2–7
$3–8 ⊞ CGX**

An **Atari computer game,** Footballer of the Year, c1986, 5½in (14cm) high.
**£1–5 / €2–7
$3–8 ⊞ CGX**

A **Nintendo Game Boy game,** 1980–90, 2½in (6.5cm) square.
**£3–7 / €4–8
$5–9 ⊞ MEx**

◀ A **Sega Game Gear portable video game system,** c1988, 8in (20.5cm) wide.
**£35–40 / €50–60
$60–70 ⊞ MEx**

A **Rainbow Arts computer game,** Turrican, c1990, 7½in (19cm) high.
**£1–5 / €2–7
$3–8 ⊞ CGX**

◀ An **SNK computer game,** Baseball Stars, and three other computer games, 1990s.
**Baseball Stars
£25–30 / €35–40 / $40–50 each
Other Games
$11–15 / €16–21 / $19–24 each
⊞ CGX**

GAMES

Playing Cards

► **A pack of Royal National Patriotic playing cards,** c1900, 3½ x 2in (9 x 5cm).
£135–150
€ 190–210
$220–250
⊞ MURR

A pack of Goodalls playing cards, depicting kings and queens, c1897, 5 x 4in (12.5 x 10cm).
£75–85 / € 105–120
$125–140 ⊞ MURR

◄ **A pack of De La Rue playing cards,** depicting lady and gentleman motorists, 1900–08, 5 x 3½in (12.5 x 9.5cm).
£75–85
€ 105–120
$125–140
⊞ MURR

A pack of Lambert & Butler The Garrick playing cards, c1910, 5 x 3¼in (12.5 x 8.5cm).
£25–30 / € 35–40
$40–50 ⊞ HUX

A pack of Alice in Wonderland playing cards, 1905, 5 x 3¼in (12.5 x 8.5cm).
£65–75 / € 90–100
$105–120 ⊞ HUX

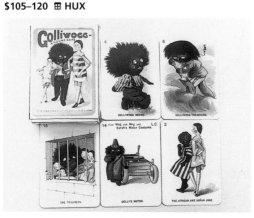

► **A pack of John Jaques & Son French for Fun playing cards,** 1910, 4 x 3in (10 x 7.5cm).
£11–15 / € 16–21
$19–24 ⊞ J&J

◄ **A pack of Florence Upton Golly snap cards,** 1910–20, 5 x 4in (12.5 x 10cm).
£90–100
€ 125–140
$150–165
⊞ MURR

A pack of Chad Valley Round Card Game of Happy
Families playing cards, c1920, 6 x 4in (15 x 10cm).
£20–25 / €30–35
$35–40 ⊞ J&J

◀ A Chad
Valley Old
Maid card
game, 1920,
4in (10cm) square.
£15–20
€20–25
$25–30 ⊞ J&J

▶ A pack of Dewar's playing
cards, 1920s, 5 x 3¾in
(12.5 x 9.5cm).
£20–25 / €30–35
$35–40 ⊞ HUX

A pack of Dewar's playing cards, 1920s, 5 x 3¾in
(12.5 x 9.5cm).
£20–25 / €30–35
$35–40 ⊞ HUX

A pack of Dewar's playing cards, 1920s, 5 x 3¾in
(12.5 x 9.5cm).
£20–25 / €30–35
$35–40 ⊞ HUX

A pack of Waddington's Black & White Whisky
playing cards, 1930s, 5 x 3¼in (12.5 x 8.5cm),
in a sealed box.
£25–30 / €35–40
$40–50 ⊞ HUX

A pack of Sadia Water Heater playing cards, 1930s,
3¼in (8.5cm) diam.
£20–25 / €30–35
$35–40 ⊞ HUX

GAMES

A pack of De La Rue playing cards, depicting a
mounted jockey, 1930s, 2½ x 3in (6.5 x 7.5cm).
£11–15 / €16–21
$19–24 ⊞ ATK

A pack of Chad Valley Knock Knock playing cards,
1930s, 4 x 3in (10 x 7.5cm).
£15–20 / €20–25
$25–30 ⊞ J&J

A pack of playing cards, depicting matches,
1930s, 3½ x 2½in (9 x 6.5cm).
£14–18 / €20–25
$23–29 ⊞ BOB

A Kum-Bak Jack of All Trades card game, 1930s,
4 x 3in (10 x 7.5cm).
£14–18 / €20–25
$23–29 ⊞ J&J

A Pepys Film Fantasy card game, 1940s, 4 x 2½in (10 x 6.5cm).
£11–15 / €16–21
$19–24 ⊞ J&J

◀ A pack of playing cards, depicting aeroplanes, 1930s,
3¼in (8.5cm) high.
£11–15 / €16–21
$19–24 ⊞ HUX

A pack of **Victory playing cards,** depicting satirical portraits of WWII figures, 1939–45, 3½ x 2½in (9 x 6.5cm).
£20–25 / €30–35
$35–40 ⊞ HUX

A pack of **Metrovick & Cosmos Lamps playing cards,** 1940s, 3½ x 2½in (9 x 6.5cm), in tax wrapper.
£30–35 / €45–50
$50–60 ⊞ BOB

A *Wizard of Oz* card game, 1940s, 5 x 3¼in (12.5 x 8.5cm).
£30–35 / €45–50
$50–60 ⊞ HUX

An **Animal Grab card game,** 1940s, 4 x 2½in (10 x 6.5cm).
£6–10 / €8–14
$10–16 ⊞ RTT

A **Pepys I Commit card game,** 1940s, 3½ x 2½in (9 x 6.5cm).
£11–15 / €16–21
$19–24 ⊞ HUX

A pack of **playing cards,** 1940s, 3½ x 2½in (9 x 6.5cm), in tax wrapper.
£20–25 / €30–35
$35–40 ⊞ BOB

A pack of **Metrovick Lamps playing cards,** 1940s, 3¼in (8.5cm) high.
£11–15 / €16–21
$19–24 ⊞ HUX

GAMES

◀ A Kargo golfing card game, 1940s, 3¼in (8.5cm) high.
£20–25
€30–35
$35–40 ⊞ HUX

▶ A Pepys Peter Cheyney Crime Club card game, c1950, 4 x 3in (10 x 7.5cm).
£11–15
€16–21
$19–24 ⊞ J&J

A Castell Brothers Progress card game, Pepys series, c1950, 4 x 2½in (10 x 6.5cm).
£15–20 / €20–25
$25–30 ⊞ J&J

A pack of 'Art Studies' plastic-coated playing cards, depicting pin-up girls, American, 1950s, 3½in (9cm) high, with original box.
£30–35 / €45–50
$50–60 ⊞ SpM

A Muffin the Mule card game, 1950s, 5 x 3¼in (12.5 x 8.5cm).
£20–25 / €30–35
$35–40 ⊞ HUX

A pack of So I Told 'Em Oldham playing cards, with Jokers, 1950s, 3½ x 2½in (9 x 6.5cm).
£25–30 / €35–40
$40–50 ⊞ BOB

A pack of Glamour Girls plastic-coated playing cards, depicting 55 different girls, 1950s, 3¾ x 2¼in (9.5 x 5.5cm).
£50–60 / €70–80
$85–95 ⊞ SpM

A Russell Manufacturing Co Disneyland Express Trainload of Walt Disney's Fantasyland Card Games, American, 1950s, 14in (35.5cm) long.
£75–85 / €105–120
$125–140   ⊞ J&J

A double pack of playing cards, with Jokers, 1950s, 5 x 3in (12.5 x 7.5cm).
£25–30 / €35–40
$40–50   ⊞ BOB

A pack of Waddington's playing cards, 1950s, 4 x 3in (10 x 7.5cm).
£6–10 / €8–14
$10–16   ⊞ COB

A pack of Guinness playing cards, 1950s, 3½ x 2½in (9 x 6.5cm).
£15–20 / €20–25
$25–30   ⊞ J&J
This pack would be valued at £25 / €35 / $40 with the original box.

A Pepys Punch & Judy card game, 1950s, 3½ x 2½in (9 x 6.5cm).
£15–20 / €20–25
$25–30   ⊞ J&J

A pack of playing cards, designed by Raymond Peynet, 1950s–60s.
£30–35 / €45–50
$50–60   ⊞ RDG

A pack of Riders of the Range playing cards, from the *Eagle* comic, late 1950s, 3¼in (8.5cm) high.
£11–15 / €16–21
$19–24   ⊞ HUX

A pack of playing cards, depicting pin-up girls, 1950–60s, 3½ x 2½in (9 x 6.5cm).
£11–15 / €16–21
$19–24   ⊞ RTT

GAMES

▶ **A Walt Disney's Alice card game,** 1960s, 5 x 3½in (12.5 x 9cm).
£20–25 / €30–35
$35–40 ⊞ HUX

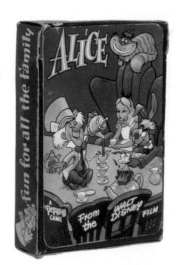

A Sooty Saves Sixpence card game, 1960, 3¼in (8.5cm) high.
£11–15 / €16–21
$19–24 ⊞ HUX

A pack of British Airways playing cards, 1960s, 4 x 2½in (10 x 6.5cm).
£6–10 / €8–14
$10–16 ⊞ RTT

A pack of Embassy Cigarettes playing cards, 1960s, 4 x 2½in (10 x 6.5cm).
£6–10 / €8–14
$10–16 ⊞ RTT

A pack of decimalization playing cards, 1971, 4 x 2½in (10 x 6.5cm).
£1–5 / €2–7
$3–8 ⊞ CMF

◀ **A pack of Roots playing cards,** 1970s, 4 x 2½in (10 x 6.5cm).
£6–10 / €8–14
$10–16 ⊞ RTT

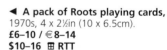

◀ **A pack of Smiling Brand playing cards,** depicting pin-up girls, 1970s, 2 x 1½in (5 x 4cm).
£6–10 / €8–14
$10–16 ⊞ RTT

A pack of Tetley's Tea playing cards, 1980s, 2½in (6.5cm) high.
£1–5 / €2–7
$3–8 ⊞ CMF

Yo-Yos

A Return Top Deluxe yo-yo, Japanese, 1940,
2in (5cm) diam.
£15–20 / €20–25
$25–30 ⊞ YO

Four Lumar pressed-metal yo-yos, c1950,
2¼in (5.5cm) diam.
£15–20 / €20–25
$25–30 each ⊞ YO

A Lumar 34 pressed-metal yo-yo,
1950s, 2¼in (5.5cm) diam.
£15–20 / €20–25
$25–30 ⊞ YO

A Lumar pressed-metal whistling
yo-yo, 1950s, 2½in (6.5cm) diam.
£70–80 / €100–115
$115–130 ⊞ YO

A yo-yo instruction book, by
Linda Sengpiel, American, 1972,
8in (20.5cm) diam.
£20–25 / €30–35
$35–40 ⊞ YO

▶ A Duncan Fire Wheels plastic
yo-yo, American, 1973,
2¼in (5.5cm) diam.
£11–15 / €16–21
$19–24 ⊞ YO

A Mondial Injection Came-yo
aluminium yo-yo, by Harry Baier,
with rubber buffers, German,
c1998, 2¼in (5.5cm) diam.
£95–110 / €135–155
$155–180 ⊞ YO

◀ An Ultimate Proyo II limited
edition yo-yo, 1999,
2¼in (5.5cm) diam.
£11–15 / €16–21
$19–24 ⊞ YO

A Team Losi Cherry Bomb yo-yo,
1998, 2in (5cm) diam.
£15–20 / €20–25
$25–30 ⊞ YO

Trains

◀ A Welker & Crosby cast-iron and wood floor train, American, c1885, 35in (89cm) long.
£2,500–3,000
€3,550–4,250
$4,150–4,950 ➤ S(NY)

A Wilkins cast-iron floor train, old repair to locomotive, American, c1890, 54in (137cm) long.
£3,300–3,950 / €4,700–5,600
$5,500–6,500 ➤ S(NY)

A painted tin train set, comprising buildings, track and figures, German, c1900.
£7,000–8,400 / €9,950–11,900
$11,600–13,900 ➤ RBB

A Karl Bub tinplate gauge 0 clockwork 4–4–0 locomotive, RN1632, with six-wheel tender and two bogie carriages with opening doors and side-hinged roof, minor damage, German, early 20thC.
£550–660 / €780–930
$910–1,050 ➤ WAL

A Güntherman American Outline 4–4–0 loco and tender, No. 101, with cow catcher, 1905–10, 13¾in (35cm) long.
£500–600 / €710–850
$830–1,000 ➤ VEC

A Carette gauge 1 eight-wheeled carriage, with opening doors, German, c1910.
£270–300 / €380–420
$450–500 ▦ WOS

A Hubley cast-iron floor train, American, c1920, 34in (86.5cm) long.
£1,100–1,300 / €1,550–1,850
$1,800–2,150 ➤ S(NY)

A clockwork 2in gauge tank locomotive, No. 112, with a coal tender and a quantity of track, 1920s, 15in (38cm) long.
£350–420 / €**500–600**
$580–680 ⚒ G(B)

A freight wagon, German, 1930s, 7in (18cm) long.
£40–45 / €**55–65**
$65–75 ⊞ WOS

A Lionel electric 2–6–2 streamlined locomotive and tender, with three-rail pick-up, American, 1930s, 18in (45.5cm) long.
£145–165 / €**200–220**
$240–270 ⊞ WOS

An LMS live steam 4–4–2 locomotive and tender, 3½in gauge, finished in GNR livery, early 1930s, 45in (114.5cm) long.
£1,000–1,200 / €**1,400–1,650**
$1,650–1,950 ⚒ ROS

A Wrenn Great Western Railways locomotive and tender, 'Devizes Castle', 1930s, 10in (25.5cm) long.
£90–100 / €**130–145**
$150–165 ⊞ DAC

A Milbro gauge 0 bogie passenger coach, RN 8173, third class, corridor, 1930s.
£110–130 / €**160–190**
$180–210 ⚒ WAL

A Leeds Model Co gauge 0 Brighton Belle Pullman coach, 'Hazel', minor wear, 1930s.
£100–120 / €**140–165**
$165–195 ⚒ WAL

A Trix Express train set, comprising locomotive, tender and three coaches, c1935, locomotive 7in (18cm) long.
£450–500 / €**640–710**
$750–830 ⊞ WOS

◀ **An American Flyer gauge 0 electric train,** roof repainted, c1935, 21in (53.5cm) long.
£180–200
€260–290
$300–330
⊞ **WOS**

▶ **An Exley restaurant car,** with Great Western crest, third class, c1935, 17in (43cm) long.
£360–400 / €510–570
$600–660 ⊞ HOB

A Bowman gauge 0 live steam tank locomotive, c1935, 9in (23cm) long.
£120–135 / €170–190
$200–220 ⊞ DQ

A tin electric train shed, No. 2E, with brick- and slate-effect decoration, 1936, 20in (51cm) long.
£400–450 / €570–630
$660–730 ⊞ HOB

A Leeds Model Co Great Western locomotive, 1937, 7in (18cm) long.
£180–200 / €260–290
$300–330 ⊞ HOB

An engine and tender, 'Princess Elizabeth', 1938, in original wooden box, 23in (58.5cm) long.
£2,000–2,300 / €2,850–3,150
$3,300–3,650 ⊞ HOB

▶ **A Crescent garage set,** with metal figures and accessories, incomplete, c1949, 14in (35.5cm) wide.
£450–500 / €780–900
$910–1,050 ⊞ MRW

A Fleischmann gauge H0 D.B. 4–6–2 mainline heavy duty locomotive and tender, German, 1950s.
£90–100 / € 125–140
$150–165 ⊞ WOS

A Pyramid Toys gauge 00 clockwork Trackmaster N2 goods train set, 1950s, in original box, 9 x 14in (23 x 35.5cm).
£65–75 / € 90–100
$105–120 ⚡ RAR

◀ **A hand-built brass engine,** No. GP7, with Tenshodo bogie, American, 1954, 7in (18cm) long.
£90–100 / € 125–145
$150–165 ⊞ WOS

A hand-built brass engine, with Tenshodo bogie, American, c1958, 9in (23cm) long.
£90–100 / € 125–140
$150–165 ⊞ WOS

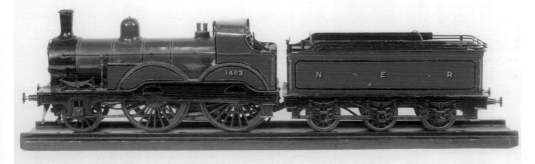

A 3½in gauge 2–4–0 coal-fired GNR Stirling locomotive and tender, No. 1463, 1950s–60s, 37in (94cm) long.
£820–980 / € 1,150–1,300
$1,350–1,500 ⚡ AH

A Lionel gauge 0 electric locomotive, No. 1668.E, with four tinplate rolling stock and track, marked, American, mid-20thC.
£80–95 / €115–135
$130–155 ✗ SWO

A Fleischmann electric locomotive, German, 1960s, 12in (30.5cm) long, boxed.
£75–85 / €105–120
$125–140 ⊞ WOS

A Rivarossi gauge H0 plastic station, No. 5511, Italian, c1965, 21in (54cm) long, boxed.
£60–70 / €85–95
$100–110 ⊞ WOS

A gauge 0 motorized fine scale LSWR Drummonds 'Bug', two rail, c1970, 10in (25.5cm) long.
£990–1,100 / €1,400–1,650
$1,650–1,950 ✗ RAR

▶ **A Wrenn gauge 00 4–6–2 West Country class locomotive and tender,** No. RN 21C109, 'Lyme Regis', 1973–78, 11½in (29cm) long, with original box.
£140–165 / €200–240
$230–270 ✗ WAL

A gauge 0 fine scale LSWR Adams Radial tank engine, two rail, electric motor, 1970s, 10in (25.5cm) long.
£490–550 / €700–770
$810–900 ✗ RAR

A Wills Finecast gauge 00 LSWR class T9 kit-built locomotive and tender, 1975, 9in (23cm) long, with original box.
£140–160 / €200–220
$230–260 ✗ RAR

▶ **A Wrenn AM2 4–6–2 locomotive and tender,** No. 46238, 'City of Carlisle', some paint chips and flakes, 1970s.
£180–210 / €250–300
$300–360 ✗ VEC

◀ A Wrenn 4–6–2 streamlined locomotive and tender, No. 35026, 'Lamport & Holt Line' 1970s.
£160–190 / €230–270
$260–310 ⚲ VEC

A J & M Toys-style gauge 1 kit model railcar, No. RN 162, diecast bogies and steel wheels, GWR roundel transfer, 1970s–80s, 16in (40.5cm) long.
£150–180 / €210–250
$250–300 ⚲ WAL

A pair of Wrenn gauge 00 Brighton Belle Pullman coaches, 1970s.
£155–175 / €220–250
$260–290 ⊞ WOS

▶ A Wrenn gauge 00 4–6–2 city class locomotive and tender, No. RN 4642, 'City of Glasgow', 1978–91, 11½in (29cm) long, with original box and paperwork.
£110–130 / €160–190
$180–210 ⚲ WAL

◀ A Wrenn gauge 00 4–6–2 A4 class locomotive and tender, No. RN 7, 'Sir Nigel Gresley', 1971–91, 11in (28cm) long, in associated original box.
£55–65 / €80–95
$90–105 ⚲ WAL

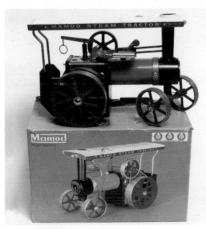

A Mamod Sherman's steam engine, c1980, 10in (25.5cm) long, boxed.
£80–90 / €115–130
$130–145 ⊞ GTM

▶ A Bachmann gauge 00 2–6–2 Branch Line V2 class locomotive, No. 8509, 1990s, 9in (23cm) long, boxed.
£40–45 / €55–65
$65–75 ⊞ GTM

A British Rail electric freight engine, 1980s, 10in (25.5cm) long.
£18–22 / €25–30
$30–35 ⊞ GTM

Bassett-Lowke

A **Carette for Bassett-Lowke gauge 1 carriage,**
1910–14, 11in (28cm) long.
£200–220 / €280–310
$330–370 ⊞ WOS

▶ A **Bing for Bassett-Lowke gauge 0 LMS 2783
passenger coach,** c1925, 13in (33cm) long.
£110–125 / €155–175
$190–210 ⊞ DQ

A **Bassett-Lowke gauge 0 clockwork LMS
locomotive and tender,** restored, 1920s,
17in (43cm) long, with original box.
£240–270 / €340–380
$400–440 ✕ BKS

◀ A **Bassett-Lowke
2–6–0 live steam Mogul,**
No. 2945, in LMS black,
only fired once or twice,
with instructions and inner
packing card, 1930s,
15in (38cm) long.
£550–650 / €780–930
$910–1,050 ✕ VEC

▶ A **Bassett-Lowke gauge 0 4–6–0 live steam
locomotive and tender,** No. 6285, 'Enterprise', c1935,
with other items including original Bassett-Lowke bill of
sale, spare wick and spring, filler, two cans each of
rocket oil and cylinder oil.
£500–600 / €710–840
$830–990 ✕ AH

A **Bassett-Lowke gauge 1 2–6–0 clockwork Mogul
locomotive and tender,** 1930s, 24in (61cm) long.
£680–750 / €960–1,100
$1,150–1,300 ✕ BKS

▶ A **Bassett-Lowke gauge 0
spirit-fired 2½in scale locomotive
and tender,** 'Flying Scotsman',
c1935, locomotive 20in (51cm) long.
£900–1,000 / €1,300–1,450
$1,500–1,650 ✕ BKS

A Bassett-Lowke 2525 gauge 0 live steam locomotive and tender, No. 2525, 'Enterprise', c1935, 18in (45.5cm) long, boxed.
£400–450 / €570–630
$660–730 ⊞ DQ

▶ **A Bassett-Lowke 4–6–2 electric locomotive and tender,** 'Flying Scotsman', c1952.
£1,000–1,200 / €1,400–1,650
$1,650–1,950 ⚸ S

A Bassett-Lowke gauge 0 BR clockwork locomotive and tender, 'Prince Charles', c1952, 16in (40.5cm) long, boxed.
£250–280 / €260–290
$410–460 ⊞ WaH

◀ **A Bassett-Lowke gauge 0 electric locomotive and tender,** 'Queen Elizabeth', c1952, 20in (51cm) long.
£1,800–2,000
€2,550–2,850
$3,000–3,300 ⊞ HOB

Bing

A Bing 240 tinplate clockwork steam engine, 1912, 16in (40.5cm) long.
£850–950 / €1,200–1,350
$1,400–1,550 ⊞ JUN

A Bing clockwork gauge 0 LMS locomotive and tender, 1920, 14in (35.5cm) long.
£190–220 / €270–300
$310–350 ⚸ RAR

Two Bing carriages, German, 1920s, 5in (12.5cm) long.
£50–55 / €70–80
$85–95 ⊞ WOS

◀ **A Bing plastic signal box,** restored, 1930s, 10in (25.5cm) high.
£40–45 / €55–65
$65–75 ⊞ WOS

Märklin

A Märklin live-steam locomotive, German, c1912, 12in (30.5cm) long.
£310–350 / €440–490
$510–570 ⊞ DQ

A Märklin gauge 0 steam locomotive and tender, German, 1935, 20in (51cm) long.
£2,700–3,200 / €3,800–4,550
$4,500–5,400 ⚒ KOLN

A Märklin tinplate signal bell, restored, German, late 1930s, 5in (12.5cm) high.
£20–25 / €30–35
$35–40 ⊞ WOS

A Märklin 4–4–0 three-rail electric locomotive and tender, No. E800, made in Germany for the UK market, c1938, locomotive 6in (15cm) long.
£25,250–30,300 / €36,000–43,000
$42,000–50,000 ⚒ VEC

A Märklin four-wheeled crane truck, No. 1668, German, 1930s.
£170–200 / €240–280
$280–330 ⚒ VEC

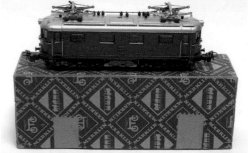

A Märklin gauge H0 Swiss railway Bo-Bo twin pantograph mainline locomotive, German, 1950s, boxed.
£190–220 / €270–300
$310–350 ⊞ WOS

Hornby

A Hornby gauge 0 Royal Scot locomotive and tender,
slight imperfections, c1920,
£300–360 / €510–610
$600–720 ↗ N

The Hornby clockwork Train,
finished in Great Northern livery,
brass numberplate 2710, 1920,
14in (35.5cm) wide, with original box.
£1,100–1,300 / €1,550–1,850
$1,800–2,150 ↗ S(S)

◀ **A Hornby gauge 0 saloon car,**
early 1920s, 13in (33cm) long.
£115–130 / €165–185
$190–210 ⊞ HAL

**A Hornby gauge 0 Coleman's Mustard
wagon,** 1923, 6in (15cm) long, with box.
£1,800–2,000 / €2,550–2,800
$3,000–3,300 ⊞ HOB

A Hornby clockwork train set,
1923, in original box, 11 x 14in
(28 x 35.5cm).
£270–300 / €380–420
$450–500 ⊞ HOB

**A Hornby clockwork
train,** No. 0, in Great
Northern livery, comprising
0–4–0 locomotive and
tender, two coaches
and track, early 1920s,
in original box,
21in (53.5cm) wide.
£310–350 / €440–490
$510–570 ⊞ BKS

◀ **A Hornby porter's
barrow and luggage
set,** c1925, in original
box, 8in (20.5cm) long.
£105–120 / €150–170
$175–195 ⊞ HOB

A Hornby Crawford's Biscuits railway wagon,
with gold crest, c1927, 7in (18cm) long.
£180–200 / €260–290
$300–330 ⊞ HOB

A Hornby gauge 0 single wine wagon, c1928,
6in (15cm) long.
£270–300 / €380–420
$450–500 ⊞ HOB

A Hornby Great Western train tender, 1928, 15in (38cm) long.
£2,250–2,500 / €3,200–3,550
$3,700–4,050 ⊞ HOB

A Hornby No. 2 gauge 0 timber wagon, 1930,
14in (35.5cm) long.
£55–65 / €80–90
$90–100 ⊞ GTM

A Hornby No. 1 gauge 0 special tank engine, c1930,
7in (18cm) long, boxed.
£200–220 / €280–310
$330–370 ⊞ GTM

A Hornby gauge 0 clockwork Southern locomotive,
c1930, 11in (28cm) long.
£360–400 / €510–570
$600–660 ⊞ HOB

A Hornby gauge 0 Pullman coach, c1930, boxed.
£135–150 / €190–210
$220–250 ⊞ GTM

A Hornby Meccano coal wagon, 1930, 7in (18cm) long.
£135–150 / €190–210
$220–250 ⊞ HOB

A Hornby No. 2 electric LNER 201 locomotive and tender, 'Bramham Moor', 1930, 16in (40.5cm) long.
£1,800–2,000 / €2,550–2,850
$3,000–3,300 ⊞ HOB

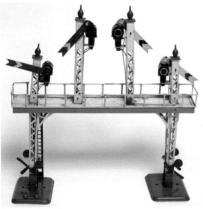

A Hornby electric signal gantry, 1932, 14in (35.5cm) high.
£900–1,000 / €1,300–1,450
$1,500–1,650 ⊞ HOB

A Hornby station, with a note indicating its history and ownership, 1930s, 33in (84cm) long, with original box.
£115–130 / €165–185
$190–210 ⚒ BKS

▶ A Hornby gauge 0 clockwork engine, 1930s, 8in (20.5cm) long.
£165–185 / €230–260
$270–300 ⊞ WOS

A Hornby gauge 0 open wagon 'B', RS 694, 1934, 7in (18cm) long, with original box.
£50–55 / €70–80
$85–95 ⊞ GTM

▶ A Hornby electric locomotive, 'Lord Nelson', with boxed tender, 1930s, 16in (40.5cm) long.
£270–300 / €380–420
$450–500 ⚒ BKS

A Hornby tinplate gauge 0 20v electric locomotive and tender, 'Flying Scotsman', damaged, 1930s,
17in (43cm) long.
£180–200 / €260–290
$300–330 ⊞ HAL

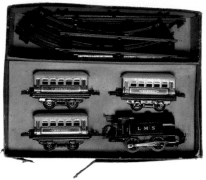

A Hornby gauge 0 clockwork train set,
1930s, in a box, 13 x 16in (33 x 40.5cm).
£195–220 / €280–310
$320–360 ⊞ HAL

A Hornby No. 1 passenger train set, 1930s, boxed.
£300–360 / €430–510
$500–600 ⋩ WAL

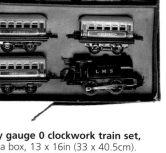

**A Hornby No. 2 gauge 0 special Pullman
car,** 'Loraine', 1930s, 15in (38cm) long,
with original box.
£200–240 / €290–340
$330–390 ⋩ DN

A Hornby No. 2 gauge 0 clockwork special LMS locomotive,
1930s, 10in (25.5cm) long.
£115–130 / €165–185
$190–210 ⊞ HAL

▶ **A Hornby No. 2 gauge 0
clockwork 4–4–2 special tank
locomotive,** No. 6, 1930s.
£280–330 / €400–480
$460–550 ⋩ VEC

A Hornby No. 2 gauge 0 corridor brake end coach, with opening windows, compensating bogies with reduced Mansell wheels, mid-1930s.
£230–270 / €330–390
$380–450 ⚒ WAL

◄ A Hornby gauge 0 E2E engine shed, with two three-rail roads, details to one side only, mid-1930s.
£370–440 / €520–620
$610–730 ⚒ WAL

A Hornby No. 2 gauge 0 4–4–0 special LNER locomotive and tender, RN 201, 'Bramham Moor' hunt class, mid-1930s, 15in (38cm) long.
£360–430 / €500–600
$580–690 ⚒ WAL

◄ A Hornby gauge 0 clockwork M3 tank locomotive, No. 2270, 1935, 8in (20.5cm) long, boxed.
£65–75 / €90–105
$105–120 ⊞ GTM

A Hornby 20v electric locomotive and tender, No. 6100, 'Royal Scot', 1935, 16in (40.5cm) long.
£460–520 / €650–720
$760–840 ⊞ HOB

► A Hornby snow plough railway wagon, 1936, 7in (18cm) long.
£75–85
€105–120
$125–140
⊞ HOB

A Hornby gauge 0 train station, No. 2E, 'Margate', with electric bracket lamps, c1936, with original box.
£320–380 / €450–540
$530–630 ⚒ DN

A Hornby No. 1 gauge 0 0–4–0 clockwork tank locomotive, c1937.
£35–40 / € 50–55
$60–70 ⊞ VJ

A Hornby clockwork locomotive, 1937, 8in (20.5cm) long.
£135–150 / € 190–210
$220–250 ⊞ HOB

▶ A Hornby electric locomotive and tender, 'Eton', 1937–39, 15in (38cm) long.
£540–600 / € 770–850
$900–990 ➤ BKS

A Hornby clockwork locomotive and tender, No. 234, c1938, 15in (38cm) long.
£810–900 / € 1,150–1,300
$1,350–1,500 ⊞ HOB

A Hornby closed-axle goods wagon, c1938, 7in (18cm) long.
£1,050–1,200 / € 1,500–1,650
$1,750–1,950 ⊞ HOB

◀ Three Hornby gauge 0 accessories, No. 1 footbridge with lattice sides, No. 1 level crossing, single track, No. 2 signal cabin with glued posters, late 1930s.
£85–100 / € 120–140
$140–165 ➤ DN

A Hornby No. 4 electric locomotive and tender, 'Eton', c1938, 13in (33cm) long.
£1,250–1,400 / € 1,800–2,000
$2,100–2,350 ⊞ HOB

A set of Hornby No. 3 gauge 0 platform machines, 1938, in original box, 8½in (21.5cm) long.
£135–150 / €190–210
$220–250 ➹ RAR

A Hornby gauge 0 Southern Railways passenger coach, late 1930s, 13in (33cm) long, boxed.
£310–350 / €450–500
$520–580 ⊞ WaH

A Hornby No. 3 4–4–2 electric locomotive and tender, No. 6100, 'Royal Scot', three rail, with smoke deflectors, 1938, 12in (30.5cm) long.
£450–540 / €640–770
$750–890 ➹ VEC

▶ **A Hornby Dublo LMS electric locomotive,** No. 6917, c1939, 5in (12.5cm) long.
£145–160 / €210–240
$240–270 ⊞ HAL

Three Hornby gauge 0 railway wagons, c1940, 6in (15cm) long, with original boxes.
£35–40 / €50–55
$60–70 each ⊞ STK

A Hornby No. 1 gauge 0 level crossing, c1940, boxed.
£35–40 / €50–55
$60–70 ⊞ STK

Three Hornby gauge 0 wagons, 1940s–50s, 6in (15cm) long, boxed.
£25–30 / €35–40
$40–45 each ⊞ HAL

A Hornby gauge 0 signal,
1940s, 9in (23cm) high.
£15–20 / €25–30
$30–35 ⊞ STK

▶ **A Hornby dublo
all-metal locomotive,**
'Cardiff Castle', 1950,
11in (28cm) long,
with original box.
£115–130 / €165–185
$190–210 ⊞ HAL

A Hornby Dublo uncoupling rail, c1952, 6½in (16.5cm) long, boxed.
£15–20 / €25–30
$30–35 ⊞ CWO

A Hornby train set, c1950, in
original box, 18 x 16in (45.5 x 40.5cm).
£310–350 / €450–500
$520–580 ⊞ HOB

▶ **A Hornby Dublo locomotive
and tender,** 'Duchess of Montrose',
three rail, 1950s, 11½in (29cm) long.
£55–65 / €80–90
$90–100 ⊞ WOS

A **first type gauge 00 locomotive and tender,** 'Duchess of Montrose', 1950s, locomotive 9in (23cm) long, boxed.
£90–100 / €125–140
$150–165 ⊞ HAL

A **Hornby tinplate No. 1 gauge 0 crane truck,** 1950s, 6½in (16.5cm) long, boxed.
£25–30 / €35–40
$40–45 ⊞ WOS

A **Hornby Dublo tank engine,** three rail, 1950s, 8in (20.5cm) long, boxed.
£50–60 / €70–80
$85–95 ⊞ HAL

A **Hornby tinplate No. 41 gauge 0 wagon,** 1950s, 8in (20.5cm) long, boxed.
£30–35 / €45–50
$50–55 ⊞ WOS

A **Hornby Dublo restaurant car,** with tin roof, 1950s, 9in (23cm) long, boxed.
£15–20 / €25–30
$30–35 ⊞ HAL

A **Hornby gauge 0 Cadbury's Chocolates box car,** 1950s, 5in (12.5cm) long.
£190–220 / €270–300
$310–350 ⊞ WOS

◀ A **Hornby No. 50 clockwork goods train set,** 1950s, in original box.
£200–240 / €280–330
$330–390 ⚒ WAL

A Hornby BR diesel locomotive, two rail, 1950s.
£65–75 / €90–105
$105–120 ⊞ WOS

A Hornby Dublo T.P.O. mail van set, 1950s,
11in (28cm) long, boxed.
£30–35 / €45–50
$50–55 ⊞ HAL

▶ **A Hornby gauge 0
tinplate station,** with
later electric lights,
bulbs missing, 1950s,
32in (81.5cm) wide.
£75–85 / €105–120
$125–140 ⊞ WOS

**A Hornby gauge 0 printed
tinplate signal box,** with pierced
windows, c1955, 7in (18cm) high.
£30–35 / €45–50
$50–55 ⊞ WaH

◀ **A Hornby Dublo gauge 00
coal wagon,** 1954–58,
4in (10cm) long, boxed.
£8–12 / €11–16
$13–18 ⊞ GTM

A Hornby Dublo LMS passenger train set, comprising 4–6–2 'Duchess of
Atholl' locomotive and tender, track, controller, spanner and oil, repaired,
1950s, with original box.
£280–330 / €400–480
$460–550 ⚚ VEC

**A Hornby Dublo gauge 00
DI tank wagon,** 1956–57,
4in (10cm) long, boxed.
£11–15 / €16–21
$19–24 ⊞ GTM

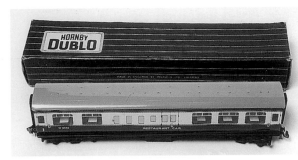

A Hornby Dublo tinplate restaurant car, 1950s, 9in (23cm) long, boxed.
£15–20 / €25–30
$30–35 ⊞ HAL

A Hornby gauge 0 LNER flat truck and container, 1956–59, 6in (15cm) long, boxed.
£35–40 / €50–55
$60–70 ⊞ GTM

▶ **A Hornby Dublo all-metal locomotive,** 'Duchess of Montrose', three rail, 1950s, 12in (30.5cm) long, with original box.
£70–80 / €100–110
$115–130 ⊞ HAL

Four Hornby Dublo wagons, 1950s–60s, 4in (10cm) long, with boxes.
£11–15 / €16–21
$19–24 ⊞ HAL

A Hornby Dublo electric LMR 8F freight locomotive and tender, 1958–61, with original box.
£110–125 / €155–175
$180–200 ⊞ GTM

A Hornby Dublo electric suburban locomotive, with a trailing coach, 1962–64, each 9in (23cm) long, boxed.
£270–310 / €380–420
$450–500 ⊞ WaH

A Hornby Dublo locomotive and tender, 'City of London', two rail, 1960s, 12in (30.5cm) long.
£115–130 / €165–185
$190–210 ⊞ HAL

A Hornby Dublo locomotive and tender, with nickel-plated wheels, three rail, c1962, 7in (18cm) long, with original box.
£190–220 / €270–300
$310–350 ⊞ WaH

▶ **A Hornby No. 50 gauge 0 gas cylinder wagon,** 1960s, 10in (25.5cm) long, boxed.
£35–40 / €50–55
$60–70 ⊞ GTM

A Hornby Minitrix N-gauge locomotive and tender, No. N203, c1980, 6½in (16.5cm) long, boxed.
£65–75 / €90–100
$105–120 ⊞ WOS

A Hornby No. 50 gauge 0 low-sided wagon with Liverpool Cables drum, 1960s,
6in (15cm) long, boxed.
£40–45 / €55–65
$65–75 ⊞ GTM

▶ **A Hornby gauge 0 4–6–2 LMS class 7P locomotive,**
'The Princess Royal', 1980s, 14in (35.5cm) long, boxed.
£45–50 / €65–75
$75–85 ⊞ GTM

A Hornby gauge 00 Battle of Britain class locomotive, R375, 'Spitfire', 1980s, 11in (28cm) long, boxed.
£65–75 / €90–100
$105–120 ⊞ GTM

A Hornby *Harry Potter and the Philosopher's Stone* electric train set, 'Hogwarts Express', 2001, in original box, 24in (61cm) wide.
£75–85 / €105–120
$125–140 ⊞ WOS

Tri-ang

A pair of Tri-ang Emu powered and non-powered suburban motor coaches, R156 and R25, RN S1-57S and S1052S, with seats, minor wear, 1950s, 9in (23cm) long, boxed.
£100–120 / € 140–165
$160–190 ⚒ WAL

A Tri-ang wooden train, c1930, 26in (66cm) long.
£135–150 / € 190–210
$220–250 ⊞ JUN

A Tri-ang Dublo locomotive, c1960, 11in (28cm) long.
£30–35 / € 45–50
$50–55 ⊞ WOS

A Tri-ang Blue Pullman electric train set, No. RS52, early 1960s, in original box, 15in (38cm) wide.
£60–70 / € 85–95
$100–110 ⊞ GAZE

▶ **A Tri-ang RS29 Local Passenger train set,** comprising 4–6–0 B12 locomotive and tender, two Mark I coaches and track, c1964, boxed.
£80–95 / € 115–135
$130–155 ⚒ VEC

Tri-ang Hornby

Tri-ang, a division of the toy giant Lines Bros, started making model trains in the 1950s, a quarter of a century after Tri-ang Toys was registered as a trade mark by William, Arthur and Walter Lines. Tri-ang had previously established itself making wooden and metal toys and, after rivalling Hornby trains throughout the 1950s, Tri-ang Railways and Hornby Dublo merged in 1965 to become Tri-ang Hornby. The Tri-ang Group was disbanded in 1971 and the model railway system was renamed Hornby Railways in 1972.

◀ **A Tri-ang Hornby Minic RMD motorail set,** comprising Dock Authority diesel shunter, rail transporter, Aston Martin, track and hand controller, c1967, boxed.
£250–300 / € 360–430
$410–490 ⚒ VEC

Sci-Fi

Space Toys

A tinplate Rocket Racer, Japanese, 1950, 7in (18cm) long.
£105–120 / €150–165
$175–195 ⊞ HUX

An SFA tinplate friction spaceship, French, 1950s,
6in (15cm) diam.
£30–35 / €45–50
$50–55 ⊞ HUX

A Kokusai Mokei Co wooden 'Rocket' boat, with
battery-powered electric motor, Japanese, 1950s,
20in (51cm) long, boxed.
£380–450 / €540–640
$630–750 ⤢ AH

◄ **A tinplate X-7
flying saucer,**
with bump-and-
go mechanism
and animated
pilot, slight
damage,
1950s–60s, 7¾in
(19.5cm) diam.
£50–60 / €70–80
$85–100 ⤢ BLH

A TM Space Control gun, Japanese, c1950,
4in (10cm) wide.
£70–80 / €100–110
$115–130 ⊞ HUX

A Merit *Dan Dare* Planet Gun, with three spinning
missiles and instructions, 1953, in original box,
7 x 11in (18 x 28cm).
£270–300 / €380–420
$450–500 ⊞ SSF

A Modern Toys tinplate Moon Rocket, Japanese,
1950s, 9in (23cm) long.
£180–200 / €260–290
$300–330 ⊞ HUX

A Dinky Toys *Captain Scarlet* **Spectrum Pursuit Vehicle,** No. 104, 1960s, 6in (15cm) long, with box.
£135–150 / €190–210
$220–250 ⊞ HAL

◀ **An S.H. tinplate and plastic battery-operated space capsule,** Japanese, c1960, 15in (38cm) high.
£90–100 / €130–145
$150–165 ⊞ GTM

A tinplate battery-operated Sonicon Rocket, Japanese, c1960, 13in (33cm) long.
£220–250 / €310–350
$360–400 ⊞ HAL

A Modern Toys tinplate battery-operated Planet Explorer, Japanese, 1960s, 9in (23cm) long.
£115–130 / €165–185
$190–210 ⊞ HAL

A *Captain Scarlet* **Lone Star diecast cap gun,** 1960s, 7in (18cm) long.
£40–45 / €55–65
$65–75 ⏇ GAZE

A tinplate clockwork Emergency Space Rocket, 1960s, 6in (15cm) long, boxed.
£75–85 / €105–120
$125–140 ⊞ CBB

A Yon battery-operated tinplate Moon Explorer, Japanese, 1960, 11in (28cm) long.
£140–160 / €200–220
$230–260 ⊞ HAL

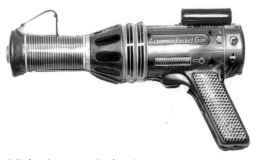

A tinplate and plastic jet car, Japanese, 1960s, 7in (18cm) long.
£20–25 / € 30–35
$35–40 ⊞ RTT

A Daiya Astronaut Rocket Gun, Japanese, 1960s, 9in (23cm) wide.
£70–80 / € 100–115
$115–130 ⊞ HUX

A tinplate battery-operated Apollo-Z spacecraft, Japanese, 1970s, 12in (30.5cm) long.
£75–85 / € 105–120
$125–140 ⊞ GTM

► **A Pedigree Toys** *Captain Scarlet* **Destiny Angel figure,** 1970, 6in (15cm) high, boxed.
£65–75 / € 90–105
$105–120 ⊞ GTM

A Dinky Toys UFO Interceptor, No. 351, 1978, 9in (23cm) long, with original box.
£145–160 / € 200–230
$240–270 ⊞ SSF

► **A Walt Disney's** *The Black Hole* **Dr Alex Durant action figure,** wearing a Palomino company uniform, 1979, 20in (51cm) high.
£400–480 / € 570–680
$660–790 ⚲ CO
This model of Dr Alex Durant (played by Anthony Perkins in the film) comes with a certificate of authenticity from the current owner, confirming that the figure was obtained from the Walt Disney Studios.

A Walt Disney's *The Black Hole* **Maximillian action figure,** 1979, 3¾in (9.5cm) high, on original card.
£20–25 / € 30–35
$35–40 ⊞ OW

SCI-FI

A *Buck Rogers in the 25th Century* Buck Rogers figure, 1979, 13in (33cm) high, with original box.
£75–85 / €105–120
$125–140 ⊞ OW

Two *Star Fleet* model kits, produced for the Japanese market, 1982, in original boxes, 4 x 6in (10 x 15cm).
£35–40 / €50–55
$60–70 ⊞ OW

► A *Space Precinct* Lieutenant Brogan action figure, 1994, in original packaging, 9 x 6in (23 x 15cm).
£1–5 / €2–7
$3–8 ⊞ CTO

A TSR *Buck Rogers in the 25th Century* role-playing game, American, 1990, 12 x 9in (30.5 x 23cm).
£15–20 / €25–30
$30–35 ⊞ SSF

A Vivid Imaginations *Captain Scarlet* action figure, wearing Spectrum astronaut kit, signed by Francis Matthews, 1994, 4in (10cm) high.
£180–200 / €250–280
$300–330 ⊞ CoC
The actor Francis Matthews was the voice of Captain Scarlet and has appeared in nearly 50 films.

► A Hasbro Signature series *Planet of the Apes* Taylor action figure, collector's edition, 1999, 12in (30.5cm) high.
£25–30 / €35–40
$40–45 ⊞ SSF

A plastic *Lost in Space* lunchbox, with metal clasps, 1998, 9in (23cm) wide.
£25–30 / €35–40
$40–45 ⊞ SSF

A *Forbidden Planet* C-57D Starcruiser model kit, reissue, 2001, 24in (61cm) long.
£45–50 / €65–75
$75–85 ⊞ SSF

Robots

A Super Moon Explorer plastic battery-operated robot, c1960, 12in (30.5cm) high.
£75–85 / €105–120
$125–140 ⊞ UCO

A Robbie the Robot, from *Return to the Forbidden Planet*, 1958, 24in (61cm) high.
£450–500 / €640–710
$750–830 ⊞ SSF

▶ **An S.Y. tinplate clockwork Spaceman robot,** Japanese, c1960, 8in (20.5cm) high.
£140–160 / €200–220
$230–260 ⊞ HAL

A tinplate Mechanical Mighty Robot, 1960s, 5in (12.5cm) high, with original box.
£100–115 / €140–165
$165–185 ⊞ PLB

A battery-operated robot, Japanese, 1960s, 12in (30.5cm) high.
£135–150 / €190–210
$220–250 ⊞ HUX

▶ **A tinplate battery-operated Rotate-O-Matic Super Astronaut robot,** Japanese, 1960s, 12in (30.5cm) high, with original box.
£175–195 / €250–280
$290–320 ⊞ GTM

A plastic battery-operated robot, 1960s, 10in (25.5cm) high.
£55–65 / €80–90
$90–105 ⊞ UCO

A robot, Japanese, 1960s,
16in (40.5cm) high.
£400–450 / €570–630
$660–730 ⊞ CWO
This robot is unusually large,
hence its high price range.

**A tinplate battery-operated
gear robot,** Japanese, 1960s,
12in (30.5cm) high.
£270–300 / €380–420
$450–500 ⊞ GTM

**A tinplate battery-operated
robot,** Japanese, 1960s,
11in (28cm) high.
£130–145 / €185–210
$210–240 ⊞ GTM

**An Ideal Toy Corp plastic
battery-operated Zeroids robot,**
American, 1968, 7in (18cm) high.
£90–100 / €125–140
$150–165 ⊞ HAL

A GEAG tin robot, Japanese, 1970,
9½in (24cm) high, with original box.
£270–300 / €380–420
$450–500 ⊞ HUX

**An Airfix Micronauts Microtron
motorized mini-robot,** 1976, in
original box, 10 x 8in (25.5 x 20.5cm).
£25–30 / €35–40
$40–45 ⊞ OW

◄ **A Calfax battery-
operated Starroid
robot and AM radio,**
Star Command series,
American, 1977,
7½in (19cm) high.
£30–35 / €45–50
$50–55 ⊞ GTM

► **An M.B.
Transformers Prowl,**
French, 1985,
5in (12.5cm) high.
£90–100 / €125–140
$150–165 ⊞ OW

A Hasbro Transformers Thrust, 1985,
8in (20.5cm) long.
£40–45 / €55–65
$65–75 ⊞ OW

▶ **An M.B. Transformers Prowl,** French,
1985, in original box, 8 x 9in (20.5 x 23cm).
£180–200 / €260–290
$300–330 ⊞ OW

**A Takara twin cast Transformers
Robot tape recorder,** Japanese,
1987, 9in (23cm) high,
with original box.
£670–750 / €950–1,050
$1,100–1,250 ⊞ OW

Three Tomy automated toys, 1980, largest 9in (23cm) high.
£1–5 / €2–7
$3–8 each ⚒ MED

**A Billiken tinplate clockwork
Mighty Atom robot,** Japanese,
c1988, 9in (23cm) high.
£135–150 / €190–210
$220–250 ⊞ TOY

A robot, from *Lost in Space*, 1997,
11in (28cm) high.
£15–20 / €25–30
$30–35 ⊞ SSF
**With its original box this robot
could be worth £35–40 / €50–55 /
$60–70.**

**A Takara Transformers Cybertron
Commander Convoy,** remould
from 1980s, Japanese version,
2002, in unopened box, 8 x 6in
(20.5 x 15cm).
£30–35 / €45–50
$50–55 ⊞ NOS

Thunderbirds

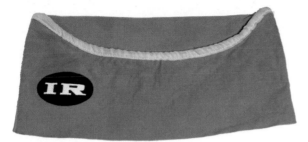

A *Thunderbirds* cloth hat, 1960, 10in (25.5cm) wide.
£25–30 / €35–40
$40–45 ⊞ HAL

A Dinky Toys Lady Penelope's Rolls-Royce
FAB 1, No. 100, from *Thunderbirds*, 1960s,
6in (15cm) long, with original box.
£220–250 / €310–350
$360–410 ⊞ CWO

A *Thunderbirds* Virgil Tracy
puppet head, on a replica body,
1960s, 21in (53.5cm) high.
£8,000–9,000 / €11,400–12,800
$13,300–15,000 ⊞ CO
This Virgil puppet is very rare as
it is the last surviving original
head complete with the old
mechanism inside. The body and
costume have been specially
made to go with the head by
Chris King, who is one of the top
professional model-makers in
Europe. Virgil was the pilot of
Thunderbird 2 and this head is
from the 1965 to 1966 episodes.

A JR 21 Toys friction-
driven plastic
Thunderbird 3, 1960s,
8in (20.5cm) high.
£50–60 / €70–80
$85–95 ⊞ HAL

A JR 21 Toys battery-operated plastic
Thunderbird 5, Hong Kong, 1960s,
11in (28cm) wide.
£220–250 / €310–350
$370–410 ⊞ HAL

▶ An Empire plastic Thunderbird
1 novelty pencil sharpener,
1960s, 5in (12.5cm) high.
£20–25 / €30–35
$35–40 ⊞ HAL

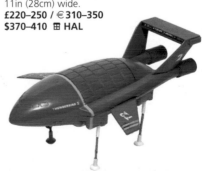

A JR 21 Toys friction-driven plastic
Thunderbird 2, 1960s, 10in (25.5cm) long.
£50–60 / €70–80
$85–95 ⊞ HAL

◀ A JR 21 Toys friction-driven plastic Thunderbird 1, c1966, 8in (20.5cm) long, boxed.
£90–100 / €130–145
$150–165 ⊞ GTM

A J. Rosenthal Toys *Thunderbirds* 3D Painting Set, 1964, 13 x 16in (33 x 40.5cm).
£50–60 / €70–80
$85–95 ⊞ OW

▶ A *Thunderbirds* resin Scott puppet, sash replaced, leg repaired, c1985, 21½in (54.5cm) high, with original box.
£900–1,050 / €1,300–1,500
$1,500–1,800 ✗ DN
This puppet was possibly made for an advertising campaign.

A *Thunderbirds* rocket station and models, 1992, 20in (51cm) wide.
£14–18 / €20–25
$25–30 ✗ GAZE

A *Thunderbirds* Parker figure, 1966, 12in (30.5cm) high.
£80–90 / €115–130
$130–145 ⊞ UCO
If Parker still had his original chauffeur's hat the price would be doubled.

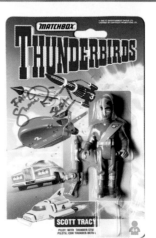

Two Matchbox *Thunderbirds* models, Lady Penelope's Rolls-Royce FAB 1 and Brains, 1992, figure 4in (10cm) high, both in original packaging signed by David Graham.
£25–30 / €35–40
$40–45 ⊞ CoC

A Matchbox *Thunderbirds* Scott Tracy figure, 1992, 4in (10cm) high, in original packaging signed by Shane Rimmer.
£25–30 / €35–40
$40–45 ⊞ CoC

An English Porcelain Classics *Thunderbirds* porcelain Parker figure, 1999, 21in (53.5cm) high, with original box.
£270–300 / €380–420
$450–500 ⊞ UCO

Dr Who

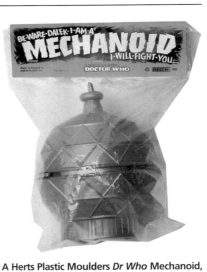

A Marx Toys *Dr Who* battery-operated Dalek, 1960s, 6in (15cm) high, with original box.
£70–80 / €100–110
$115–130 🪓 RAR

A Herts Plastic Moulders *Dr Who* Mechanoid, 1965, 8in (20.5cm) high, unopened.
£360–400 / €510–570
$600–660 ⊞ WHO
In 1965, this Mechanoid sold for 4s 11d (just under 25p). Today it is extremely rare to find an unopened example. Smaller versions were produced by Cherilea Toys and these now attract a price range of **£90–100 / €125–140 / $150–165.**

◄ **A Mego Cop *Dr Who* figure,** c1966, 9in (23cm) high.
£40–45 / €55–65
$65–75 ⊞ UD

◄ **A Dekker Toys *Dr Who* tardis play house tent,** 1982, 48in (122cm) high.
£90–100 / €125–140
$150–165 ⊞ WHO

Cross Reference
See Games (pages 161–185)

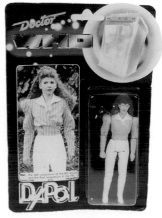

◄ **A Palitoy battery-operated BBC Talking Dalek,** 1975, 7½in (19cm) high, boxed.
£125–140 / €175–195
$200–220 ⊞ CBB

A Dapol *Dr Who* Mel figure, 1987, on original card, 7¾ x 5¼in (19.5 x 13.5cm).
£1–5 / €2–7
$3–8 ⊞ UNI

Star Trek

A Mego *Star Trek* Mr Scott 'Scottie' action figure, American, 1974, on original card, 9 x 8in (23 x 20.5cm).
£135–150 / €190–210 $220–250 ⊞ OW

A Mego *Star Trek* Klingon action figure, American, 1974, 8in (20.5cm) high.
£35–40 / €50–55 $60–70 ⊞ OW

Two Mego *Star Trek* action figures, Gorn and Cheron, American, 1974, 8in (20.5cm) high.
£65–75 / €90–100 $105–120 ⊞ OW

A Mego *Star Trek* Captain Kirk action figure, American, 1979, 8in (20.5cm) high, with original packaging.
£65–75 / €90–100 $105–120 ⊞ OW

◄ **A Mego *Star Trek* Dr McCoy 'Bones' action figure,** American, 1974, on original card, 9 x 8in (23 x 20.5cm).
£135–150 / €190–210 $220–250 ⊞ OW

An ERTL *Star Trek III* Captain Kirk action figure, 1984, 6in (15cm) high, with original packaging.
£135–150 / €190–210 $220–250 ⊞ OW

A Playmates *Star Trek The Next Generation* Captain Jean Luc Picard action figure, 1992, on original card, 10 x 8in (25.5 x 20.5cm).
£15–20 / €25–30 $30–35 ⊞ OW

◄ **A Mego *Star Trek* Mr Spock action figure,** American, produced in Hong Kong, 1979, 12in (30.5cm) high, with original box.
£60–70 / €85–95 $100–110 ⊞ HAL

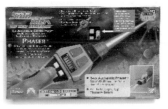

A Playmates *Star Trek The Next Generation* phaser electronic toy, 1993, 10in (25.5cm) long, boxed.
£40–45 / €55–65
$65–75 ⊞ OW

Three *Star Trek The Next Generation* Worfs medals, 1992–93, 4in (10cm) high.
£310–350 / €440–490
$510–580 each ⊞ OW

A Playmates *Star Trek The Next Generation* Tricorder electronic toy, 1993, 6 x 10in (15 x 25.5cm).
£70–80 / €100–110
$115–130 ⊞ OW

A Playmates *Star Trek* Space Talk Series Borg talking figure, 1995, 7in (18cm) high, with original packaging.
£30–35 / €45–50
$50–55 ⊞ SSF

Further reading

Miller's Sci-Fi & Fantasy Collectibles, Miller's Publications, 2003

A Playmates *Star Trek* General Chang action figure, 1995, on original card, 10 x 8in (25.5 x 20.5cm).
£25–30 / €35–40
$40–45 ⊞ OW

A Playmates *Star Trek* Space Talk Series Captain Jean Luc Picard talking figure, 1995, 7in (18cm) high, with original packaging.
£30–35 / €45–50
$50–55 ⊞ SSF

▶ A Playmates *Star Trek* USS Voyager Star Ship, 1995, 17in (43cm) long, boxed.
£270–300 / €380–420
$450–500 ⊞ OW

SCI-FI

Star Wars

A Palitoy *Star Wars* Land Speeder, 1977, 8 x 10in (20.5 x 25.5cm), boxed.
£180–200 / €260–290
$300–330 ⊞ OW

A Palitoy *Star Wars* Death Star playset, 1977, 12in (30.5cm) high.
£135–150 / €190–210
$220–250 ⊞ OW

▶ A Parker *Star Wars* Adventures of R2D2 board game, 1977, 9 x 17in (23 x 43cm).
£25–30 / €35–40
$40–45 ⊞ SSF

A Palitoy *Star Wars* Escape from Death Star board game, 1977, boxed, 9 x 18in (22 x 45.5cm).
£30–35 / €40–50
$50–55 ⊞ SSF

A Palitoy *Star Wars* Death Star playset, 1977, boxed, 12 x 17in (30.5 x 43cm).
£360–400 / €510–570
$600–660 ⊞ OW

◀ Two *Star Wars* figures, R2D2 and C3PO, 1977, larger 4in (10cm) high.
£6–10 / €8–14
$10–16 each ⊞ SSF

▶ A Palitoy *Star Wars* C3PO figure, No. 12BK, first issue British release, 1977, on original card, 9 x 6in (23 x 15cm).
£270–300 / €380–420
$450–500 ⊞ OW

SCI-FI

◄ **Three** *Star Wars* **figures,** Storm Trooper, Darth Vader and Snow Trooper, 1977, largest 4in (10cm) high.
£6–10 / €8–14
$10–16 ⊞ SSF

A Kenner *Star Wars* **X-Wing Aces electronic target game,** American, 1978, 26in (66cm) wide.
£1,800–2,000 / €2,550–2,850
$3,000–3,300 ⊞ SSF

A *Star Wars* **Hammerhead action figure,** 1977, 4½in (11.5cm) high.
£3–7 / €4–8
$5–9 ⊞ UNI

A *Star Wars* **Greedo action figure,** gun missing, 1978, 4in (10cm) high.
£2–6 / €3–8
$4–9 ⊞ UNI

► **A Kenner** *Star Wars* ***The Empire Strikes Back* Han Solo action figure,** No. 21BK, American, 1979, on original card, 9 x 6in (23 x 15cm).
£270–300 / €380–420
$450–500 ⊞ OW

A *Star Wars* **Boba Fett action figure,** 1979, 12in (30.5cm) high, boxed.
£490–550 / €700–770
$810–900 ⊞ OW
This is a very rare figure to find mint and boxed, hence its high value.

◄ **A Kenner** *Star Wars* **action figure display stand,** 1979, 20in (51cm) wide.
£630–700 / €890–980
$1,000–1,150 ⊞ OW
This stand was originally made as a white mailing box, then released in this format in two American states.

► A Palitoy *Star Wars The Empire Strikes Back* AT-AT all-terrain armoured transport vehicle, 1980, boxed, 23 x 9in (58.5 x 23cm).
£270–300
€380–420
$450–500
⊞ OW

◄ A collection of *Star Wars The Empire Strikes Back* action figures, c1982, 2in (5cm) high.
£1–5 / €2–7
$3–8 ⊞ Ada

A Palitoy *Star Wars* Boba Fett action figure, 1979, 12in (30.5cm) high, with original box.
£490–550 / €700–770
$810–900 ⊞ OW

► A Kenner *Star Wars Return of The Jedi* Ben (Obi-Wan) Kenobi action figure, American, 1983, on original card, 9 x 6in (23 x 15cm).
£90–100 / €125–140
$150–165 ⊞ OW

A Palitoy *Star Wars Return of The Jedi* Princess Leia action figure, produced for the European market, 1983, on tri-logo card, 9 x 6in (23 x 15cm).
£310–350 / €440–490
$510–570 ⊞ OW

► A *Star Wars* Boba Fett action figure, signed by Jeremy Bullock, 1980s, 8in (20.5cm) high, with original box.
£50–55 / €70–80
$85–95 ⊞ CoC

A *Star Wars* Chewbacca action figure, 1980, 3¾in (9.5cm) high.
£2–6 / €3–8
$4–9 ⊞ UNI

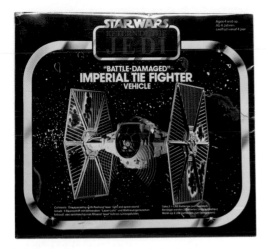

A Palitoy *Star Wars Return of The Jedi* 'Battle-Damaged' Imperial Tie Fighter Vehicle, produced for the European market, 1983, boxed, 12 x 11in (30.5 x 28cm).
£90–100 / €125–140
$150–165 ⊞ OW

A Palitoy battery-operated *Star Wars Return of The Jedi* Rebel Armoured Snowspeeder Vehicle, 1983, boxed, 11 x 13in (28 x 33cm).
£55–65 / €80–90
$90–100 ⊞ OW

A Kenner *Star Wars Return of The Jedi* Jabba the Hutt action playset, American, 1983, 13in (33cm) wide, with original box.
£65–75 / €90–100
$105–120 ⊞ TBoy

A Kenner *Star Wars* The Power of The Force Special Collector's Coin, with B-Wing Pilot action figure, American, 1983, 4in (10cm) high, with original packaging.
£140–160 / €200–220
$230–260 ⊞ SSF

A Kenner *Star Wars Return of The Jedi* Chewbacca action figure, American, 1983, 4in (10cm) high, with original packaging.
£90–100 / €125–140
$150–165 ⊞ SSF

A Palitoy *Star Wars Return of the Jedi* X-Wing Fighter Vehicle, 1983, boxed, 14 x 13in (35.5 x 33cm).
£50–60 / €70–80
$85–95 ⊞ OW

► Two Kenner *Star Wars Return of The Jedi* action figures, B-Wing Pilot and Chewbacca, American, 1983, 4in (10cm) high, with original packaging.
£90–100
€125–140
$150–165 each
⊞ SSF

Two Kenner *Star Wars Return of The Jedi* **action figures,** C3PO and Biker Scout, American, 1983, 4in (10cm) high, with original packaging.
£90–100 / €125–140
$150–165 ⊞ SSF

A Recticel Sutcliffe *Star Wars* **playmat,** 1983, 24 x 38in (61 x 96.5cm).
£220–250 / €310–350
$370–410 ⊞ SSF

A Palitoy *Star Wars Return of The Jedi* **EV-9D9 action figure,** 1983, 4in (10cm) high, on tri-logo card.
£140–160 / €200–220
$230–260 ⊞ SSF

A Palitoy *Star Wars Return of The Jedi* **Anakin Skywalker action figure,** 1983, 4in (10cm) high, on tri-logo card.
£140–160 / €200–220
$230–260 ⊞ SSF

A Palitoy *Star Wars Return of The Jedi* **A-Wing Pilot action figure,** 1983, 4in (10cm) high, on tri-logo card.
£140–160 / €200–220
$230–260 ⊞ SSF

A Palitoy *Star Wars Return of The Jedi* **Luke Skywalker in battle poncho action figure,** 1983, 4in (10cm) high, on tri-logo card.
£140–160 / €200–220
$230–260 ⊞ SSF

◀ An Acamas Toys *Star Wars* **Darth Vader costume set,** 1983, in original box.
£45–50 / €65–75
$75–85 ⊞ CTO

A Palitoy battery-operated *Star Wars Return of The Jedi* **Millennium Falcon Vehicle,** 1983, 16 x 22in (40.5 x 56cm), boxed.
£135–150 / €190–210
$220–250 ⊞ OW

A Kenner *Star Wars* **The Power of the Force Special Collector's Coin,** with Lando Calrissian action figure, American, 1984, on original card, 9 x 6in (23 x 15cm).
£90–100 / €125–140
$150–165 ⊞ OW

A Kenner *Star Wars Return of The Jedi* **AST-5 Mini-Rig,** American, 1980s, 6¼in (16cm) high, unopened.
£11–15 / €16–21
$19–24 ⊞ UNI

A Hasbro Toys *Star Wars Return of The Jedi* **Princess Leia action figure,** 1984, 4in (10cm) high.
£11–15 / €16–21
$19–24 ⊞ CoC

▶ A *Star Wars* TV series **Ewok figure,** Wicket W. Warwick, 1984, 2in (5cm) high.
£4–8 / €5–11
$6–12 ⊞ UNI

◀ A *Star Wars The Empire Strikes Back* **carbonite chamber Han Solo figure,** 1980s, 4in (10cm) high.
£70–80
€100–110
$115–130
⊞ HAL

A *Star Wars The Return of The Jedi* **Anakin Skywalker Vintage action figure,** 1984, 4in (10cm) high.
£14–18 / €20–25
$25–30 ⊞ CoC

◀ Two Kenner *Star Wars* **Collector Series figures,** Han Solo and Tauntaun, American, 1997, in original box, 18in (45.5cm) square.
£135–150
€ **190–210**
$220–250
⊞ **OW**

A Hasbro Toys *Star Wars* **Darth Vader action figure,** 1997, in original packaging signed by Dave Prower, 10in (25.5cm) high.
£35–40 / € 50–55
$60–70 ⊞ **CoC**

A Hasbro Toys *Star Wars* Luke Skywalker **Vintage action figure,** 1997, 4in (10cm) high.
£15–20 / € 25–30
$30–35 ⊞ **CoC**

A Kentucky Fried Chicken *Star Wars The Phantom Menace* **plastic life-size advertising figure of Yoda,** 1999, 56in (142cm) high.
£1,350–1,500 / € 1,900–2,150
$2,250–2,600 ⊞ **WAm**

◀ A *Star Wars* The Power of the Force **plastic model of R2D2,** with holographic Princess Leia, 1999, on unopened card, 9 x 6in (23 x 15cm).
£30–35 / € 45–50
$50–55 ⊞ **NOS**
This toy was taken off the market due to small parts and is therefore rare.

A Kentucky Fried Chicken *Star Wars The Phantom Menace* **plastic life-size advertising figure of Darth Maul,** 1999, 74in (188cm) high.
£1,350–1,500 / € 1,900–2,150
$2,250–2,600 ⊞ **WAm**

◀ **Two Hasbro** *Star Wars* **action figures,** Clone Trooper and Saesee Tiin Jedi Master, 2002, 4in (10cm) high, in original packaging.
£6–10 / €8–14
$10–16 ⊞ CoC

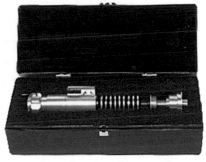

A Lucasfilm *Star Wars Return of The Jedi* **replica Skywalker light sabre,** limited edition of 2,500, 2002, 11in (28cm) long.
£270–300 / €380–420
$450–500 ⊞ OW

◀ **A Lucasfilm** *Star Wars* **Episode IV replica Han Solo blaster,** limited edition of 1,500, 2002, 12in (30.5cm) long.
£450–500 / €640–710
$750–830 ⊞ OW

Alien

A Kenner KB Toys Aliens vs Corp Hicks figure, limited edition of 25,000, American, 1997, 12in (30.5cm) high.
£180–200 / €250–280
$300–330 ⊞ SSF

A Hasbro Signature series *Alien Resurrection* **call figure,** reissue, 1997, 7in (18cm) high, with original box.
£15–20 / €25–30
$30–35 ⊞ SSF

A Hasbro Signature series *Alien Resurrection* **newborn Alien figure,** reissue, 1997, 7in (18cm) high.
£15–20 / €25–30
$30–35 ⊞ SSF

Kenner produced the first *Alien* toy in 1979, with the release of the first *Alien* movie, starring Sigourney Weaver as Ripley. At 18in (45.5cm) high, the figure was deemed too scary for children and was removed from store shelves. Action figures have continued to be popular with each of the *Alien* sequels: *Aliens, Alien 3* and *Alien Resurrection*.

▶ **A Hasbro Signature series** *Alien Resurrection* **Ripley figure,** reissue, 1997, 7in (18cm) high.
£15–20
€25–30
$30–35 ⊞ SSF

Characters

▶ **A Chad Valley Mickey Mouse Scatter Ball game,** 1930s, 11½in (29cm) wide.
£70–80
€100–115
$115–130
⊞ ARo

A painted tinplate wind-up walking figure of *Popeye*, c1935, 8in (20.5cm) high.
£350–420 / €500–600
$580–680 ⚒ BAu

A Louis Marx & Co tinplate wind-up figure of Pinocchio, c1939, 8in (20.5cm) high.
£800–900 / €1,150–1,300
$1,350–1,500 ⊞ HOB

A Mickey Mouse tea service, 1940s, plate 6in (15cm) diam.
£100–115 / €140–155
$165–185 ⊞ HYP

◀ **An Enid Blyton stencil and painting set,** c1950, in original box, 13in (33cm) wide.
£18–22
€26–30
$30–35 ⊞ J&J

A Louis Marx & Co plastic wind-up Mickey the Musician xylophone player, c1950, 12in (30.5cm) high, with original box.
£180–200 / €260–290
$300–330 ⊞ HOB

A Louis Marx & Co tinplate Disney Dipsy Car, American, c1950s, 6in (15cm) long.
£470–530 / €660–750
$780–880 ⊞ CBB

◀ **Two Walt Disney plastic pez holders,** 1960–70, larger 4½in (11.5cm) high.
£6–10 / €8–14
$10–16 ⊞ RTT

An Aurora *King Kong* glow-in-the-dark plastic assembly kit, 1960, 10in (25.5cm) square.
£180–200 / €260–290
$300–330 ⊞ SSF

A Berwick *Bugs Bunny* Tiddley Winks game, 1963, 8 x 11in (20.5 x 28cm).
£6–10 / €8–14
$10–16 ⊞ J&J

A Corgi Toys *The Saint* Volvo P1800, No. 258, black Saint logo to bonnet, 1965–68, 4in (10cm) long, with box.
£140–160 / €200–230
$230–260 ⋗ B(Ch)

▶ **A Corgi Toys *Daktari* gift set,** 1967, 7½in (19cm) long, with box.
£75–85 / €105–120
$125–140 ⊞ GTM

Cross Reference
See Diecast (pages 120–152)

A Corgi Toys Comics *Popeye* Paddle Wagon, No. 802, with five figures, 1969–72, with original box.
£420–500 / €600–710
$700–830 ⋗ VEC

◀ **A Mattel Truly Scrumptious doll,** from the film *Chitty Chitty Bang Bang,* c1968, in original unopened box, 15 x 6in (38 x 15cm).
£450–500 / €640–710
$750–830 ⊞ T&D

A Gilbert *The Man from U.N.C.L.E.* action figure, Illya Kuryakin, Hong Kong, 1960s, 13in (33cm) high, with original box.
£180–200 / €260–290
$300–330 ⊞ HAL

CHARACTERS

A Milton Bradley Co *The Man from U.N.C.L.E.* **card game,** American, 1960s, 6 x 10in (15 x 25.5cm).
£45–50 / €60–70
$75–85 ⊞ HAL

A Dinky Toys *Joe 90* **Joe's Car,** No. 102, 1960s, 7in (18cm) long, with box.
£155–175 / €220–250
$260–290 ⊞ GTM

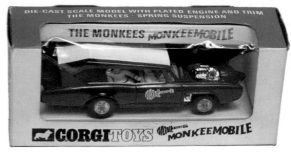

A Corgi Toys *The Monkees* **Monkeemobile,** No. 277, with figures, 1969–70, 6in (15cm) long, with original box.
£340–380 / €480–550
$560–630 ⊞ UCO

A Corgi Toys *Magic Roundabout* **clockwork carousel,** c1972, 7in (18cm) high.
£135–150 / €190–210
$220–250 ⚲ RAR

▶ **A Marx Toys** *Lone Ranger* **Tonto figure,** 1973, 10in (25.5cm) high.
£45–50 / €60–70
$75–85 ⊞ TOY

A Corgi Toys *The Green Hornet* **car,** No. 268, Black Beauty, early 1970s, 5in (12.5cm) long, with box.
£340–380 / €480–540
$560–630 ⊞ UCO

A Kenner *Bionic Woman* **outfit,** Designer Collection Fashions for Jaime Sommers, American, 1974, in original packaging, 12in (30.5cm) wide.
£11–15 / €16–21
$19–24 ⊞ TOY

A Corgi Toys *The Man from U.N.C.L.E.* **Thrush-Buster car,** No. 497, early 1970s, with original box, 12in (30.5cm) long.
£270–300 / €380–430
$450–500 ⊞ UCO
A white version of this model could be worth £900–1,000 / €1,300–1,400 / $1,500–1,650.

▶ A General Mills *Six Million Dollar Man* **figure,** Hong Kong, 1970s, 13in (33cm) high.
£35–40 / €50–60
$60–70 ⊞ HAL

A Corgi Toys **Kojak's Buick,** No. 290, 1975, in original box, 8in (20.5cm) long.
£110–125 / €155–175
$180–210 ⊞ GTM

Two composition **Sooty money boxes,** 1970s, 7in (18cm) high.
£75–85 / €105–120
$125–140 ⊞ HYP

◀ A Combex Models squeaky **rubber Womble,** c1974, 6in (15cm) high.
£15–20 / €20–25
$25–30 ⊞ CWO

Two Marx Toys *Lone Ranger* **action figures,** Danny Reid and Little Bear, fully jointed, 1975, 9in (23cm) high, with original boxes.
£65–75 / €90–105
$105–120 ⊞ TOY

A Kenner *Bionic Woman* **figure,** American, 1977, 12in (30.5cm) high, with original box.
£90–100 / €125–140
$150–165 ⊞ TOY

A Galoob *Starsky & Hutch* **radio-controlled Ford Torino,** 1970s, 11in (28cm) long.
£50–55 / €70–80
$80–90 ⊞ OW

◀ A plastic **Rupert Bear money box,** 1970s–80s, 20in (51cm) high.
£50–55 / €70–80
$80–90 ⊞ HYP

Three plastic Mr Men figures, Mr Noisy, Mr Tickle and Mr Strong, c1980, 2in (5cm) high.
£1–5 / €2–7
$3–8 each ⊞ STa

A Urago diecast and plastic model of Donald Duck with a Jaguar SS100, 1:18 scale, c1980, 10in (25.5cm) long.
£20–25 / €30–35
$35–40 ⤢ MED

◄ **Four plastic Mr Men pencil ends,** Mr Cheerful, Mr Silly, Mr Funny and Mr Greedy, c1980, 1in (2.5cm) high.
£1–5 / €2–7
$3–8 each ⊞ STa

◄ **A Rupert Bear money box,** 1982, 6in (15cm) high.
£15–20 / €20–25
$25–30 ⊞ HYP

A plastic Care Bears Cloud Keeper figure, fluffy cloud broom missing, c1983, 4in (10cm) high.
£1–5 / €2–7
$3–8 ⊞ STa

A Care Bears Cheer Bear soft toy, c1983, 6in (15cm) high.
£1–5 / €2–7
$3–8 ⊞ STa
All official Care Bear soft toys have a plastic heart-shaped button attached to the right hip.

◄ **A plastic Postman Pat figure,** 1983, 2in (5cm) high.
£1–5 / €2–7
$3–8 ⊞ STa

► **A Galoob The A-Team Murdock action figure,** with accessories, 1983, 13in (33cm) high.
£35–40 / €50–60
$60–70 ⊞ CTO

A Daisy Toys *The A-Team* cap pistol, 1983, in original packaging, 12 x 7in (30.5 x 18cm).
£35–40 / €50–60
$60–70 ⊞ CTO

Cross Reference
For more action figures see Sci-Fi (pages 208–227)

▶ A Kenner Toys plastic Centurions figure, Jake Rockwell and Fireforce, American, 1986, 10in (25.5cm) high.
£15–20 / €20–25
$25–30 ⊞ STa

Three plastic Care Bears badges, 1986, 3in (7.5cm) high.
£1–5 / €2–7
$3–8 each ⊞ STa

▶ A Corgi Toys *Spider-Man* Spiderbike, No. 266, 1984, in box, 6¼in (16cm) wide.
£50–55 / €70–80
$80–90 ⊞ GTM

A plastic Paddington Bear figure, 1984, 2in (5cm) high.
£1–5 / €2–7
$3–8 ⊞ STa

◀ A Games Workshop *Golden Heroes* super heroes role-playing game, 1984, 12 x 9in (30.5 x 23cm).
£20–25 / €30–35
$35–40 ⊞ SSF

A Hasbro plastic Keyper, Baby Scamper the Squirrel, c1985, 4in (10cm) high.
£1–5 / €2–7
$3–8 ⊞ STa

A Kenner Toys pack of Mask Action figures, Miles Mayhem with Python mask and Nash Gorey with Powerhouse mask, American, 1986, on card, 9 x 6in (23 x 15cm).
£11–15 / €16–21
$19–24 ⊞ STa

Five plastic Battle Beasts action figures, 1987, 3in (7.5cm) high.
£1–5 / €2–7
$3–8 each ⊞ STa

Two pairs of Pizza Hut *Back to the Future* **solar shades,** 1989, 6in (15cm) wide, with original packaging.
£6–10 / €8–14
$10–16 each ⊞ STa

A Ronald McDonald toy car, c1989, 2½in (6.5cm) long.
£1–5 / €2–7
$3–8 ⊞ CMF

A set of seven Dwarfs rubber squeeze toys, from *Snow White and the Seven Dwarfs*, with original clear PVC carry case, 1980s–90s, 5½in (14cm) high.
£25–30 / €35–40
$40–45 ⚒ MED

A Hasbro plastic Bucky O'Hare and Dead-Eye Duck, in the Toad Croaker, 1989, 10in (25.5cm) long.
£15–20 / €20–25
$25–30 ⊞ STa

A Playmates plastic *Teenage Mutant Ninja Turtles* **Ray Fillet figure,** 1990, 4in (10cm) high, on card.
£11–15 / €16–21
$19–24 ⊞ STa

A Playmates *Teenage Mutant Ninja Turtles* **April O'Neil figure,** 1990, 4in (10cm) high, on card.
£11–15 / €16–21
$19–24 ⊞ STa

◄ A Playmates plastic *Teenage Mutant Ninja Turtles* Sewer Sand Cruiser, 1990, boxed, 11in (28cm) wide.
£11–15
€16–21
$19–24 ⊞ STa

Four McDonald's Happy Meal plastic *Back to the Future* toys, 1991, 2in (5cm) wide.
£6–10 / €8–14
$10–16 ⊞ STa

A *Judge Dredd* Judge Hunter gun, 1995, 46in (117cm) long.
£1,000–1,200 / €1,400–1,650
$1,650–1,950 ✂ CO

► A Ronald McDonald plastic clock-work Big Mac, c1995, 1¼in (3cm) high.
£1–5 / €2–7
$3–8 ⊞ CMF

A Sega *The Nightmare Before Christmas* Jack figure, Japanese, 2001, 8in (20.5cm) high.
£20–25 / €30–35
$35–40 ⊞ NOS

◄ A Mezco Living Dead Dolls Sheena figure, 2001, 12in (30.5cm) high, unopened.
£35–40
€50–60
$60–70 ⊞ NOS

A Jun Planning *The Nightmare Before Christmas* Santa Jack figure, limited edition of 800, American, 1998, 48in (122cm) high.
£80–95 / €115–135
$130–155 ✂ CBP

◄ A Playmates *The Simpsons* Convention Comic Book Guy, with Intelli-tronic voice activation, 2001, in unopened box, 7 x 6in (18 x 15cm).
£60–70
€85–100
$100–115 ⊞ NOS

A Marvel Spider-Man plush figure, 2002, 15in (38cm) high.
£6–10 / €8–14
$10–16 ⊞ CoC

Batman

A **Corgi Toys Batmobile,** first series, 1960s, 6in (15cm) long, with box.
£400–450 / €570–640
$670–750 ⊞ CBB

A polythene plastic **Bat Jet! Batman's Catapult Glider,** 1966, 12in (30.5cm) long.
£45–50 / €60–70
$75–85 ⊞ HAL

▶ A **Corgi Toys Batmobile,** No. 267, 1960s, 6in (15cm) long, with box.
£360–400 / €510–570
$600–660 ⊞ UCO

A **Corgi Toys Batboat,** No. 107, second series, early 1970s, in unopened box, 6in (15cm) long.
£85–95 / €120–135
$140–160 ⊞ UCO

A **Corgi Toys Batmobile,** No. 267, 1972, with original box, 6½in (16.5cm) long.
£200–230 / €280–320
$330–380 ⊞ GTM

▶ A **Corgi Toys Batmobile and Batboat,** 1979, 11½in (29cm) long, with original box.
£300–330 / €420–470
$500–550 ⊞ GTM

James Bond

A Corgi Toys James Bond Aston Martin DB5, No. 261, with inner stand and secret instructions, 1965, 4in (10cm) long, with original box.
£90–105 / €130–150
$150–175 ⚒ B(WM)

A Solido James Bond Goldfinger's Rolls-Royce, with Oddjob and Goldfinger, No. 8 of 100, French, c1965, with gold outer tube.
£500–600 / €710–850
$830–1,000 ⚒ VEC

Cross Reference

See Diecast (pages 120–152)

A Corgi Toys James Bond Aston Martin DB5, No. 261, with wire wheels, Bond at the wheel with passenger, with box containing pictorial inner car, special instructions, envelope with spare bandit and adhesive badge, 1965–69, 4in (10cm) long.
£240–280 / €340–400
$400–460 ⚒ B(Ch)

▶ A Spear's Games James Bond 007 Secret Service Game, 1966, 15in (38cm) square.
£35–40 / €50–60
$60–70 ⊞ HAL

A Corgi Toys James Bond Aston Martin DB5, No. 270, with tyre-slashers, unopened secret instruction pack, 1968–76, 4in (10cm) long, with box.
£360–430 / €510–610
$600–710 ⚒ VEC

A Corgi Toys James Bond Toyota 2000GT, No. 336, with two figures, in a pictorial box with inner card and unopened special instructions, 1967–69, 4in (10cm) long.
£200–240 / €280–340
$330–400 ⚒ B(Ch)

▶ A Corgi James Bond Toyota 2000GT, 1960s, 4in (10cm) long.
£90–100 / €130–140
$150–165 ⊞ HAL
With its original box this item could be worth £180–200 / €250–280 / $300–330.

A Corgi Toys James Bond Aston Martin, second type, with tyre-slashers and revolving number plates, 1973, 6in (15cm) long, with box.
£180–200 / €250–280
$300–330 ⊞ HAL

A Corgi Toys James Bond Toyota 2000GT, No. 336, 1976, 4in (10cm) long, with original box.
£85–95 / €120–135
$140–155 ⊞ UCO

A Corgi Toys James Bond Lotus Esprit, No. 269, from *The Spy Who Loved Me*, 1977, in box, 7in (18cm) long.
£110–125 / €155–175
$180–210 ⊞ GTM

A Corgi Toys James Bond Aston Martin, No. 271, with gold bumpers and grille, Bond driving and two seated bandits, inner card, 1:36 window tag, 1978, 4in (10cm) long, with box.
£120–140 / €170–200
$195–230 ⚒ B(Ch)

A Lone Star James Bond *Moonraker* space gun, 1979, 12in (30.5cm) long, with original box.
£45–50 / €60–70
$75–85 ⊞ TOY

The Reel to Reel Picture Show, 007 Movie Trivia Game, 1997, 8in (20.5cm) diam.
£8–12 / €11–16
$13–18 ⊞ GRa

G.I. Joe

A Plastirama G.I. Joe Cobra Glider, made for the Mexican market, 1982, boxed, 12 x 21in (30.5 x 53.5cm).
£220–250 / €310–350
$370–420 ⊞ OW

A Hasbro G.I. Joe battery-operated Mauler M.B.T. Tank, with G.I. Joe driver, 1985, boxed, 14 x 13in (35.5 x 33cm).
£110–125 / €155–175
$180–200 ⊞ OW

A plastic G.I. Joe The Baroness figure, 1986, 3¼in (10cm) high.
£15–20 / €20–25
$25–30 ⊞ STa

A plastic G.I. Joe General Hawk figure, 1987, 3¼in (10cm) high.
£6–10 / €8–14
$10–16 ⊞ STa

A plastic G.I. Joe Raptor figure, 1987, 3¼in (10cm) high.
£11–15 / €16–21
$19–24 ⊞ STa

A plastic G.I. Joe Storm Shadow figure, 1986, 3¼in (10cm) high.
£15–20 / €20–25
$25–30 ⊞ STa

▶ A Plastirama plastic G.I. Joe Persuader vehicle, with variant Back-Stop figure, made for the Mexican market, 1987, boxed, 9 x 11in (23 x 28cm).
£15–20 / €20–25
$25–30 ⊞ STa

Masters of the Universe

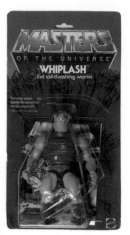

A Mattel plastic *Masters of the Universe* Skeletor figure, 1981, 5in (12.5cm) high.
£20–25 / €30–35
$35–40 ⊞ STa
This is a first issue figure with half-painted boots, all the others have fully-painted boots.

A Mattel plastic *Masters of the Universe* Wind Raider Assault Lander, 1981, in a sealed box, 10in (25.5cm) square.
£40–45 / €55–65
$65–75 ⊞ STa
Fantasy artwork was only used on early boxes.

A Mattel plastic *Masters of the Universe* Whiplash figure, battle-thrasher tail whips round when waist is twisted, 1983, 6in (12.5cm) high, on original card.
£35–40 / €50–60
$60–70 ⊞ STa

◄ A Mattel plastic *Masters of the Universe* Modulok The Ultimate Transforming Creature figure, 1984, in unopened box, 11 x 9in (28 x 23cm).
£45–50 / €60–70
$75–85 ⊞ STa

A Mattel plastic *Masters of the Universe* Skeletor Lord of Destruction action figure, 1983, 5in (12.5cm) high, on original card.
£70–80 / €100–115
$115–130 ⊞ OW

► A Mattel *Masters of the Universe* Mini Comic, 'Spikor Strikes', 1984, 5 x 4in (12.5 x 10cm).
£1–5 / €2–7
$3–8 ⊞ STa

A Mattel plastic *Masters of the Universe* Hordak figure, swings back with a punch when waist is twisted, 1984, 6in (12.5cm) high, on original card.
£35–40 / €50–60
$60–70 ⊞ STa

A Mattel plastic *Masters of the Universe* **Modulok The Ultimate Transforming Creature figure,** 1984, 5in (12.5cm) high.
£11–15 / €16–21
$19–24 ⊞ STa

A Mattel plastic *Masters of the Universe* **Beast Man figure,** 1984, 5in (12.5cm) high.
£11–15 / €16–21
$19–24 ⊞ STa

A Mattel *Masters of the Universe* **Mantenna action figure,** 1984, on original card, 11 x 6in (28 x 15cm).
£11–15 / €16–21
$19–24 ⊞ SAND

▶ **Three Mattel** *Masters of the Universe* **action figures,** Hordak, Tri-Klops and Roboto, 1984, on original cards, 11 x 6in (28 x 15cm).
£11–15
€16–21
$19–24 each
⊞ SAND

A Mattel *Masters of the Universe* **The Evil Horde Slime Pit,** 1985, 11 x 16in (28 x 40.5cm).
£45–50 / €60–70
$75–85 ⊞ OW

▶ **A Mattel plastic** *Masters of the Universe* **Snout Spout figure,** 1986, 5in (12.5cm) high.
£8–12 / €11–16
$13–18 ⊞ STa

▶ **Two Mattel Commemorative series** *Masters of the Universe* **action figures,** He-Man and Battle Cat, limited edition of 10,000, reissue, 2000, 13 x 17in (33 x 43cm).
£25–30 / €35–40
$40–45 ⊞ SSF

My Little Pony

Five My Little Pony Collector ponies, including Butterscotch, Cotton Candy, Lilac Blossom and Minty, with concave feet, 1982, 5in (12.5cm) high.
£1–5 / €2–7
$3–8 ⊞ RAND

A Minty My Little Pony, with concave feet, 1982, 5in (12.5cm) high.
£25–30 / €35–40
$40–50 ⊞ RAND

Two My Little Ponies, Bubbles and Seashell, 1983, 5in (12.5cm) high.
£6–10 / €8–14
$10–16 ⊞ RAND
These are the only sitting ponies ever made.

Two My Little Pony Sea ponies, Seaspray and Wavebreaker, non-American versions, with standing shells, 1983, 4in (10cm) high.
£15–20 / €20–25
$25–30 ⊞ RAND

▶ **A set of three My Little Pony Ember mail order club ponies,** 1983, 3in (7.5cm) high.
£6–10 / €8–14
$10–16 ⊞ RAND

A Majesty My Little Pony and Spike, part of the Dream Castle set, 1983, 2in (5cm) high.
£3–7 / €4–9
$5–11 ⊞ RAND
The complete Dream Castle set would cost **£70–80 / €100–110 / $115–130.**

A Baby Sea Pony My Little Pony, Surf Rider, 1984, 4in (10cm) high.
£6–10 / €8–14
$10–16 ⊞ RAND

A Baby Cuddles Beddy Byes Eyes My Little Pony, 1984, 3in (7.5cm) high.
£1–5 / €2–7
$3–8 ⊞ STa

A Sundance My Little Pony, with Megan, 1984, 8in (20.5cm) high.
£20–25 / €30–35
$35–40 ⊞ RAND
Megan and Sundance were characters from the *My Little Pony* film.

A My Little Pony Baby Pony with Pram, c1985, pram 8in (20.5cm) high.
£75–85 / €105–120
$125–140 ⊞ STa

◀ A Dancing Butterflies Party pony My Little Pony, 1987, 5in (12.5cm) high.
£1–5 / €2–7
$3–8 ⊞ STa

Four Flutter My Little Ponies, Peach Blossom, Honeysuckle, Rosedust and Morning Glory, 1985, 4in (10cm) high.
£1–5 / €2–7
$3–8 ⊞ RAND
Flutter ponies came with very delicate iridescent wings which were easily damaged. Examples with wings are worth about £30–35 / €45–50 / $50–60.

Two Twinkle-Eyed My Little Ponies, Gingerbread and Whizzer, 1985, 5in (12.5cm) high.
£4–8 / €5–11
$16–12 ⊞ RAND

Two My Little Pony EP records, French, 1986.
£6–10 / €8–14
$10–16 each
⊞ STa

A Magic Hat Message My Little Pony, 1987, 5in (12.5cm) high.
£1–5 / €2–7
$3–8 ⊞ STa

A Sand Digger Sunshine My Little Pony, 1988, 5in (12.5cm) high.
£1–5 / €2–7
$3–8 ⊞ STa

A My Little Pony Activity Club baby pony, with birth certificate, 1989, 3in (7.5cm) high.
£6–10 / €8–14
$10–16 ⊞ RAND
This pony came free when you renewed your membership of the My Little Pony Club.

◄ **A Teeny Tiny My Little Pony,** Baby Rattles, 1990, 2½in (6.5cm) high.
£4–8 / €5–11
$6–12 ⊞ RAND
This is the smallest My Little Pony.

A Drink and Wet My Little Pony, Baby Rainfeather, with bottle, changing table, diapers, brush and ribbon, 1989, 3in (7.5cm) high.
£1–5 / €2–7
$3–8 ⊞ RAND

A My Little Pony Playset pony, Lemon Drop, sold individually, made in Hong Kong, 1989–90, 4in (10cm) high.
£4–8 / €5–11
$6–12 ⊞ RAND

A Sweet Delight Cookery My Little Pony, 1991, 5in (12.5cm) high.
£1–5 / €2–7
$3–8 ⊞ STa

◄ **A Rollerskates My Little Pony,** Melody, 1992, 6in (15cm) high.
£1–5 / €2–7
$3–8 ⊞ RAND

Muppets

◀ **A Fisher Price** *Muppet Show*
character, Fozzie Bear, c1976,
13½in (34.5cm) high.
£8–12 / € 11–16
$13–18 ⊞ CMF

A *Muppet Show* **character,** Kermit
the Frog, 1976, 19in (48.5cm) high.
£14–18 / € 20–25
$25–30 ⊞ CMF

A *Muppet Show* **character,**
Scooter, c1976, 17in (43cm) high.
£8–12 / € 11–16
$13–18 ⊞ CMF

◀ **A** *Muppet Show* **Bendy Toy,** Miss
Piggy, 1970–80, 16in (40.5cm) high.
£22–26 / € 32–37
$36–42 ⊞ TAC

▶ **A** *Muppet show* **character,**
Miss Piggy, with cloth body,
plastic head and realistic hair,
1981, 13½in (34.5cm) high.
£20–25 / € 30–35
$35–40 ⊞ UNI

Noddy

◀ **A pack of**
Noddy snap
cards, c1955,
3½ x 2in (9 x 5cm).
£11–15
€ 16–21
$19–24 ⊞ HUX

▶ **A tinplate**
Noddy's Jack in
the Box, 1956,
6in (15cm) wide.
£50–60
€ 70–80
$85–95 ⚒ GAZE

A Merrythought figure of
Noddy, with sprung neck,
1950s, 12in (30.5cm) high.
£270–300 / € 380–420
$450–500 ⊞ RBB

▶ **A Budgie Toys Noddy train,** containing figures of Noddy and Big Ears, 1950s–60s, engine 4in (10cm) long.
£135–150
€190–210
$220–250
⊞ BBe

A tinplate Noddy and Friends kaleidoscope, 1950s, 8in (20.5cm) high.
£35–40 / €50–60
$60–70 ⊞ MRW

A Corgi Noddy car, containing figures of Noddy, Big Ears and Golly, 1950s–60s, 4in (10cm) long.
£145–165 / €200–230
$240–270 ⊞ BBe

A plastic model of Noddy, with jointed limbs and painted face, 1950s–60s, 6in (15cm) high.
£90–100 / €125–140
$150–165 ⊞ BBe

A Marx Toys Noddy figure, with watering can, 1950s–60s, 6in (15cm) high, with original box.
£90–100 / €125–145
$150–165 ⊞ BBe

▶ **An Emco model of Noddy,** 1950s–60s, 12in (30.5cm) high.
£45–50 / €65–75
$75–85 ⊞ BBe

An Emco model of Noddy, with rubber face and nylon plush body, 1950s–60s, 10in (25.5cm) high.
£25–30 / €35–40
$40–45 ⊞ BBe

A Spear's Games Noddy's Ring Game, 1960, 6 x 13in (15 x 33cm).
£20–25 / €30–35
$35–40 ⚘ GAZE

A foam rubber model of Noddy in his car, 1970s, 5in (12.5cm) long.
£25–30 / €35–40
$40–45 ⚘ GAZE

◄ A bendy rubber Noddy figure, with bell, 1970s, 12in (30.5cm) high.
£25–30 €35–40
$40–45 ⊞ BBe

◄ A Marx Toys plastic clockwork Noddy's horse and cart, 1976, 7in (18cm) long.
£55–65 / €80 95
$90–105 ⊞ UD

► A Dekkertoys plastic self-winding Noddy in his car, 1990s, 8in (20.5cm) high.
£20–25 / €30–35
$35–40 ⊞ CBB

The Simpsons

A Burger King Kid's Meal plastic *The Simpsons* Lisa figure, 2000, 6in (15cm) high.
£1–5 / €2–7
$3–8 ⊞ STa

Three Burger King Kid's Meal plastic *The Simpsons* figures, Marge with vacuum cleaner, Sideshow Bob and Marge baking, 2000, 6in (15cm) high.
£1–5 / €2–7
$3–8 each ⊞ STa

◀ A Playmates plastic *The Simpsons* Sideshow Mel interactive figure, Series 5, American, 2000, 5in (12.5cm) high, on card.
£6–10 / €8–14
$10–16 ⊞ STa

◀ A Playmates plastic *The Simpsons* Officer Marge interactive figure, Series 7, American, 2001, 5in (12.5cm) high, on card.
£6–10 / €8–14
$10–16 ⊞ STa

The Simpsons

Created by Matt Groening, previously known for his cartoon strip *Life in Hell*, *The Simpsons* were first seen in 1987 as shorts on *The Tracey Ullman Show*. *The Simpsons* first stand-alone series was aired in 1990 and is now as well known for celebrity cameos as the characters themselves. All official Simpsons toys are marked in some way, depending on the manufacturer, and unofficial copies of figures often lack the accessories included with authorized toys.

A Playmates plastic *The Simpsons* Sunday Best Grandpa interactive figure, Series 9, American, 2002, 5in (12.5cm) high.
£6–10 / €8–14
$10–16 ⊞ STa

Smurfs

A Schleich Smurf, Angry, c1964, 2in (5cm) high.
£3–7 / €4–10
$5–12 ⊞ CMF

A Schleich Smurf on a leaf skateboard, 1960s–70s, 2¾in (7cm) high.
£7–11 / €10–16
$12–18 ⊞ CMF

A Smurf, Bully with umbrella, 1960s–70s, 3in (7.5cm) high.
£7–11 / €10–16
$12–18 ⊞ CMF

A Schleich Smurf in a car, 1960s–70s, 3in (7.5cm) long.
£7–11 / €10–16
$12–18 ⊞ CMΓ

A Smurf, Emperor, 1978, 2½in (6.5cm) high.
£3–7 / €4–10
$5–12 ⊞ CMF

A Schleich French Fries Smurf, 1981, 2in (5cm) high.
£4–8 / €5–11
$6–12 ⊞ CMF

Snoopy

A Mattel Snoopy pop-up music box, c1960, 11in (28cm) high.
£75–85 / €105–120
$125–140 ⊞ CWO

A Snoopy money box, 1970s, 6in (15cm) high.
£25–30 / €35–40
$40–45 ⊞ HYP

◀ **A Snoopy money box,** 1970s, 6in (15cm) high.
£30–35 / €45–50
$50–60 ⊞ HYP

A Snoopy money box, 1970s, 6in (15cm) high.
£25–30 / €35–40
$40–45 ⊞ HYP

A Snoopy money box, 1970s, 4½in (11.5cm) high.
£30–35 / €45–50
$50–60 ⊞ HYP

A Snoopy money box, 1970s, 6in (15cm) high.
£30–35 / €45–50
$50–60 ⊞ HYP

Trade Cards

Stingray **Cadet Sweet cards,** set of 50, 1964.
£60–70 / €85–100
$110–115 ⊞ SSF

Batman, A & BC bubble gum cards, set of 55,
American, 1966.
£540–600 / €770–850
$900–990 ⊞ SSF

Land of the Giants, bubble gum cards, set of 55, 1968.
£540–600 / €770–850
$900–990 ⊞ SSF

Joe 90, Primrose Confectionery trade cards,
set of 50, 1968.
£60–70 / €85–95
$100–115 ⊞ SSF

Star Trek, A & BC bubble gum cards, set of 55, 1969.
£720–800 / €1,000–1,100
$1,200–1,350 ⊞ SSF

Space 1999, bubble gum cards, trade box, 1970s.
£60–70 / €85–95
$100–115 ⊞ HAL

Star Wars, bubble gum cards, set of 66, 1977.
£50–60 / €70–80
$85–95 ⊞ SSF

Star Wars, wax bubble gum cards, series
three, 1977.
£90–100 / €130–145
$150–165 ⊞ OW

Star Wars, Topps bubble gum cards, series one and two, 1977–78.
£55–65 / €80–95
$90–105 ⊞ OW

◄ ***Star Wars,*** bubble gum cards, The little
droid, Artoo-Detoo, set of 66, 1977.
£50–60 / €70–80
$85–95 ⊞ SSF

Star Wars, Topps bubble
gum cards, series three
and four, 1978.
£90–100 / €130–145
$150–165 ⊞ OW

CHARACTERS

◀ **Star Wars,** Widevision chase cards, set of 10, 1995.
£180–200 / €260–290
$300–330 ⊞ SSF

Star Wars, Widevision chase cards, set of 120, 1995.
£65–75 / €90–105
$105–120 ⊞ SSF

◀ **Star Trek Voyager,** Skybox trade cards, series one,
set of 98, 1995.
£11–15 / €16–21
$19–24 ⊞ SSF

◀ **Independence Day,** Topps
Widevision trade cards, set of
72, 1996.
£6–10 / €8–14
$10–16 ⊞ SSF

James Bond 007, Inkworks trade
cards, Volume 3, set of 270, 1997.
£2–6 / €3–8
$4–10 ⊞ SSF

Buffy the Vampire Slayer, Inkworks
trade cards, series one, contains 36
packs of seven cards, 1998, unopened.
£270–300 / €380–420
$450–500 ⊞ SSF

Mars Attacks!, Topps Widevision
trade cards, set of 72, 1998.
£6–10 / €8–14
$10–16 ⊞ SSF

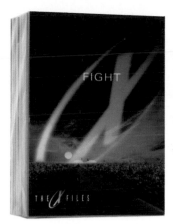

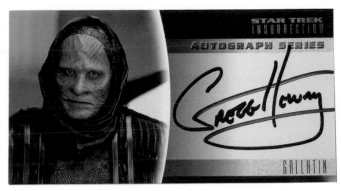

The X-Files Fight, Topps trade cards, set of 72, 1998.
£6–10 / €8–14
$10–16 ⊞ SSF

Star Trek Insurrection, autograph series trade card, Gregg Henry as Gallatin, 1998.
£30–40 / €45–50
$50–60 ⊞ SSF

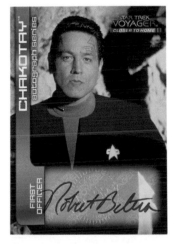

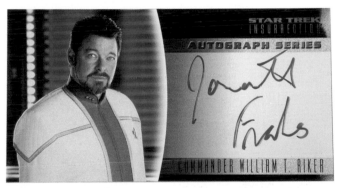

Star Trek Insurrection, autograph series trade card, Jonathon Frakes as Commander William T. Riker, 1998.
£135–150 / €190–210
$220–250 ⊞ SSF

Star Trek Voyager, autograph series trade card, First Officer Robert Beltran as Chakotay, 1998.
£50–60 / €70–80
$85–95 ⊞ SSF

▶ *Star Trek Deep Space Nine,* autograph series trade card, Max Grodénchik as Rom, 1999.
£35–40 / €50–60
$60–70 ⊞ SSF

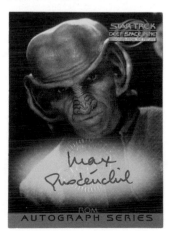

◀ *Star Trek Voyager,* profiles card, Species 8472 Ship, 1998, 3 x 4in (7.5 x 10cm).
£30–35 / €45–50
$50–60 ⊞ SSF

Star Wars Episode I, chase cards, set of 8, 1999.
£45–50 / €60–70
$75–85 ⊞ OW

CHARACTERS

▶ *Babylon 5,* trade cards, set of 100, 1999.
£135–150
€190–210
$220–250
⊞ **SSF**

◀ *Alien Legacy,* Inkworks trade cards, set of 90, 1999.
£6–10 / €8–14
$11–16 ⊞ **SSF**

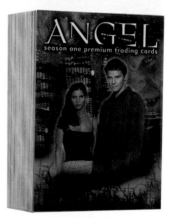

X-Men The Movie, Topps trade cards, set of 72, 2000.
£6–10 / €8–14
$11–16 ⊞ **SSF**

Buffy the Vampire Slayer, trade cards, series four, set of 90, 2000.
£11–15 / €16–21
$19–24 ⊞ **SSF**

Angel, trade cards, season one, set of 90, 2000.
£15–20 / €20–25
$25–30 ⊞ **SSF**

Lord of the Rings, trade cards, set of 90, 2001.
£11–15 / €16–21
$19–24 ⊞ **SSF**

Lord of the Rings, five autograph cards, 2001.
£90–100 / €125–140
$150–165 each ⊞ **SSF**

Lord of the Rings, prismatic foil trade cards,
set of 10, 2001.
£25–30 / €35–40
$40–50 ⊞ SSF

Lord of the Rings, foil trade cards, bonus set of 2, 2001.
£11–15 / €16–21
$19–24 ⊞ SSF

Star Wars, Evolution cards, set of 12, 2001.
£15–20 / €20–25
$25–30 ⊞ SSF

▶ **Star Wars,**
Topps autograph
card, Jeremy
Bullock as Boba
Fett, 2001.
£70–80
€100–110
$115–130
⊞ SSF

Star Wars, Topps autograph card, Ian
McDiarmid as Senator Palpatine, 2001.
£360–400 / €510–570
$600–660 ⊞ SSF

Star Wars, Topps autograph card,
James Earl Jones as Darth Vader, 2001.
£90–100 / €130–145
$150–165 ⊞ SSF

Buffy the Vampire Slayer,
Angelus Vampire, from the card
game, 2002, 3½ x 2½in (9 x 6.5cm).
£11–15 / €16–21
$19–24 ⊞ NOS

Puppets

Two Pelham Punch and Judy glove puppets, 1950s, Punch 12in (30.5cm) high.
£70–80 / € 100–110
$115–130 ⊞ J&J

A cat hand puppet, 1950–60, 11in (28cm) high.
£30–35 / € 45–50
$50–55 ⊞ LBe

A Soo glove puppet, from *Sooty & Sweep,* 1950s, 9in (23cm) high.
£11–15 / € 16–21
$19–24 ⊞ CCO

Two Chad Valley Sooty and Sweep glove puppets, c1960, 10in (25.5cm) high.
£55–65 / € 80–90
$90–100 ⊞ BINC

◄ **A set of Sooty, Sweep, Soo and Scampi hand puppets,** 1980s, 12in (30.5cm) high.
£25–30 / € 35–40
$40–45 ⊞ UD
Scampi is Sooty's cousin.

A papier-mâché glove puppet, 1950s, 10in (25.5cm) high.
£45–50 / € 60–70
$75–85 ⊞ AnS

A Picot schoolboy string puppet, c1960, 8in (20.5cm) high.
£70–80 / € 100–110
$115–130 ⊞ ARo

A Shillabeer wooden circus horse string puppet, c1960, 13in (33cm) long.
£180–200 / € 260–290
$300–330 ⊞ STK

Pelham

A Pelham Mexican string puppet, with lead hands and original box, c1950, 12in (30.5cm) high.
£70–80 / €100–110
$115–130 ⊞ ARo

A Pelham Mrs Macboozle string puppet, 1947 52, 12in (30.5cm) high.
£210–240 / €300–330
$350–390 ⊞ ARo
This is the female version of Macboozle, and is particularly sought after.

◄ A Pelham Pinocchio string puppet, 1947–52, 12in (30.5cm) high.
£190–220 / €270–300
$320–360 ⊞ ARo
This is the rare pre-Disney version.

A Pelham Duchess string puppet, with standard control and metal knee joints, pre-1955, 11¾in (30cm) high, with original box.
£200–240 / €280–340
$330–390 ⚒ B(Ch)

A Pelham Big Ears string puppet, 1950s, 12in (30.5cm) high.
£50–60 / €70–85
$85–100 ⊞ ARo

A Pelham Cinderella string puppet, 1950s, 12in (30.5cm) high.
£45–50 / €60–70
$75–85 ⊞ J&J

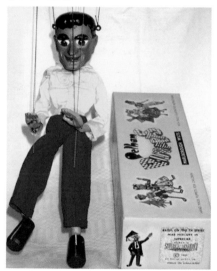

A Pelham Mike Mercury string puppet, from *Superstars,* c1960, 12in (30.5cm) high.
£135–150 / €190–210
$220–250 ⊞ ARo

Collecting puppets

In recent years prices for Pelham puppets have been at an all time high. The rarer characters can sell for exceptional amounts, although prices for the lesser ones are now levelling out. Generally speaking, the earliest puppets, made during the first five to eight years of production, are the most sought after and command the highest prices. Many collectors will only consider buying puppets in brown boxes, but this does not indicate rarity – only an early date.

▶ **A Pelham Pinky string puppet,** c1960, 13in (33cm) high.
£40–45
€55–65
$65–75 ⊞ TOY

◀ **A Pelham Walt Disney's Donald Duck character string puppet,** 1960, 10in (25.5cm) high, with original box.
£55–65
€80–90
$90–100 ⊞ J&J

▶ **A Pelham Walt Disney's Mickey Mouse character string puppet,** c1960, 10in (25.5cm) high, with original box.
£155–175 / €220–250
$260–290 ⊞ Beb

A Pelham string puppet, 1960, 12in (30.5cm) high.
£35–40 / €50–55
$60–70 ⊞ J&J

▶ **A Pelham Noddy string puppet,** 1960s, 9in (23cm) high.
£70–80 / €100–110
$115–130 ⊞ BBe

A Pelham Professor Popkiss string puppet, from Jerry Anderson's *Supercar* series, 1960s, 10in (25.5cm) high.
£135–150 / €190–210
$220–250 ⊞ ARo

A Pelham MacBoozle string puppet, 12in (30.5cm) high, with original box.
£55–65 / €80–90
$90–100 ⊞ STK

A Pelham Fido puppet, 1960s, 26in (66cm) high.
£85–95 / €120–135
$140–155 ⊞ POLL

A Pelham Dopey shop display string puppet, 1960s, 18in (45.5cm) high.
£135–150 / €190–210
$220–250 ⊞ BBe

▶ **A Pelham Prince Charming string puppet,** No. 122, slight damage, 1960s, 12in (30.5cm) high, with original box.
£15–20 / €20–25
$25–30 ⊞ J&J

◀ **A pair of Pelham Pinky and Perky string puppets,** 1960s, 10in (25.5cm) high.
£60–70 / €85–95
$100–110 ⊞ J&J

A Pelham Beatles string puppet, 1960s, 12½in (32cm) high, with original box.
£60–70 / €85–95
$100–110 ⊞ ARo

PUPPETS

◀ **A Pelham Mother Dragon string puppet,** 1960s, 20in (51cm) long.
£45–50
€60–70
$75–80 ⊞ ARo

A Pelham frog string puppet, 1960s, 12½in (32cm) high, with original box.
£45–50 / €60–70
$75–80 ⊞ ARo

A Pelham Schoolmaster string puppet, c1970, 12in (30.5cm) high, with original box.
£60–70 / €85–95
$100–110 ⊞ UD

◀ **A Pelham Mrs Oblige the Char string puppet,** 1970s, 12in (30.5cm) high, with original window box.
£30–35 / €45–50
$50–55 ⊞ ARo

A Pelham Gretel string puppet, with plastic arms and legs, restrung, 1970s, 11in (28cm) high.
£11–15 / €16–21
$19–24 ⊞ J&J

A Pelham Queen string puppet, 1970s, 12in (30.5cm) high, with original window box.
£40–45 / €55–65
$65–75 ⊞ ARo

A Pelham Indian Snake Charmer string puppet, 1970s, 13in (33cm) high, with original box.
£45–50 / €60–70
$75–85 ⊞ ARo

A Pelham plastic Walt Disney's Mickey Mouse string puppet, c1980, 12in (30.5cm) high.
£65–75 / €90–100
$105–120 ⊞ UD

Soft Toys

A plush miniature monkey, with tin face, jointed head and limbs, early 20thC, 2¼in (5.5cm) high.
£75–90 / €105–125
$125–150 ✗ SWO

▶ **A mohair teddy bear,** possibly by the Ideal Toy Co, with boot-button eyes and felt pads, American, 1910–20, 18in (45.5cm) high.
£500–550 / €710–780
$830–910 ⊞ BBe

A mohair teddy bear, possibly by Schuco, with glass eyes, stitched nose and mouth, felt pads, swivel head and jointed shoulders and hips, ears missing, German, c1920, 24in (61cm) high.
£120–140 / €170–200
$200–230 ✗ Bon(C)

A mohair dog, with boot-button eyes, early 20thC, 4¾in (12cm) high.
£50–55 / €70–80
$80–90 ⊞ BBe

A mohair teddy bear, possibly by the Ideal Toy Co, with boot-button eyes, replacement pads, American, 1910–20, 18in (45.5cm) high.
£350–400 / €500–570
$580–660 ⊞ BBe

A Chad Valley velvet Bonzo dog, with painted features, swivel head, jointed limbs, card-lined feet and original collar with button, c1920, 10¼in (26cm) high.
£280–330 / €400–480
$460–550 ✗ DA

◀ **A straw-filled mohair dog on wheels,** with original eyes, c1920, 12¼in (31cm) long.
£270–300 / €380–420
$450–500 ⊞ BaN

A mohair teddy bear, with glass eyes, 1920s, 18in (45.5cm) high.
£590–650 / €840–930
$980–1,100 ⊞ BBe

A mohair dog, with glass eyes and leather collar, 1920s–30s, 10in (25.5cm) high.
£85–95 / €120–135
$140–155 ⊞ BBe

A velvet Mickey Mouse, slightly worn, some repair, c1930, 9in (23cm) high.
£140–165 / €200–240
$230–270 ⚒ DA

A plush teddy bear, with glass eyes and shaven snout, 1930s, 26in (66cm) high.
£150–180 / €210–250
$250–300 ⚒ G(L)

A Chiltern musical bear, 1930s, 14in (35.5cm) high.
£220–250 / €310–350
$360–410 ⊞ POLL

A mohair teddy bear, possibly by Schuco, with glass eyes, stitched nose and mouth, felt pads, swivel head and jointed shoulders and hips, 1930s, 7in (18cm) high.
£120–140 / €170–200
$200–230 ⚒ Bon(C)

Further reading

Miller's Teddy Bears: A Complete Collector's Guide, Miller's Publications, 2001

◄ **A Scottie dog nightdress case,** with tartan collar, 1930s, 22in (56cm) long.
£85–95 / €120–135
$140–155 ⊞ DOL

A straw-filled mohair Felix the Cat, with original boot-button eyes, c1930, 19in (48.5cm) high.
£270–300 / €380–420
$450–500 ⊞ BaN

A plush Felix the Cat, with velvet eyes and nose, felt mouth and stitched teeth, 1930s, 15¼in (38.5cm) high.
£280–330 / €400–470
$460–540 ↗ B(MW)

A Tri-ang push-along dog on wheels, 1930s, 18in (45.5cm) high.
£25–30 / €35–40
$45–50 ⊞ JUN

▶ **A Chad Valley Snow White and the Seven Dwarfs,** late 1930s, Snow White 16in (40cm) high, in original boxes with names and price tags.
£1,600–1,900 / €2,250–2,700
$2,650–3,150 ↗ Bon(C)

A wool poodle nightdress case, 1930s, 18in (45.5cm) long.
£30–35 / €45–50
$50–60 ⊞ DOL

▶ **A Berg cat,** Austrian, 1930s, 5½in (14cm) high.
£85–95
€120–135
$140–155
⊞ LBe

◀ **A West Highland White terrier dog,** 1930s, 17in (43cm) long.
£85–95
€120–135
$140–155
⊞ DOL

SOFT TOYS

An Alpha Barnell monkey tea cosy, 1940,
10in (25.5cm) wide.
**£100–110 / €140–155
$165–185 ⊞ BINC**

A Roullet & Decamps rabbit-fur cat, French, c1940,
15in (38cm) long.
**£1,050–1,200 / €1,500–1,650
$1,750–1,950 ⊞ AUTO**

► **A Chiltern dog on wheels,**
1940s, 24in (61cm) high.
**£145–165 / €200–220
$240–270 ⊞ POLL**

◄ **A Pedigree dog on wheels,**
1940s, 22in (56cm) high.
**£115–130 / €165–185
$190–210 ⊞ POLL**

A panda, possibly by Dean's,
1940s, 15in (38cm) high.
**£220–250 / €310–350
$360–410 ⊞ POLL**

► **A mohair Scottie dog,**
with glass eyes and felt collar,
1940s–50s, 8in (20.5cm) high.
**£45–50 / €60–70
$75–85 ⊞ BBe**

A felt Mickey and Minnie Mouse,
post-WWII, 13½in (34.5cm) high.
**£35–40 / €50–60
$60–70 ↗ G(L)**

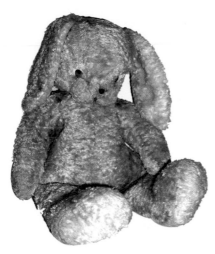

A **silk plush rabbit,** 1940s–50s, 20in (51cm) high.
£65–75 / €90–100
$110–125 ⊞ BBe

A **poodle nightdress case,** 1950, 20in (51cm) long.
£30–35 / €45–50
$50–55 ⊞ POLL

A **Wendy Boston mohair dog nightdress case,** with plastic eyes, leather collar and original label, 1950s, 16in (40.5cm) long.
£60–70 / €85–95
$100–110 ⊞ BBe

A **mohair teddy bear,** with glass eyes, stitched nose and mouth, jointed shoulders and hips, red metal heart attached to chest, 1950s, 4in (10cm) high.
£50–60 / €75–85
$85–100 ⚒ Bon(C)

A **plush teddy bear,** with plastic eyes and growler, 1950s, 25in (63.5cm) high.
£45–50 / €60–70
$75–85 ⚒ G(L)

◄ A **cloth lion,** with glass eyes, 1950s, 12in (30.5cm) high.
£25–30 / €35–40
$40–45 ⊞ YC

A **silk plush teddy bear,** wearing a vintage dress, 1950s, 27in (68.5cm) high.
£140–155 / €200–220
$230–260 ⊞ POLL

SOFT TOYS

A Chad Valley cloth golly, small hole to back of head, one felt nostril missing, with cardboard label 'By Appointment to HM Queen Elizabeth the Queen Mother', late 1950s–early 1960s, 24in (61cm) high.
£140–165 / €200–240
$230–270 ⚒ VEC

A fur monkey, with glass eyes, c1960, 14in (35.5cm) high.
£20–25 / €30–35
$35–40 ⊞ YC

A cloth golly, c1960, 19in (48.5cm) high.
£18–22 / €25–30
$30–35 ⊞ UD

A mohair poodle, c1960, 18in (45.5cm) high.
£35–40 / €50–55
$60–70 ⊞ POLL

A cloth golly, c1960, 14in (35.5cm) high.
£25–30 / €35–40
$40–50 ⊞ UD

A cloth and vinyl monkey, Jacko, c1960, 20in (51cm) high.
£15–20 / €20–25
$25–30 ⊞ UD

A Pedigree Walt Disney's Eeyore, 1960, 8in (20.5cm) high.
£30–35 / €45–50
$50–55 ⊞ POLL

Five soft toy characters, from *Jungle Book*, c1966, 6in (15cm) high.
£20–25 / €30–35
$35–40 each ⊞ HYP

◀ **A battery-operated poodle,** with remote control, some damage, Japanese, 1960s, with original box, 9in (23cm) square.
£6–10 / €8–14
$10–16 ⊞ RTT

A Walt Disney's Hissing Sid soft toy, made in Japan under licence to Disney, 1960s, 6in (15cm) high.
£25–35 / €35–40
$40–45 ⊞ GrD

A Wendy Boston synthetic machine-washable bear, with nylon eyes, 1960s, 24in (61cm) high.
£50–60 / €75–85
$85–100 ⊞ BBe
Wendy Boston created the first machine-washable bear in 1954.

◀ **A Chad Valley Chiltern golly,** 1970s, 15in (38cm) high.
£25–30 / €35–40
$40–45 ⊞ CMF

Three Nisbet Beatrix Potter Miniatures, Mrs Tiggywinkle, Jemima Puddleduck and Peter Rabbit, c1970, 7in (18cm) high.
£15–20 / €20–25
$25–30 ⊞ UD

▶ **A Wendy Boston Basil Brush,** 1970, 16in (40.5cm) high.
£55–65 / €80–90
$90–100 ⊞ POLL

A PG Tips toy monkey,
1970s, 14in (35.5cm) high.
£15–20 / €20–25
$25–30 ⊞ HUX

**A La Verne and Shirley stuffed
cat,** Kitty, American, 1970s,
22in (56cm) high.
£125–140 / €180–200
$210–240 ⊞ SpM

A mohair Paddington Bear, with plastic eyes
and nose, felt hat and coat and Wellington
boots, 1970s, 18½in (47cm) high.
£80–95 / €115–135
$135–160 ⚒ Bon(C)

◀ **A James Blackmore Guinness Toucan,**
with original labels, 1980, 20in (51cm) high.
£55–65 / €80–90
$90–100 ⊞ POLL

A Womble soft toy,
Madame Cholet, 1970s,
9in (23cm) high.
£6–12 / €8–14
$10–16 ⊞ CMF

**A Street Kids Corporation 'Socks the
White House Cat',** 1993, 14in (35.5cm) long.
£50–60 / €75–85
$85–100 ⊞ TBoy

A Roland Rat soft toy,
c1983, 16in (40.5cm) high.
£8–12 / €11–16
$13–19 ⊞ CMF

A Tolitoy Gordon the Gopher,
c1985, 16in (40.5cm) high.
£18–22 / €25–30
$30–35 ⊞ UD

▶ **A Beanie Baby,** Weenie, 1995,
8in (20.5cm) long.
£2–6 / €3–8
$4–10 ⊞ BeG

Dean's

▶ **A Dean's Dismal Desmond Dalmation,** 1930s, 6½in (16.5cm) high.
£150–180
€210–250
$250–300
⚒ **FHF**

◀ **A Dean's felt Mickey Mouse,** c1928, 18in (45.5cm) high.
£460–520 / €650–720
$760–840 ⊞ **DAn**

A Dean's dog, 1940, 22in (56cm) long.
£85–95 / €120–135
$140–155 ⊞ **POLL**

◀ **A Dean's mohair Scottie dog,** 1940, 14in (35.5cm) long.
£45–50 / €60–70
$75–85 ⊞ **POLL**

A Dean's monkey, c1950, 12in (30.5cm) high.
£35–40 / €50–55
$60–70 ⊞ **UD**

A Dean's Mr Golly, 1950s, 13in (33cm) high.
£60–70 / €85–95
$100–110 ⊞ **TAC**

A Dean's golly, 1950s, 16in (40.5cm) high.
£30–35 / €45–50
$50–55 ⊞ **A&J**

Merrythought

A **Merrythought terrier nightdress case,** 1930s, 20in (51cm) long.
£85–95 / € 120–135
$140–155 ⊞ POLL

A **Merrythought rabbit,** 1940s,
25in (63.5cm) high.
£135–150 / € 190–210
$220–250 ⊞ BINC

◀ A **Merrythought Walt
Disney's Thumper** 1956–80,
22in (56cm) high.
£110–125 / € 155–175
$180–200 ⊞ POLL

A **Merrythought Cheshire cat,**
c1950, 8in (20.5cm) high.
£25–30 / € 35–40
$40–45 ⊞ UD

A **Merrythought beach donkey,**
late 1960s, 15½in (39.5cm) high.
£20–25 / € 30–35
$35–40 ⊞ UNI

A **Merrythought Cheeky Bear
synthetic plush muff,** with plastic
eyes, velvet muzzle and stitched
nose and mouth, original label,
1960s, 13in (33cm) high.
£180–210 / € 250–300
$300–350 ➶ Bon(C)

A **Merrythought monkey,** 1980,
17in (43cm) high.
£45–50 / € 60–70
$75–85 ⊞ POLL

Schuco

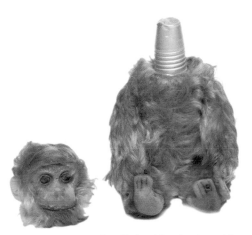

A Schuco mohair monkey flask, with painted metal face and metal eyes, swivel head and jointed shoulders and hips, felt ears, hands and feet, c1920, 9in (23cm) high.
£360–430 / €510–610
$600–720 ✗ Bon(C)
The head lifts off to reveal a glass bottle within the body, with a cork and a metal cup.

A Schuco mohair Yes/No monkey, German, 1920s, 4¾in (12cm) high.
£145–170 / €200–240 $240–280 ✗ JDJ

A Schuco plush monkey scent bottle, worn, German, c1920, 4in (10cm) high.
£135–150 / €190–210 $220–250 ⊞ A&J

A Schuco Goofy, German, 1950s, 14in (35.5cm) high.
£160–190 / €220–260
$260–310 ✗ TQA

A Schuco bigo-bello Apache Samson Jr, 1950s, 10½in (26.5cm) high, with original box.
£45–50 / €60–70
$70–80 ✗ TQA

Mueller & Schreyer

Heinrich Mueller and Heinrich Schreyer founded Schreyer & Co in Nuremberg in 1912, initially making a range of plush- and felt-covered toys. The Schuco brand did not appear until 1921 after the company had been reformed following WWI. Although production also halted during WWII, the Schuco brand is now as well known for their early witty monkeys with hidden features and Disney plush toys as for their mechanical and diecast items. Reissues of their classic toys continue to be made using the original techniques where possible.

Steiff

A Steiff fur monkey on a bicycle, with felt face and bead eyes, the wire bicycle with wooden seat and wheels, German, 1920, 5in (12.5cm) high.
£140–165 / €200–240
$230–270 ↗ **AH**

▶ **A Steiff mohair family of cows,** with glass eyes, velvet muzzles, chests and horns, ear buttons to the bull, German, c1950, largest 3in (7.5cm) high.
£200–240 / €280–330
$330–390 ↗ **Bon(C)**

A Steiff goat, German, c1948, 7in (18cm) high.
£40–45 / €55–65
$65–75 ⊞ **UD**

◀ **A Steiff squirrel,** German, 1940s, 6in (15cm) high.
£45–50 / €60–70
$75–85 ⊞ **BINC**

A Steiff mohair squirrel, Pirri, with acorn and boot-button eyes, German, 1950s, 5in (12.5cm) high.
£35–40 / €50–55
$60–70 ⊞ **BBe**

▶ **A Steiff mohair giraffe,** with original buttons, squeaker, boot-button eyes and ear tag, German, 1950s, 11in (28cm) high.
£55–65 / €80–90
$90–100 ⊞ **BBe**

A Steiff mohair hedgehog, Joggi, with button eyes and original label, German, 1950s, 5in (12.5cm) high.
£45–50 / €60–70
$75–85 ⊞ **BBe**

A Steiff mohair lion, well worn, German, 1950s, 9in (23cm) high.
£25–30 / €35–40
$40–45 ⊞ A&J

A Steiff plush kitten, with glass eyes, German, 1950s, 3½in (9cm) high.
£50–60 / €75–85
$85–100 ➴ FHF

A Steiff velvet zebra, with card chest tag, 1950s, 4¾in (12cm) high.
£55–65 / €80–90
$90–100 ⊞ BBe

A Steiff golden plush dog, Waldi, German, 1950s, 21in (53.5cm) long
£135–150 / €190–210
$220–250 ⊞ GrD

Two Steiff wool plush and mohair poodles, the black dog with glass eyes and chest tag, the grey dog with glass eyes, chest tag and ear button, German, 1956–58, 4in (10cm) high.
Black Dog
£55–65 / €80–90 / $90–100
Grey dog
£75–85 / €105–120 / $125–140 ⊞ BBe

A Steiff Jumbo, part jointed, with card tag, 1950s–60s, 8¾in (22cm) high.
£115–130 / €165–185
$190–210 ⊞ BBe

A Steiff mohair Bambi, German, 1950s, 6in (15cm) high.
£35–40 / €50–55
$60–70 ⊞ A&J

A Steiff velvet Bambi, with mohair chest and tail, button missing, German, 1950s–60s, 5½in (14cm) high.
£30–35 / €45–50
$50–55 ⊞ BBe

SOFT TOYS

A Steiff cat, Suzi, German,
1959–69, 4in (10cm) high.
£50–60 / €75–85
$85–100 ⊞ TED

A Steiff cat, with glass eyes and ear button,
fully jointed, 1950s–60s, 6¾in (17cm) high.
£110–125 / €155–175
$185–210 ⊞ BBe

A Steiff penguin, Peggy,
with chest tag but no
button, German, c1960,
19½in (49.5cm) high.
£135–150 / €190–210
$220–250 ⊞ TED

A Steiff plush dog, Waldi, with glass eyes
and stitched nose, the leather collar with
original paper label, German, 1960,
17¼in (44cm) long.
£140–165 / €200–240
$230–270 ✦ DN

A Steiff kangaroo, with ear button
and chest tag, joey missing, German,
1960s, 6in (15cm) high.
£45–50 / €60–70
$75–85 ⊞ BBe

A Steiff mohair rabbit,
Manni, with glass eyes
and ear button, German,
1960s, 4½in (11.5cm) high.
£55–65 / €80–90
$90–100 ⊞ BBe

A Steiff lion, German, 1960s, 13in (33cm) high.
£70–80 / €100–110
$115–130 ⊞ POLL

A Steiff Pekinese dog, Peky,
with original ribbon and chest tag,
no button, German, 1960s,
3¼in (8.5cm) high.
£35–40 / €50–55
$60–70 ⊞ TED

▶ **A Steiff Toad of Toad Hall,** limited
edition, German, 1999, 11in (28cm) high.
£130–145 / €185–210
$210–240 ⊞ Ann

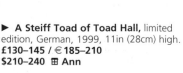

Dolls

◄ **A carved wood doll,** with glass eyes, painted mouth, eyebrows and cheeks, jointed hips and knees, with cloth and leather arms, early 18thC, 20in (51cm) high.
£1,000–1,200
€1,400–1,650
$1,700–2,000 ⚒ Bon(C)

► **A carved wood doll,** with glass eyes and carved features, jointed hips and knees, leather arms, mid-18thC, 23in (58.5cm) high.
£260–310 / €370–440
$430–510 ⚒ Bon(C)

◄ **A pair of wooden dancing wrestler dolls,** with painted composition heads, jointed arms and legs, early 20thC, 8½in (21.5cm) high.
£50–60 / €75–85
$85–100 ⚒ AH

A woodentop peg doll, with jointed legs, wearing a floral print dress, German, 19thC, dress 20thC, 11¾in (30cm) high.
£60–70 / €85–100
$100–120 ⚒ G(L)

A Mabel Lucie Attwell celluloid Diddums doll, with egg timer, c1930, 4in (10cm) high.
£85–95 / €120–135
$140–155 ⊞ MEM

A Schultz celluloid doll, with flirty eyes, wearing original dress, c1930, 22in (56cm) high, with extra dress.
£340–380 / €480–530
$560–620 ⊞ DOL

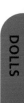

DOLLS

A doll, with flirty eyes, wearing an original outfit, c1930, 16½in (42cm) high.
£55–65 / €80–90 $90–100 ⊞ DOL

A celluloid doll, with moulded hair, French, 1930s, 21in (53.5cm) high.
£140–155 / €200–220 $230–260 ⊞ POLL

▶ **A Käthe Kruse Du Mein sand baby doll,** with magnesite head, painted eyes and closed mouth, the foam-filled body covered with stockinet, stamped on right foot, German, c1940, 21in (53.5cm) high.
£1,300–1,550 / €1,850–2,200 $2,150–2,550 ⚒ B(Ch)

A celluloid doll, on a bent-limbed body, German, 1930s, 16in (40.5cm) high.
£45–50 / €60–70 $75–85 ⊞ A&J

A pot doll, possibly by Diamond Doll Company, with original hair, 1940, 23in (58.5cm) high.
£105–120 / €150–170 $175–200 ⊞ POLL

▶ **A Roddy vinyl doll,** 1950s, 27in (68.5cm) high.
£175–195 / €250–280 $290–320 ⊞ POLL

A Rosebud Suck-A-Thumb doll, wearing original outfit, 1950s, 6in (15cm) high.
£50–55 / €70–80 $85–95 ⊞ POLL

A Pedigree vinyl baby doll, with moulded hair, late 1950s, 11in (28cm) high
£30–35 / € 40–45
$50–55 ⊞ POLL

A Madame Alexander hard plastic Cissy doll, with vinyl limbs, wearing a tagged taffeta dress, c1958, 21in (53.5cm) high.
£460–550 / € 650–780
$760–910 ⚒ HAYS

A Madame Alexander Jo doll, from *Little Women*, American, c1958, 5in (12.5cm) high, with original box.
£220–250 / € 310–350
$360–400 ⊞ UD

A Moon McDare doll, with accessories by Gilbert, 1960, 12in (30.5cm) high.
£105–120 / € 150–165
$175–195 ⊞ HAL

A Chiltern vinyl doll, wearing original outfit, 1958–67, 12in (30.5cm) high.
£25–30 / € 35–40
$40–50 ⊞ POLL

A Roddy vinyl doll, 1950s–60s, 21in (53.5cm) high.
£45–50 / € 60–70
$75–85 ⊞ POLL

▶ **A Palitoy vinyl Patsy doll,** c1960, 16in (40.5cm) high, boxed.
£65–75 / € 95–105
$110–130 ⊞ UD

DOLLS

A Dam Things vinyl troll, 1964,
11in (28cm) high.
£35–40 / €50–60
$60–70 ⊞ UD

A Pedigree vinyl doll,
wearing original outfit, 1962,
27in (68.5cm) high.
£85–95 / €120–135
$140–155 ⊞ UD

A Pedigree vinyl Melanie doll,
1962, 36in (91.5cm) high.
£160–180 / €230–260
$270–300 ⊞ UD

Vinyl dolls

Be aware that saggy, split,
sticky or powdery surfaces
signal degrading vinyl,
which cannot be reversed.

► **A Palitoy Teeny Tiny Tears
doll,** 1966, 12in (30.5cm) high.
£35–40 / €50–60
$60–70 ⊞ POLL

A Palitoy Tiny Tears doll, 1960s,
16in (40.5cm) high.
£40–45 / €55–65
$65–75 ⊞ UD

◄ **A Palitoy
vinyl Tiny
Tears doll,**
1966, 15in
(38cm) high.
£30–35
€45–50
$50–60 ⊞ POLL

► **A Pedigree
Patch's Pony,**
c1968, 8in
(20.5cm) high,
with original box.
£20–25
€30–35
$35–40 ⊞ CMF

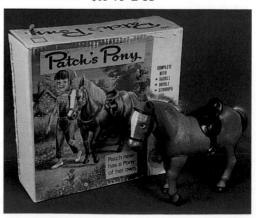

An Amanda Jane doll, *wearing original outfit,* 1960s, 7in (18cm) high.
£60–70 / €85–95
$100–110 ⊞ POLL

A Palitoy vinyl doll, 1960s, 14in (35.5cm) high.
£30–35 / €45–50
$50–60 ⊞ POLL

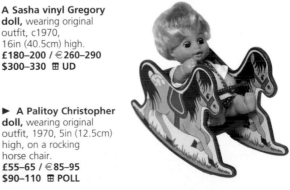

A Flair Toys Mary Quant Daisy series doll, 1970, 10in (25.5cm) high, with original packaging.
£45–50 / €60–70
$75–85 ⊞ CTO

A Sasha vinyl Gregory doll, *wearing original outfit,* c1970, 16in (40.5cm) high.
£180–200 / €260–290
$300–330 ⊞ UD

A Palitoy Carrie doll, *wearing original outfit,* 1970, in a carrying cot, 7in (18cm) wide.
£40–45 / €55–65
$65–75 ⊞ POLL

Three vinyl Mandy Jane dolls, c1970, 6in (15cm) high.
£4–8 / €5–11
$6–12 each ⊞ UD

► **A Palitoy Christopher doll,** *wearing original outfit,* 1970, 5in (12.5cm) high, on a rocking horse chair.
£55–65 / €85–95
$90–110 ⊞ POLL

DOLLS

An Amanda Jane doll, wearing original outfit, 1970, 8in (20.5cm) high.
£35–40 / €50–60
$60–70 ⊞ POLL

A vinyl Pillsbury doughboy, Poppin Fresh, 1971, 7in (18cm) high.
£11–15 / €16–21
$19–24 ⊞ RTT

◀ **Two Peggy Nisbet Wallis Simpson and Edward VIII costume dolls,** c1972, 8in (20.5cm) high, unopened.
£28–32
€40–45
$45–50 ⊞ UD

A plastic Sweet April doll, in a plastic carry case/swing by Remco, 1972, 10in (25.5cm) high.
£25–30 / €35–40
$40–50 ⊞ UD

A vinyl Shirley Temple doll, wearing original outfit, 1973, 19in (48.5cm) high.
£90–100 / €130–145
$150–165 ⊞ BGC

A Dennis Fisher vinyl Katie Kiss doll, 1974, 17in (43cm) high.
£18–22 / €25–30
$30–35 ⊞ UD

A First Love doll, with jointed waist, 1974, 15in (38cm) high.
£35–40 / €50–60
$60–70 ⊞ POLL

A Flair Toys Daisy Long Legs Sugarpie outfit, by Mary Quant, 1978, in original packaging, 14 x 10in (35.5 x 25.5cm).
£35–40 / €50–60
$60–70 ⊞ CTO

A Flair Toys Daisy Long Legs Buster outfit, by Mary Quant, 1978, in original packaging, 14 x 10in (35.5 x 25.5cm).
£25–30 / €35–40
$40–50 ⊞ CTO

◀ **A vinyl Aborigine doll,** 1970s, 16in (40.5cm) high.
£25–30 / €35–40
$40–50 ⊞ UD

A Sasha baby doll, wearing original outfit, 1970s, 11in (28cm) high.
£140–155 / €200–220
$230–260 ⊞ POLL

A Flair Toys Daisy Long Legs Follies outfit, by Mary Quant, 1978, in original packaging, 14in (35.5cm) high.
£25–30 / €35–40
$40–50 ⊞ CTO

Two Sasha dolls, wearing original outfits, 1970s, 16in (40.5cm) high.
£175–195 / €250–280
$290–320 each ⊞ POLL

◀ **A Flair Toys Daisy Long Legs Checkmate trouser suit,** by Mary Quant, 1978, in original packaging, 12in (30.5cm) high.
£25–30 / €35–40
$40–50 ⊞ CTO

DOLLS

◄ **An Amanda Jane doll,** wearing original outfit, 1970s, 7in (18cm) high.
£60–70 / €85–100
$100–115 ⊞ POLL

An Amanda Jane doll, wearing original outfit, 1970s–80s, 7½in (19cm) high.
£55–65 / €85–95
$90–110 ⊞ POLL

► **A Sunshine Sindy doll,** wearing Casual Dress outfit, 1982, 12in (30.5cm) high, with Sindy scooter.
£30–35 / €40–45
$50–55 ⊞ CMF

A Sleeping Sindy doll, wearing Sweet Dreams outfit, 1980s, 12in (30.5cm) high.
£45–50 / €60–70
$75–85 ⊞ CMF

◄ **A Sigikid artists' doll,** 'Michelle', limited edition, German, 2000, 30in (76cm) high.
£360–400 / €510–570
$600–660 ⊞ Ann

► **A Gene Marshall King's Daughter doll,** limited edition of 5,000, 1997, 15in (38cm) high.
£220–250 / €310–350
$360–400 ⊞ SAND

Composition

An Oriental jointed doll, with cloth body and composition hands and feet, wearing original outfit, Japanese, 1890, 11in (28cm) high.
£130–145 / €185–210
$210–240 ⊞ **Ann**

An Oriental souvenir boy doll, 1912, 7in (18cm) high.
£55–65 / €85–95
$90–110 ⊞ **Ann**

A Buddy Lee doll, with a painted face and five-piece body, wearing denim dungarees labelled 'Lee-Union Made', American, c1922, 12in (30.5cm) high.
£190–220 / €270–300
$310–350 ⊞ **THE**

A composition and cloth St Trinian's doll, wearing a labelled outfit, c1930, 16in (40.5cm) high.
£310–350 / €440–490
$510–570 ⊞ **Beb**
Character dolls are always worth more if they have all the original accessories. If in doubt, research items in design catalogues before purchasing.

A musical doll, with painted features and straw-stuffed body containing a pump musical movement, c1930, 20½in (52cm) high.
£70–80 / €100–115
$115–130 ⊞ **YC**

▶ **A Cameo Doll Co Rose O'Neill Scootles doll,** with painted eyes and original outfit, c1930, 15¼in (39.5cm) high.
£400–450 / €570–630
$660–730 ⊞ **DOL**

DOLS

A doll, with painted
features, on a cloth
body with composition
arms, French, c1930,
12½in (32cm) high.
£65–75 / €90–100
$105–120 ⊞ YC

A Dee Cee baby doll, on a bent-limbed
body, Canadian, 1930s, 12in (30.5cm) high.
£70–80 / €100–110
$115–130 ⊞ POLL

A doll, with original wig, 1930s,
18in (45.5cm) high.
£210–240 / €300–330
$350–390 ⊞ POLL

▶ **An Ideal Novelty & Toy
Company Shirley Temple doll,** shoes
missing, 1930s, 13in (33cm) high.
£310–370 / €440–520
$510–610 ⋌ HAYS

A Topsy doll, American, c1940,
11in (28cm) high.
£85–95 / €120–135
$140–155 ⊞ UD

**A pair of Armand Marseille
animated dolls,** mould 1353,
on a basket pram, 1930s–40s,
18in (45.5cm) long.
£720–800 / €1,000–1,100
$1,200–1,300 ⊞ UD

▶ **A Pedigree baby doll,** with
bent-limbed body, minor wear,
1960s, 12in (30.5cm) high.
£75–85 / €105–120
$125–140 ⊞ POLL

Plastic

A Terri Lee hard plastic doll, with painted eyes, wearing a tagged satin wedding gown by the Terri Lee Sales Corporation, c1946, 16in (40.5cm) high.
£240–280 / €340–400
$400–480 🔨 HAYS

A Pedigree hard plastic doll, late 1940s, 12in (30.5cm) high.
£85–95 / €120–135
$140–155 ⊞ UD

A Madame Alexander hard plastic bride doll, c1948, 18in (45.5cm) high.
£850–1,000 / €1,200–1,400
$1,400–1,650 🔨 HAYS

▶ **A hard plastic Roddy doll,** c1950, 21in (53.5cm) high.
£65–75 / €95–105
$110–125 ⊞ UD

A Pedigree baby doll, c1950, 10in (25.5cm) high.
£45–50 / €65–75
$75–85 ⊞ A&J

A Pedigree hard plastic Elizabeth doll, c1950, 19in (48.5cm) high.
£110–125 / €160–180
$180–200 ⊞ UD

▶ **A Tudor Rose hard plastic doll,** c1950, 9in (23cm) high.
£40–45 / €55–65
$65–75 ⊞ POLL

DOLLS

A Polyflex doll, French, c1950, 16in (40.5cm) high.
£60–70 / €85–95
$100–110 ⊞ T&D

A Käthe Kruse doll, 'Little German Child', with hard plastic head and painted eyes, on a cloth body, German, c1950, 18in (45.5cm) high.
£450–540 / €640–760
$750–900 ⚒ B(Ch)

A Rosebud hard plastic doll, c1950, 16in (40.5cm) high, with original box.
£150–165 / €210–240
$250–280 ⊞ UD

A Palitoy hard plastic walking talking doll, c1950, 21in (53.5cm) high.
£65–75 / €95–105
$110–125 ⊞ UD

A Pedigree hard plastic walking talking doll, c1950, 20in (51cm) high.
£65–75 / €95–105
$110–125 ⊞ UD

A B. N. D. plastic walker doll, with original wig, 1952, 21in (53.5cm) high.
£150–165 / €210–240
$250–280 ⊞ POLL

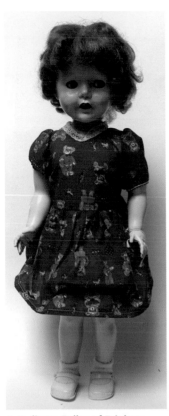

A plastic doll, with sleeping eyes, a knitted doll in the pocket of her dress, 1950s, 12in (30.5cm) high.
£20–25 / €30–35
$35–40 ⊞ GRa

A Pedigree walker doll, with original wig, 1955–56, 16in (40.5cm) high.
£150–165 / €210–240
$250–280 ⊞ POLL

A Pedigree Belles of Brighton walking talking doll, 1955, 28in (71cm) high.
£140–160 / €200–220
$230–260 ⊞ UD

A Roddy walker doll, wearing original outfit and wig, 1950s, 13in (33cm) high.
£45–50 / €60–70
$75–85 ⊞ POLL

A Roddy plastic baby doll, 1950s, 21in (53.5cm) high.
£130–145 / €185–210
$210–240 ⊞ POLL

◄ A Pedigree walker doll, wearing original wig and outfit, 1950s, 20in (51cm) high.
£175–195 / €250–280
$290–320 ⊞ POLL

DOLLS

A Rosebud doll, wearing original mohair wig, 1950s, 11in (28cm) high.
£30–35 / €40–45
$50–55 ⊞ POLL

A Pedigree plastic doll, with bent-limbed body and mohair wig, 1950s, 10in (25.5cm) high.
£50–60 / €75–85
$85–100 ⊞ POLL

A Roddy walker doll, wearing a Scottish outfit, 1950s, 12in (30.5cm) high.
£30–35 / €45–50
$50–60 ⊞ POLL

◄ **A Rosebud Suck-A-Thumb doll,** with Victorian bed, 1950s, 13in (33cm) high.
£70–80 / €100–115
$115–130 ⊞ POLL

Two Rosebud Twins dolls, 1950s, 6in (15cm) high, with knitting pattern book.
£11–15 / €16–21
$19–24 ⊞ POLL

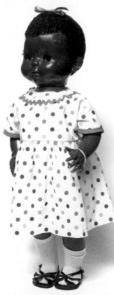

A Roddy doll, 1950s, 6in (15cm) high.
£30–35 / €45–50
$50–60 ⊞ POLL

A Pedigree hard plastic doll, 1950s, 20in (51cm) high.
£220–250 / €320–360
$370–410 ⊞ POLL

A Rosebud Suck-A-Thumb doll, 1950s, 7in (18cm) high.
£50–55 / €70–85
$85–95 ⊞ POLL

A Rosebud hard plastic doll,
wearing later outfit, 1950s,
13in (33cm) high.
£45–50 / €60–70
$75–85 ⊞ UD

A Pedigree plastic doll, c1960,
20in (51cm) high.
£70–80 / €100–110
$120–135 ⊞ PAR

A Pedigree plastic walker doll,
with moveable eyes, c1960,
22in (56cm) high.
£90–100 / €130–145
$150–165 ⊞ PAR

A B. N. D.
plastic doll,
c1960, 9in
(23cm) high.
£40–45
€55–65
$65–75 ⊞ PAR

An Old Cottage Toys
tartan doll, with hard plastic
head and felt jointed body,
c1960, 9in (23cm) high.
£35–40 / €50–60
$60–70 ⊞ A&J

A Rosebud plastic doll, c1960,
11in (29cm) high.
£40–45 / €55–65
$65–75 ⊞ PAR

▶ **A Rosebud**
plastic doll,
wearing original
outfit, c1960,
7½in (19cm) high.
£35–40
€50–55
$55–65 ⊞ PAR

Barbie & Friends

A Mattel Barbie tote and records, c1961, tote 9in (23cm) high.
£250–280 / €350–390
$410–460 ⊞ T&D

▶ **A Mattel Barbie No. 5 doll,** wearing 'Outdoor Life' outfit, 1961, 11½in (29cm) high.
£155–170 / €220–240
$260–280 ⊞ SAND

A Mattel Barbie doll, damaged, c1960, 11in (28cm) high.
£65–75 / €90–105
$110–125 ⊞ POLL

A Mattel Skipper outfit, 'Press Coat', c1962, in unopened box, 10in (25.5cm) square.
£145–160 / €200–220
$240–270 ⊞ T&D

A Mattel Bubblecut Barbie doll, 'Career Girl', c1962, 9in (23cm) high.
£115–130 / €160–185
$190–220 ⊞ T&D

A Mattel Freckles Midge doll, wearing 'Country Club Dance' outfit, American, c1962, 11½in (29cm) high.
£450–500 / €640–710
$750–830 ⊞ T&D
Midge is Barbie's friend.

A Mattel Skipper doll and vanity set,
c1962, in box, 10in (25.5cm) high.
**£400–450 / €570–640
$670–750 ⊞ T&D**

Four outfits for Ken, c1962,
largest 9in (23cm) long, all in
original packaging.
**£40–45 / €55–65
$65–75 ⊞ T&D**

▶ A Mattel Ken doll, wearing
'Play Ball' outfit and carrying a bat,
American, c1962, 12in (30.5cm) high.
**£150–165 / €215–240
$250–280 ⊞ T&D
Ken is Barbie's boyfriend.**

◀ A Barbie Little Theatre, with
Midge as Cinderella and Bubblecut
Barbie as Guinevere, c1963,
22 x 19½in (56 x 49.5cm).
**£1,850–2,100 / €2,600–3,000
$3,100–3,500 ⊞ T&D**
**If purchased without the dolls
this theatre would cost £1,300 /
€1,850 / $2,350.**

A Mattel Alan doll,
wearing 'Dream Boat'
outfit, American, c1962,
12in (30.5cm) high.
**£140–155 / €200–220
$230–260 ⊞ T&D
Alan is Midge's boyfriend.**

A Mattel Midge doll, straight-leg
version, American, c1963, 12in
(30.5cm) high, with original box.
**£240–270 / €340–380
$400–440 ⊞ T&D**

◀ A Skipper outfit, 'Tarn Togs',
c1964, in unopened box,
7in (18cm) square.
**£140–160 / €200–230
$230–260 ⊞ T&D**

DOLLS

A Skipper outfit, 'Tarn Togs', c1964, in unopened box, 7in (18cm) square.
£140–160 / €200–230 $230–260 ⊞ **T&D**

A Skipper outfit, 'Happy Birthday', c1964, in unopened box, 10in (25.5cm) square.
£450–500 / €640–710 $750–830 ⊞ **T&D**

A Mattel American Girl Barbie doll, wearing 'Shimmering Magic' outfit, c1965, 11½in (29cm) high.
£900–1,000 / €1,250–1,400 $1,500–1,650 ⊞ **T&D**

A Mattel Bendable Leg Francie doll, wearing 'Combination' outfit, c1966, 6in (15cm) high.
£330–370 / €470–530 $550–620 ⊞ **T&D**

A Mattel American Girl Barbie doll, wearing 'Golden Glamour' outfit, c1965, 11½in (29cm) high.
£950–1,100 / €1,350–1,550 $1,550–1,800 ⊞ **T&D**

▶ **A Mattel American Girl Barbie doll,** wearing 'Fraternity Dance' outfit, 1965–66, 11½in (29cm) high.
£110–125 / €155–175 $180–200 ⊞ **SAND**

A Mattel Bendable Leg Skipper doll, c1966, 9in (23cm) high, in a box.
£220–250 / €310–350
$370–420 ⊞ T&D

A Mattel Tutti doll, wearing 'Clowning Around' outfit, 1966–67, 6¼in (16cm) high.
£45–50 / €60–70
$75–85 ⊞ SAND
Tutti is Barbie's smallest sister.

◄ **A Mattel Bubblecut Barbie doll,** wearing 'Matinée' outfit, c1967, 11in (28cm) high.
£360–400 / €510–570
$600–660 ⊞ T&D

A Mattel long-haired American Girl Barbie doll, wearing 'Saturday Matinée' outfit, American, c1966, 11½in (29cm) high.
£1,250–1,400 / €1,550–2,000
$2,100–2,350 ⊞ T&D
The outfit worn by this doll is available separately at £540–600 / €770–850 / $900–990.

A Mattel Stacey doll, c1967, 11in (28cm) high.
£220–250 / €310–350
$360–400 ⊞ T&D
Barbie's friend Stacey was introduced c1967. Inspired by swinging London, Stacey was a British model. She also came in a talking version which, in an English accent, said 'Being a model is terribly exciting,' and 'I think mini-skirts are smashing.'

► **Two Twist 'n Turn Barbie dolls,** one wearing 'Peasant Pleasant' outfit, the other 'Funshine' outfit c1967, 11½in (29cm) high.
£510–570 / €720–810
$850–950 each ⊞ T&D

DOLLS

A Mattel Twist 'n Turn Barbie doll, c1967, 12½in (32cm) high, with original box.
£630–700 / €900–1,000 $1,050–1,150 ⊞ T&D

A Mattel Barbie doll, wearing 'Made for Each Other' outfit, c1967, 11½in (29cm) high.
£270–300 / €380–420 $450–500 ⊞ T&D

A Mattel Twist 'n Turn Stacey doll, American, c1967, 12in (30.5cm) high, unopened.
£630–700 / €900–1,000 $1,050–1,150 ⊞ T&D

A Mattel Walking Jamie doll, wearing 'Pepsi' outfit, American, c1968, 11½in (29cm) high.
£250–280 / €350–390 $400–450 ⊞ T&D

A Barbie carrying case, 1960s, 14in (35.5cm) high.
£11–15 / €16–21 $19–24 ⊞ SAND

A Mattel Walking Jamie doll, wearing an original outfit, c1968, 11½in (29cm) high.
£175–195 / €250–280 $290–320 ⊞ T&D
Jamie is Barbie's friend.

► **A Mattel Talking Stacey doll,** wearing a beach outfit, American, c1968, in original box, 13 x 4½in (33 x 11.5cm), unopened.
£370–420 / €540–600 $630–700 ⊞ T&D

A Barbie case, c1968, 14 x 17in (35.5 x 43cm).
£45–50 / €60–70
$75–85 ⊞ T&D

Two Mattel Skipper outfits, 'Twice as Nice', in two colourways,
c1969, in packaging, 7in (18cm) square.
£175–195 / €250–280
$290–320 each ⊞ T&D

Six Barbie booklets, c1970,
largest 4in (10cm) high.
£6–10 / €8–14
$10–16 each ⊞ T&D

▶ **A Mattel Malibu Barbie doll,** wearing a
velvet outfit, c1975, 9in (23cm) high.
£155–175 / €220–250
$250–280 ⊞ T&D

Two Mattel talking dolls, Brad and
Julia 1968–69, 11½in (29cm) high.
£280–310 / €400–440
$460–510 ⊞ T&D
Julia was based on Diahann
Carroll's character from the
popular prime-time television
show *Julia* (1968–71). The singer
was the first black female to star
in her own comedy series. She also
provided the voice for the doll.
Brad was the boyfriend of Barbie's
friend Christie, and the couple
were among the first African-
American dolls to be produced
as girlfriend and boyfriend.

▶ **A Mattel Malibu Skipper doll,**
wearing 'Wooly Winner' outfit,
c1975, 9in (23cm) high.
£140–160 / €200–230
$230–260 ⊞ T&D

A Mattel Barbie Loves Elvis doll, collector's
edition, 1996, 14in (35.5cm) high, with
original box.
£45–50 / €60–70
$75–85 ⊞ CTO

DOLLS

Action Man

A Palitoy Action Man outfit, Army Officer uniform, c1970, in unopened packaging, 14 x 11in (35.5 x 28cm).
£350–400 / €500–570 $580–660 ⊞ GTM

A Palitoy Action Man outfit, Red Devil parachutist, second issue, 1972, with original packaging, 14in (35.5cm) high.
£155–175 / €220–250 $260–290 ⊞ GTM

A Palitoy Action Man, wearing 'Underwater Explorer' outfit, with realistic hair, fixed eyes and hard fixed hands, 1972, 12in (30.5cm) high.
£50–60 / €75–85 $85–100 ⊞ CY

▶ Three sets of Palitoy Action Man accessories, 1970s, 8in (20.5cm) high.
£11–15 / €16–21 $19–24 ⊞ HAL

A Palitoy Action Man, wearing 'Red Devil' outfit, 1973, 12in (30.5cm) high.
£50–60 / €75–85 $85–100 ⊞ CY
This Red Devil uniform was used on dolls produced between 1973 and 1976. The dolls had realistic hair, rubber gripping hands and fixed eyes.

◀ A Palitoy Action Man, wearing 'Lifeguard' outfit, with reproduction sword and spurs, 1978, 12in (30.5cm) high.
£70–85 / €100–115 $115–130 ⊞ CY
This Lifeguard's uniform is displayed on an Action Man figure that was first issued in 1978 with realistic hair, moving eagle eyes and gripping hands. The uniform first appeared in the early 1970s and remained unchanged until the line was discontinued in 1984. The reproduction sword and spurs reduce the value of this doll; had these items been original the value could be approximately £125 / €175 / $210.

An Action Man Combat Division soldier, 1981, 13in (33cm) high, with original box.
£100–110 / €140–155 $165–185 ⊞ GTM

Dolls' Prams

A doll's pram, with two large and two small wheels, hood damaged, c1900, 20in (51cm) long.
£110–130 / € 155–185
$180–210 ⊞ BWL

A doll's pram, with two large and two small wheels, c1900, 28in (71cm) high.
£400–450 / € 570–630
$660–730 ⊞ JUN

A doll's pram, with new lining, hood and apron, 1930s, 33in (84cm) long.
£340–380 / € 480–530
$560–620 ⊞ POLL

▶ A Royal doll's pram, with loose bottom section and padded interior, 1940s, 43in (109cm) long.
£490–550
€ 700–770
$810–900
⊞ POLL

A Lines Brothers Tri-ang doll's pram, 1950s, 28in (71cm) long.
£175–195 / € 250–280
$290–320 ⊞ POLL

▶ A Silver Cross pram, with original canopy and bag, early 1970s, 28in (71cm) long.
£430–480
€ 610–680
$710–790
⊞ POLL

DOLLS

Dolls' Houses

▶ **A wooden doll's house on a stand,** with painted brick-effect façade and sides, balustrade added at a later date, early 19thC, 26in (66cm) wide.
£2,800–3,300
€ **4,000–4,800**
$4,650–5,500
⚒ **Bon**

A doll's house, Farnham House, with brick-effect façade, restored, late 18thC, 49in (124.5cm) high.
£20,000–24,000 / € **28,500–34,000**
$33,000–39,000 ⚒ **Bon**
Ex-Vivien Greene (widow of Graham Greene) collection.

▶ **A doll's house,** Strawberry Hill Gothick, with four bedrooms, hallway and landing, some restoration, 1820–30, 25in (63.5cm) high.
£4,000–4,800 / € **5,700–6,800**
$6,650–7,950 ⚒ **Bon**
Ex-Vivien Greene collection.
The pink paintwork is a reference to Horace Walpole's Gothick Villa at Strawberry Hill, Twickenham.

A painted wood doll's house, with painted tile roof, the front opening to reveal six rooms, hallways and staircase, mid-19thC, 38in (97cm) wide.
£1,000–1,200 / € **1,400–1,650**
$1,650–1,950 ⚒ **B(Ch)**

A painted wood doll's house, the front opening in two sections to reveal four rooms, c1860, 30in (76cm) wide.
£480–570 / € **680–810**
$800–980 ⚒ **B(Ch)**

A wooden doll's house, with four furnished rooms, c1870, 29in (73.5cm) wide.
£3,150–3,500
€ **4,450–5,300**
$5,250–6,300 ⊞ **Beb**

◀ **A wooden doll's house,** with a painted stone-effect façade, late 19thC, 23½in (59.5cm) wide.
£2,000–2,400
€2,850–3,400
$3,300–3,950
🔨 Bon

▶ **A wooden doll's house,** damaged, late 19thC, 29in (73.5cm) wide.
£400–480
€570–680
$660–790
🔨 S(O)

A doll's painted stable house, with a terrace and outside staircase, two stuffed pull-along horses and a tin horse-drawn roller, c1900, 20¾in (52.5cm) wide.
£520–620 / €740–880
$860–1,000 🔨 HOLL

A painted wood doll's house, with stonework-effect façade, contains a quantity of doll's house furniture, c1900, 47¼in (120cm) wide.
£3,000–3,600 / €4,250–5,100
$5,000–6,000 🔨 B&L

A Moritz Göttschalk painted wood doll's house, the single opening front revealing two rooms, with original wallpaper and floor coverings, German, c1900, 11in (28cm) wide.
£600–720 / €850–1,000
$1,000–1,200 🔨 B(Ch)

◀ **A Georgian-style doll's house,** early 20thC, 38in (96.5cm) high.
£900–1,000 / €1,300–1,450
$1,500–1,650 ⊞ CLE

▶ **A Lines Brothers doll's house,** with a flat roof, four rooms, staircase, butler's sink and four fireplaces, c1910, 24in (61cm) high.
£530–630 / €750–900
$900–1,050 ⊞ G(L)

DOLLS

A painted wood doll's house, with lift-off front and side opening, dated 1914, 23¾in (60.5cm) wide.
£350–420 / €500–600
$580–680 S(O)

A Lines Brothers doll's house, 1923, 27in (68.5cm) high.
£540–600 / €770–900
$900–1,050 HOB

A wooden doll's house, with detachable roof and sliding back opening, c1920, 33in (84cm) high.
£120–140 / €170–200
$200–240 SWO

A Tudor-style suburban detached doll's house, with fixed front bay window and opening front door, the four rooms with electric lighting and period furniture and fittings, removable rear panel, late 1920s, 16½in (42cm) high.
£270–320 / €380–450
$450–540 WAL

A Lines Brothers 'Queen Mary's Doll's House', in the Tudor style, with thatched-effect roof, four rooms, hall, staircase, landing, two fireplaces, dresser, sink and tinplate cooker, wired for electricity, on a garden plinth, 1930s, 24in (61cm) high, including a quantity of 1930s doll's house furniture and accessories.
£700–840 / €990–1,150
$1,150–1,300 G(L)

◀ **A Tri-ang Ultra Modern Series Art Deco-style doll's house,** No. 53, with integral garage, glass windows, balconies and removable sun room, three fitted fireplaces, decorated rooms and curtains and a simulated crazy paving base, 1930s, 40in (101.5cm) wide.
£650–780 / €920–1,100
$1,100–1,300 WAL

A wooden doll's house, rendered in stucco, the front opening in two sections to reveal four rooms, hallways, staircase and landing, all with original floor coverings and fireplaces, 1920s, 36in (91.5cm) wide.
£130–160 / €**185–220**
$210–260 ⚒ B(Ch)

A Tri-ang Tudor-style wooden doll's house, No. 77, Albert Cottage, the exterior painted with flowers to the walls, the front opening in two sections to reveal four rooms, hall, staircase and built-in garage with double doors, 1930s, 33½in (85cm) wide.
£200–240 / €**280–330**
$330–390 ⚒ WAL

A Tudor Toys doll's house, with balcony and shutters, late 1960s, 17½in (44.5cm) wide.
£40–45 / €**55–65**
$65–75 ⊞ UNI

▶ **A Mettoy tinplate Cottage Hospital,** with interior furniture and figures, 1950s–60s, 19½in (49.5cm) wide, with original box.
£60–70 / €**85–100**
$100–120 ⚒ BLH

◀ **A doll's house,** Amersham, with painted exterior and *faux*-slate roof, the front opening to reveal two rooms with fitted fireplace, late 1930s, base 16½in (42cm) square.
£80–95
€**115–135**
$130–155
⊞ WAL

▶ **A Tudor-style two-storey doll's house,** with battery-operated lighting, partly furnished, 1940s, 29in (73.5cm) wide.
£135–150
€**190–220**
$220–260
⚒ GAZE

A Tri-ang wooden doll's house, No. 93, Fashionable Tudor House, the exterior painted with flowers to the walls and half-timbered gables, the front opening in four sections to reveal five rooms, hall and staircase, built-in garage with opening double doors, with original wall and floor coverings and electric lighting, including a quantity of furniture and accessories, c1950, 47in (119.5cm) wide.
£800–960 / €**1,150–1,350**
$1,350–1,600 ⚒ B(Ch)

DOLLS

Doll's House Furniture

A set of wooden doll's house furniture, decorated with flowers, cherubs and birds, slight damage, German, mid-19thC, sofa 3in (7.5cm) high.
£600–720 / €850–1,000
$1,000–1,200 ⚒ Bon

▶ **A doll's house pine bureau,** inlaid with walnut, with four small and three large drawers, German, 1860, 5in (12.5cm) high.
£200–230 / €280–310
$330–370 ⊞ YC

A doll's house simulated rosewood and ebony French-style writing desk, with three drawers above a marble top, German, 1860, 4in (10cm) high.
£90–100 / €130–145
$150–165 ⊞ YC

A doll's house simulated rosewood and gilt French-style sofa and two chairs, with original upholstery, German, 1860–70, 2¼in (5.5cm) high.
£135–150 / €190–210
$220–250 ⊞ YC

A doll's house simulated mahogany and gilt French-style sewing table, with sewing accessories in drawer compartments, German, 1860–70, 3in (7.5cm) high.
£135–150 / €190–210
$220–250 ⊞ YC

A doll's house gilt-metal rocking chair, French, 1880–1900, 2¾in (7cm) high.
£35–40 / €50–60
$60–70 ⊞ YC

A doll's house painted metal sewing machine, c1900, 2in (5cm) high.
£35–40 / €50–60
$60–70 ⊞ YC

◀ **A set of doll's house wicker chairs and a table,** with leatherette papered seats, 1900–10, 7in (18cm) high.
£160–180 / €230–260
$270–300 ⊞ YC

A doll's house brass four-poster bed, with original bedding, 1910–15, 23in (58.5cm) high.
£190–220 / €270–300
$310–350 ⊞ BaN

A doll's house ceramic bathroom set, Japanese, 1900–20, in original box, 4in (10cm) wide.
£45–55 / €65–75
$75–85 ⊞ HUM

Tootsietoy boxed sets of doll's house diecast metal furniture, for the bedroom, living room and kitchen, 1920s–30s.
£105–125 / €150–190
$175–210 each ➴ HAYS

A doll's house tin washstand, with mirror, jug, bowl and pail, some damage, c1915, 21in (53.5cm) high.
£135–150 / €190–210
$220–250 ⊞ DOL

▶ **A doll's house tin bath and bucket,** on a wooden stand, transfer-decorated with pictures of swans, c1920, 22in (56cm) high.
£180–200 / €260–290
$300–330 ⊞ DOL

A Tri-ang doll's house mangle set, with buckets and washboard, 1930s, 19in (48.5cm) high.
£135–150 / €190–210
$220–250 ⊞ SMI

DOLLS

◀ **A doll's house trunk,** with later airline labels, 1930s–40s, 15½in (39.5cm) high.
£85–95
€ **120–135**
$140–155
⊞ **MCa**

▶ **A Lines Brothers Tri-ang doll's house high chair,** with original padded seat, 1940s, 23in (58.5cm) high.
£60–70
€ **85–95**
$100–110
⊞ **POLL**

A Brimtoy doll's house tinplate dresser, 1950s, 4in (10cm) wide.
£11–15 / € **16–21**
$19–24 ⊞ **A&J**

A Tri-ang doll's house high chair, 1950s, 20in (51cm) high.
£30–35 / € **45–50**
$50–55 ⊞ **UD**

A doll's house mahogany pulpit, 2000, 8in (20.5cm) high.
£150–170 / € **210–240**
$250–280 ⊞ **CNM**

A doll's house wooden tool cupboard, by Terry McAllister, with tools, 2002, 7in (18cm) high.
£140–160 / € **200–240**
$230–260 ⊞ **CNM**

Four pieces of doll's house kitchen furniture, by Jane Newman, comprising a dresser, two chairs and a table, 2000, dresser 7in (18cm) high.
£70–80 / € **100–110**
$115–130 ⊞ **CNM**

Directory of Specialists

If you require a valuation for an item it is advisable to check whether the dealer or specialist will carry out this service, and whether there is a charge. Please mention Miller's when making an enquiry. Having found a specialist who will carry out your valuation, it is best to send a description and photograph of the item to them, together with a stamped addressed envelope for the reply. A valuation by telephone is not possible. Most dealers are only too happy to help you with your enquiry, however, they are very busy people and consideration of the above points would be welcomed.

Berkshire
Special Auction Services,
Kennetholme, Midgham,
Reading RG7 5UX
Tel: 0118 971 2949
www.invaluable.com/sas/
Commemoratives, pot lids, Prattware,
Fairings, Goss & Crested, Baxter and Le
Blond prints. Also toys for the collector.

Buckinghamshire
Yesterday Child
Tel/Fax: 01908 583403
djbarrington@btinternet.com
Antique dolls and dolls house miniatures.

Cambridgeshire
Antique Amusement Co,
Mill Lane, Swaffham Bulbeck CB5 0NF
Tel/Fax: 01223 813041
Mobile: 07802 666755
mail@aamag.co.uk
www.aamag.co.uk
Vintage amusement machines, also
auctions of amusement machines,
fairground art and other related
collectables. Monthly collectors magazine.

Cheshire
Dollectable, 53 Lower Bridge Street,
Chester CH1 1RS
Tel: 01244 344888/679195
Antique dolls.

Cleveland
Vectis Auctions Ltd, Fleck Way,
Thornaby, Stockton-on-Tees TS17 9JZ
Tel: 01642 750616
admin@vectis.co.uk www.vectis.co.uk
Toy auctions.

Cumbria
Symon Brown Tel: 01900 825505
sheshops123@aol.com
Marbles, solitaire boards.

Dorset
Murrays' Antiques & Collectables
Tel: 01202 309094
Shipping, motoring, railway, cycling
items always required. Also advertising
related items, eg showcards, enamel
signs, tins, packaging and general
quality collectables. Anything old and
interesting. No valuations given.

Essex
Haddon Rocking Horses Ltd,
5 Telford Road, Clacton-on-Sea
CO15 4LP Tel: 01255 424745

millers@haddonrockinghorses.co.uk
www.haddonrockinghorses.co.uk
Rocking horses made and restored.

Starbase-Alpha, Unit 19–20,
Rumford Shopping Halls, Market Place,
Romford, Essex RM1 3AT
Tel: 01708 765633
starbasealpha1@aol.com
www.starbasealpha.cjb.net
Specialists in TV and film related collectables,
toys and props. From the 1970s–present.

Flintshire
Old Bears 4 U, 45 Chester Close,
Shotton, Deeside CH5 1AX
Tel: 01244 830066
debbie&paul@oldbears4u.co.uk
www.oldbears4u.co.uk
Buying, selling, repairing and cleaning
old bears.

Gloucestershire
Bourton Bears Tel: 01451 821466
www.bourtonbears.com
Teddy bears.

Gloucester Toy Mart, Ground Floor,
Antique Centre, Severn Road,
Old Docks, Gloucester GL1 2LF
Mobile: 07973 768452
Buying and selling obsolete toys
and collectables.

Hampshire
Classic Amusements
Tel: 01425 472164
pennyslot@aol.com
www.classicamusements.net
Vintage slot machines.

Solent Railwayana Auctions,
9 Wildern Close, Locks Heath,
Southampton SO31 7EZ
Tel: 01489 574029
nigel@solentrailwayana.com
www.solentrailwayana.com
Railwayana and transport related auctions.

Herefordshire
Brightwells Ltd, The Fine Art Saleroom,
Easters Court, Leominster,
Herefordshire HR6 0DE
Tel: 01568 611122
Fax: 01568 610519
fineart@brightwells.com

Isle of Wight
Nostalgia Toy Museum,
High Street, Godshill,
Ventnor PO38 3HZ

Tel: 01983 522148
toyman@nostalgiatoys.com
Diecast toys specialist and museum.

Kent
Barbara Ann Newman,
London House Antiques,
4 Market Square, Westerham,
Kent TN16 1AW
Mobile: 07850 016729
Antique dolls, teddy bears
and collectables.

The Collector's Toy & Model Shop,
49 Canterbury Road, Margate,
Kent CT9 5AS
Tel: 01843 232301
Fax: 01843 291905
k.limbert@btinternet.com

Lincolnshire
Junktion, The Old Railway Station,
New Bolingbroke, Boston PE22 7LB
Tel: 01205 480068/480087
Mobile: 07836 345491
Advertising and packaging, automobilia,
slot machines, pedal cars, etc.

London
The Antique Dealer,
115 Shaftesbury Avenue,
WC2H 8AD Tel: 020 7420 6684
info@theantiquedealer.co.uk
Monthly guide to antiques
and collectables.

Colin Baddiel, Gray's Antiques Market,
1–7 Davies Mews, London W1Y 1AR
Tel: 020 7408 1239 or 020 8452 7243

Comic Book Postal Auctions Ltd,
40–42 Osnaburgh Street,
NW1 3ND Tel: 020 7424 0007
comicbook@compuserve.com
www.compalcomics.com
Comic book auctions.

Murray Cards (International) Ltd,
51 Watford Way,
Hendon Central, NW4 3JH
Tel: 020 8202 5688
murraycards@ukbusiness.com
www.murraycard.com/
Cigarette and trade cards.

Piccypicky.com
Tel: 020 8204 2001/020 8206 2001
www.piccypicky.com
Artwork, autographs, bubblegum
cards, comics, posters, records and toys.

Toys & Dolls, 367 Fore Street,
Edmonton, London N9 0NR
Tel: 020 8807 3301

Unique Collections,
52 Greenwich Church Street,
London SE10 9BL Tel: 020 8305 0867
Fax: 020 8853 1066
glen@uniquecollections.co.uk
www.uniquecollections.co.uk
Old toys bought and sold.

Wheels of Steel,
Gray's Antiques Market,
Stand A12–13, Unit B10 Basement,
1–7 Davies Mews, London W1Y 2LP
Tel: 020 7629 2813

Oxfordshire
Alvin's Vintage Games & Toys
Tel: 01865 772409
vintage.games@virgin.net
Pelham puppets.

Mike Delaney
Tel: 01993 840064
Mobile: 07979 919760
mike@vintagehornby.co.uk
www.vintagehornby.co.uk
*Buying and selling Hornby 'O' gauge
and other vintage toy trains.*

Teddy Bears of Witney,
99 High Street, Witney OX28 6HY
Tel: 01993 702616 or 706616
www.teddybears.co.uk
*Steiff, Merrythought, Deans, Hermann,
artists' bears.*

Somerset
J & J's, Paragon Antiquities,
Antiques & Collectors Market,
3 Bladud Buildings, The Paragon,
Bath Somerset BA1 5LS
Tel: 01225 463715

The London Cigarette Card Co Ltd,
Sutton Road, Somerton TA11 6QP
Tel: 01458 273452
cards@londoncigcard.co.uk
www.londoncigcard.co.uk
Cigarette and trade cards.

Suffolk
W. L. Hoad, 9 St Peter's Road,
Kirkley, Lowestoft NR33 0LH
Tel: 01502 587758
William@whoad.fsnet.co.uk
www.cigarettecardsplus.com
Cigarette cards.

Suffolk Sci-Fi and Fantasy,
17 Norwich Road, Ipswich
Tel: 01473 400655
Mobile: 07885 298361
mick@suffolksci-fi.com
www.suffolksci-fi.com
Science fiction.

Surrey
eBay (UK) Ltd, PO Box 659,
Richmond upon Thames TW9 1EJ
Tel: 020 8605 3000

ggriffit@ebay.com
www.ebay.co.uk
Antiques and collectables online.

East Sussex
Rin Tin Tin, 34 North Road,
Brighton BN1 1YB
Tel: 01273 672424
rick@rintintin.freeserve.co.uk
*Original old advertising and
promotional material, magazines, early
glamour, games, toys, plastics and
miscellaneous 20thC collectables.
Open Mon–Sat 11am–5.30pm.*

Soldiers of Rye,
Mint Arcade,
71 The Mint, Rye TN31 7EW
Tel: 01797 225952
rameses@supanet.com
chris@johnbartholomewcards.co.uk
www.rameses.supanet.com
*Military badges, prints, medals,
collectors figurines, dolls'
house miniatures.*

Wallis & Wallis,
West Street Auction Galleries,
Lewes BN7 2NJ
Tel: 01273 480208
auctions@wallisandwallis.co.uk
grb@wallisandwallis.co.uk
www.wallisandwallis.co.uk
*Specialist auctioneers of militaria,
arms, armour, coins and medals.
Also diecast and tinplate toys, teddy
bears, dolls, model railways, toy
soldiers and models.*

West Sussex
Pollyanna, 34 High Street,
Arundel, West Sussex, BN18 9AB
Tel: 01903 885198
Mobile: 07949 903457

Wales
A.P.E.S. Rocking Horses,
20 Tan-y-Bwlch,
Mynydd Llandygai, Bangor,
Gwynedd LL57 4DX
Tel: 01248 600773
macphersons@apes-rocking-horses.co.uk
www.apes-rocking-horses.co.uk
Rocking horses.

Wiltshire
Dominic Winter Book Auctions,
The Old School, Maxwell Street,
Swindon SN1 5DR
Tel: 01793 611340
info@dominicwinter.co.uk
www.dominicwinter.co.uk
*Auctions of antiquarian and general
printed books and maps, sports books
and memorabilia, art reference and pictures,
photography and ephemera (including
toys, games and other collectables).*

Upstairs Downstairs,
40 Market Place, Devizes,
Wiltshire SN10 1JG

Tel: 01380 730266
Mobile: 07974 074220
devizesantiques@amserve.com
*Open Mon–Sat 9.30am–4.30pm,
Sun 9.30am–3pm, closed Wed.
Antiques and collectables centre on
4 floors with 30 traders.*

Yorkshire
Gerard Haley, Hippins Farm,
Black Shawhead,
Nr Hebden Bridge HX7 7JG
Tel: 01422 842484
Toy soldiers.

John & Simon Haley,
89 Northgate,
Halifax HX1 1XF
Tel: 01422 822148/360434
toysandbanks@aol.com
Old toys and money boxes.

Sheffield Railwayana Auctions,
43 Little Norton Lane,
Sheffield S8 8GA
Tel: 0114 274 5085
Mobile: 07860 921519
ian@sheffrail.freeserve.co.uk
www.sheffieldrailwayana.co.uk
Railwayana, posters and models auctions.

USA
The Calico Teddy
Tel: 410 366 7011
CalicTeddy@aol.com
www.calicoteddy.com

Randy Inman Auctions Inc,
PO Box 726, Waterville,
Maine 04903–0726
Tel: 207 872 6900
inman@inmanauctions.com
www.inmanauctions.com
*Auctions specializing in advertising,
coin-op, gambling devices, automata,
soda pop, Coca-Cola, breweriana,
robots and space toys, C. I. and tin toys,
Disneyana, mechanical music, mechanical
and still banks, quality antiques.*

Joyce M. Leiby, PO Box 6048,
Lancaster PA 17607 USA
Tel: 717 898 9113
joyclei@aol.com

Theriault's, PO Box 151,
Annapolis MD 21404 USA
Tel: 410 224 3655
Fax: 410 224 2515
info@theriaults.com
www.theriaults.com

Treasure Quest Auction Galleries Inc,
2581 Jupiter Park Drive,
Suite E 9 Jupiter, Florida 33458 USA
Tel: 561 741 0777
Fax: 561 741 0757
www.tqag.com

Directory of Collector's Clubs

Action Toy Organization of Michigan
Michael Crawford, 2884 Hawks,
Ann Arbour, MI 48108 USA
Tel: 734 973 1904

American Toy Emergency Vehicle (ATEV) Club
President Jeff Hawkins, 11415 Colfax Road,
Glen Allen, Virginia 23060 USA

Association of Game and Puzzle Collectors
PMB 321, 197M Boston Post Road West,
Marlborough, MA. 01752 USA
agca@agca.com www.agca.org

B.E.A.R. Collector's Club
Linda Hartzfeld, 16901 Covello Street, Van Nuys,
California 91406 USA

Barbie Collectors Club of Great Britain
Elizabeth Lee, 17 Rosemont Road, Acton,
London W3 9LU

Bearly Ours Teddy Club
Linda Harris, 54 Berkinshaw Crescent, Don Mills,
Ontario M3B 2T2 Canada

The Enid Blyton Society
93 Milford Hill, Salisbury, Wiltshire SP1 2QL
Tel: 01722 331937
info@enidblytonsociety.co.uk

The James Bond Collectors Club
PO Box 1570, Christchurch, Dorset BH23 4XS
solopublishing@firenet.uk.com

British Doll Collectors Club
Publisher & Editor Mrs Francis Baird,
The Anchorage, Wrotham Road, Culverstone,
Meopham, Gravesend,
Kent DA13 0QW
www.britishdollcollectors.com

British Teddy Bear Association
Sec Penny Shaw-Willett, PO Box 290, Brighton,
East Sussex BN2 1DR

Cabbage Patch Kids Collectors Club
P. O. Box 714, Cleveland, GA 30528 USA
Tel: 706-865-2171, Ext 291
www.cabbagepatchkids.com/

Canadian Toy Collectors Club
91 Rylander Blvd, Unit 7, Suite 245, Scarborough,
Ontario, MIB 5MS Canada Tel: 905 3898047
www.ctcs.org/ctcshp.htm

Corgi Collector Club
c/o Corgi Classics Ltd, Meridian East, Meridian Business Park,
Leicester LE19 1RL Tel: 0870 607 1204
susie@collectorsclubs.org.uk
www.corgi.co.uk

Cracker Jack Collectors Association
Theresa Richter, Membership Chairperson,
5469 S. Dorchester Avenue, Chicago, IL 60615
Information: WaddyTMR@aol.com

The Dean's Collectors Club
Euro Collectibles, PO Box 370565, 49 NE 39th Street,
Miami FL33 137 USA Tel: US toll free 1 800 309 8336
www.deansbears.com

Die Cast Car Collectors Club
c/o Chairman Jay Olins, PO Box 67226, Los Angeles,
California 90067–0266 USA Tel: 1 310 629 7113
jay@diecast.org www.diecast.org

Dinky Toy Club of America
c/o Jerry Fralick, 6030 Day Break Circle,
Suite A 150/132, Clarksville, Maryland 21029 USA
Tel/Fax: 301 854 2217
mrdinky@erols.com
www.erols.com/dinkytoy

The English Playing Card Society
Sec John Sings, PO Box 29, North Walsham,
Norfolk NR28 9NQ Tel: 01692 650496
Secretary@EPCS.org www.wopc.co.uk/epcs

Fisher-Price Collectors Club
Jeanne Kennedy, 1840 N. Signal Butte Road,
Mesa, AZ 85207 USA
www.fpclub.org

The Followers of Rupert
Membership Sec Mrs Shirley Reeves, 31 Whiteley,
Windsor, Berkshire SL4 5PJ
followersofrupert@hotmail.com www.rupertbear.info

G.I. Joe Official Collectors Club
Brian Savage, 225 Cattle Barron Parc Drive, Ft Worth,
TX 76108 Tel: 800 772 6673
www.gijoeclub.com

A. C. Gilbert Heritage Society
1440 Whalley, Suite 252, New Haven, CT 06515 USA
www.acghs.com

Golly Collectors' Club
Keith Wilkinson, 18 Hinton Street, Fairfield,
Liverpool, Merseyside L6 3AR

Hopalong Cassidy Fan Club International
Laura Bates 6310 Friendship Drive, New Concord,
OH 43762-9708 USA
www.hopalong.com

Hornby Collectors Club
PO Box 35, Royston, Hertfordshire SG8 5XR
www.hornby.co.uk

The Hornby Railway Collectors' Association
John Harwood, PO Box 3443, Yeovil,
Somerset BA21 4XR

Howdy Doody Memorabilia Collectors Club
Jeff Judson, 8 Hunt Court, Flemington,
NJ 08822-3349 Tel: 908-782-1159
jjudson@postoffice.ptd.net

International Playing Card Society
PR Officer Yasha Beresiner, 43 Templars Crescent,
London N3 3QR 100447.
3341@compuserve.com

The International Society of Meccanomen
Adrian Williams, Bell House, 72a Old High Street,
Headington, Oxford OX3 9HW
www.dircon.co.uk/meccano/

The International Wizard of Oz Club
PO Box 26249, San Francisco, CA 94126-6249 USA
membership@ozclub.org
www.ozclub.org

The M&M'S Collectors Club
c/o Kirsten Tucker (Treasurer) PMB 253, 8325 Broadway,
Ste 202 Pearland, TX 77584
www.mnmclub.com

**Matchbox International Collectors Association (MICA)
of North America**
c/o Stewart Orr and Kevin McGimpsey,
PO Box 28072, Waterloo, Ontario N2L 6J8, Canada

The Matchbox Toys International Collectors' Association
Kevin McGimpsey, PO Box 120, Deeside,
Flintshire CH5 3HE Tel: 01244 539414
kevin@matchboxclub.com
www.matchboxclub.com

The Matchbox USA Club
Mr C. Mack, Matchbox USA, 62 Saw Mill Road,
Durham, CT46022 TEL: 860-349-1655
MTCHBOXUSA@aol.com
www.charliemackonline.com

McDonald's Collector's Club
PMB 200, 1153 S Lee Street, Des Plaines,
IL 60016-6503
www.mcdclub.com/
membership@mcdclub.com

Merrythought International Collector's Club
Club Sec Peter Andrews, Ironbridge,
Telford, Shropshire TF8 7NJ
Tel: 01952 433116
contact@merrythought.co.uk
www.merrythought.co.uk

Merrythought International Collector's Club
PO Box 577, Oakdale, California 95361, USA

The Model Railway Club
The Hon Sec, Keen House, 4 Calshot Street,
London N1 9DA

Muffin the Mule Collectors' Club
12 Woodland Close, Woodford Green, Essex IG8 0QH
Tel/Fax: 020 8504 4943
adrienne@hasler.gotadsl.co.uk
www.Muffin-the-Mule.com

NFFC The Club for Disneyana Enthusiasts
PO Box 19212, Irvine, CA 92623-9212 USA
info@nffc.org nffc.org

The Official Betty Boop Fan Club
Ms Bobbie West, 10550 Western Avenue #133,
Stanton CA 90680–6909,
USA BBOOPFANS@aol.com

The Ohio Star Wars Collectors Club
PO Box 251, Lebanon, OH 45036 USA
www.oswcc.com

Peanuts Collectors Club Inc
539 Sudden Valley, Bellingham, WA 98229 USA
www.peanutscollectorclub.com

Pedal Car Collectors' Club (P.C.C.C.)
Sec A. P. Gayler, 4/4a Chapel Terrace Mews,
Kemp Town, Brighton, East Sussex BN2 1HU
Tel/Fax: 01273 601960
www.brmmbrmm.com/pedalcars

Pelham Puppets Collectors Club
Sue Valentine Tel: 01234 363 336
sue.valentine@ntlworld.com

The Russian Doll Collectors' Club
Gardener's Cottage, Hatchlands, East Clandon,
Surrey GU4 7RT www.russiandolls.co.uk

The Smurf Collectors Club
c/o Club Sec, PO Box 5737, Swanage BH19 3ZX

Smurf Collectors Club International
Dept 115 NR, 24 Cabot Road West, Massapeque,
New York 11758, USA

South Florida Toy Soldier Club
southfloridatoysoldier.com
secretary@southfloridatoysoldier.com

Southern New England HotWheelers
144 Mill Rock Road East, Old Saybrook, CT 06475
www.SNEHW.com/

Steiff Club
(not including North America) Margarete Steiff GmbH,
Postfach 15 60, D-89530 Giengen / Brenz, Germany
Telefax: +49 7322 / 131-476

Steiff USA Club
PO Box 460, Raynham Center, MA 02768-0460 USA
Tel: 1-800-830-0429 Fax: 1-508-821-4477
www.steiffusa.com/club/

**TEAMS Club – The official club for Brooke Bond
Card Collectors**
PO Box 1, Market Harborough,
Leicestershire LE16 9HT Tel: 01858 466441
sales@teamsclub.co.uk www.teamsclub.co.uk

The Toy Car Collectors Association
Dana Johnson Enterprises, PO Box 1824,
Bend OR 97709-1824 USA
www.toynutz.com/

Train Collectors Society
Membership Sec James Day, PO Box 20340,
London NW11 6ZE Tel/Fax: 020 8209 1589
tcsinformation@btinternet.com
www.traincollectors.org.uk

UK McDonald's & Fast Food Collectors Club
c/o Lawrence Yap, 110 Tithelands, Harlow, Essex CM19 5ND
bigkidandtoys@ntlworld.com

United Federation of Doll Clubs
10900 North Pomona Avenue, Kansas City,
MO 64153 Tel. 816-891-7040 Fax 816-891-8360
www.ufdc.org

Vintage Model Yacht Group
Trevor Smith, 1A Station Avenue, Epsom,
Surrey KT19 9UD Tel: 020 8393 1100

Museums & Websites

Alvin's Vintage Games and Toys
freespace.virgin.net/hidden.valley
London-based Alvin's Vintage Games,
offering board games, toys from 1950s,
'60s and '70s and Pelham puppets.

Baba Bears
www.bababears.co.uk
Dealer specializing in soft toys and
teddy bears from c1904 to 1970s.
Makes include Chad Valley, Merrythought,
Farnell and Steiff and also includes links
to various bear sites and museums.

Barbie Collectibles Directory
www.barbiecollectibles.com
Official Barbie website with a history of
the doll, an official collectors club and
a family tree among other features.

Big Red Toy Box
www.bigredtoybox.com
Web resource page featuring a toy
encyclopaedia, a message board and
online flea market.

Buenos Aires Toy Museum
www.ba-toymuseum.com.ar
Website featuring toys made or found
in Argentina, mainly from the 1980s
onwards. Features a photo gallery and
links page.

Collector's X-Change
www.f-t-l.com
Science fiction and fantasy TV and film
collectibles including autographs, toys,
dolls, games, props and comic books.

Disneyana.com
www.disneyana.com
Online mall featuring specialist
Disneyana stores selling a mixture of
vintage and modern Disneyana.

The Forgotten Toyshop
www.forgottentoys.co.uk
Online toy shop featuring Action Man,
diecast vehicles from *Batman, James
Bond, The Man From Uncle* and a
range of other toys such as *Dr Who,
Star Trek, Star Wars, The A-Team,
Knight Rider, Thundercats, Lone Ranger*
and *Masters of the Universe*. Staff
speak Japanese as well as English.

The Great Teddy Bear Hug
www.teddybears.com
Information, addresses and some links
to websites of magazines, shows and
collecting clubs feature on this site.
Also a section on the International
Golliwog Collectors' Club.

GPCC Toy Collectors Club
www.ultranet.com/~ed
Collectors' site dedicated to finding toys
from 1950s to '70s. Links to auction
and dealers websites.

Hornby
www.hornby.com
Official website for British model railway
manufacturer Hornby. Includes a company
history and Hornby Club online.

Isle of Skye Toy Museum
www.toy-museum.co.uk
Site for the Isle of Skye Toy Museum,
UK, destroyed in 2002 by fire but due
to reopen in 2004.

Jim's TV Collectibles
www.jimtvc.com
TV show related collectibles from shows
such as *The A-Team, Star Trek* and
Starsky and Hutch. Books, magazines,
and toys available for online purchase.

Master Collector Online
www.mastercollector.com
Selection of links to the sites of toy
dealers and manufacturers, mainly
dolls and action figures, also features
classified ads section which costs
£5 / €7 / $8 a month to access.

The Mouse Man Ink
www.mouseman.com
Established in December 1996, this
dealer's website specializes in vintage
Disneyana and has a reference gallery
of sold items.

My Little Pony Collectors
www.hallelnet.com/von/
Site on *My Little Pony* including
identification tips, research resources
and other 1980s childhood toys.

Neatstuff
www.neatstuff.net
American-based dealer site includes
vintage board games, tinplate robots
and sci-fi toys available to order online
via a secure server.

The Official Marx Toy Museum
www.marxtoymuseum.com
Website for The Official Marx Toy
Museum, Glen Dale, WV. Features
photos, visitor information and
Marx history.

The Old Bear Company
www.oldbear.co.uk
Shop that deals exclusively in old bears
and soft toys. Also a links page to
various bear-related sites.

Old Toy Soldier Home
www.oldtoysoldierhome.com
California-based toy dealer, featuring
Britains, Mignot and other toy soldier
makers. Numerous links to toy dealers,
clubs, magazines and manufacturers.

Pollocks Toy Museum
www.pollocksweb.co.uk
Website of Pollocks Toy Museum, UK,
featuring toys and toy theatres, visiting
information, links and details of
upcoming exhibitions.

Raving Toy Maniac
www.toymania.com
Action figures site with a list of links to
the sites of collectors' clubs, image
archives, manufacturers and toy dealers.
Also includes news from the toy
industry, advice and hints for collectors.

The Skaro Toy Museum
www.skaro.org
Virtual museum of *Dr Who* toys and
collectibles. Also features links to other
Dr Who websites.

Teddy Bear UK
www.teddy-bear-uk.com
Web resource for UK bear collectors
featuring biographical information
on famous bears such as Pooh and
Paddington, how to identify and care
for bears, online museum, bear makers
and their histories, an online shopping
mall, listings of bear shops and links to
clubs, societies and bear repairers.

Teddy Bears on the Net
www.tbonnet.com
Teddy bear resource site, providing
information on bear artists, galleries,
books, a history of the world's
favourite soft toy, information about
the care and repair of toys and a
research facility to submit details and
a picture of bears for identification.

**Toy and Miniature Museum of
Kansas City**
www.umkc.edu/tmm/
Site for the Toy and Miniature Museum
of Kansas City, MO. Features opening
times and a virtual tour of the museum.

TV Toys
www.tvtoys.com
Toys from TV shows including *The
Munsters* and *The Six Million-Dollar Man*.

Vintage Toy Train Shop
www.vintagetoys.co.uk
UK dealer specializing in Bassett-
Lowke, Hornby and Bing toy trains.

World's Largest Toy Museum
www.worldslargesttoymuseum.com
Website of World's Largest Toy Museum,
Branson, MO. Features toys from the
1800s to present. Site includes a slide
show, gift shop and visitor information.

A Wrinkle in Time
www.awit.com
California-based dealer selling TV and
film collectible merchandise online,
in particular TV science fiction and
fantasy series.

Directory of Markets & Centres

Derbyshire

Alfreton Antique Centre, 11 King Street,
Alfreton DE55 7AF Tel: 01773 520781
*30 dealers on 2 floors. Antiques, collectables, furniture,
books, militaria, postcards, silverware. Open 7 days
Mon–Sat 10am–4.30pm, Sundays 11am–4.30pm.*

Chappells Antiques Centre, King Street,
Bakewell DE45 1DZ Tel: 01629 812496
ask@chappellsantiquescentre.com
www.chappellsantiques centre.com
*Over 30 dealers inc BADA and LAPADA members. Quality
period furniture, ceramics, silver, plate, metals, treen, clocks,
barometers, books, pictures, maps, prints, textiles,
kitchenalia, lighting, furnishing accessories, scientific,
pharmaceutical and sporting antiques from the 17th–20thC.
Open Mon–Sat 12noon–5pm, Sun 11am–5pm. Closed
Christmas Day, Boxing Day, New Years Day. Please ring
for brochure.*

Heanor Antiques Centre, 1–3 Ilkeston Road,
Heanor DE75 7AE Tel: 01773 531181/762783
sales@heanorantiquescentre.co.uk
www.heanorantiquescentre.co.uk
*Open 7 days 10.30am–4.30pm including Bank Holidays.
Now 200 independent dealers in new 3 storey extension
with stylish cafe.*

Matlock Antiques, Collectables & Riverside Café,
7 Dale Road, Matlock DE4 3LT Tel: 01629 760808
bmatlockantiques@aol.com
www.matlock-antiques-collectable.cwc.net
*Proprietor W. Shirley. Over 70 dealers.
Open every day 10am–5pm.*

Devon

Quay Centre, Topsham, Nr Exeter EX3 0JA
Tel: 01392 874006
office@antiquesontopshamquay.co.uk
www.antiquesontopshamquay.co.uk
*80 dealers on 3 floors. Antiques, collectables and traditional
furnishings. Ample parking. Open 7 days, 10am–5pm.
All major credit cards accepted.*

Gloucestershire

Durham House Antiques Centre, Sheep Street,
Stow-on-the-Wold GL54 1AA Tel: 01451 870404
*30+ dealers. Town and country furniture, metalware, books,
ceramics, kitchenalia, sewing ephemera, silver, jewellery and
samplers. Mon–Sat 10am–5pm, Sunday 11am–5pm. Stow-
on-the-Wold, Cotswold home to over 40 antique shops,
galleries and bookshops.*

Gloucester Antiques Centre, The Historic Docks,
1 Severn Road, Gloucester GL1 2LE Tel: 01452 529716
www.antiques.center.com
Open Mon–Sat 10am–5pm, Sun 1pm–5pm.

Hampshire

Dolphin Quay Antique Centre, Queen Street,
Emsworth PO10 7BU Tel: 01243 379994
*Open 7 days a week (including Bank Holidays)
Mon–Sat 10am–5pm, Sun 10am–4pm. Marine, naval
antiques, paintings, watercolours, prints, antique clocks,*
*decorative arts, furniture, sporting apparel, luggage,
specialist period lighting, conservatory, garden antiques, fine
antique/country furniture, French/antique beds.*

Lymington Antiques Centre, 76 High Street,
Lymington SO41 9AL Tel: 01590 670934
*Open Mon–Fri 10am–5pm, Sat 9am–5pm. 30 dealers,
clocks, watches, silver, glass, jewellery, toys, dolls, books,
furniture, textiles.*

Kent

Castle Antiques, 1 London Road (opposite Library),
Westerham TN16 1BB
Tel: 01959 562492
*Open 10am–5pm 7 days. 4 rooms of antiques, small
furniture, collectables, rural bygones, costume, glass, books,
linens, jewellery, chandeliers, cat collectables. Services:
advice, valuations, theatre props, house clearance,
talks on antiques.*

Malthouse Arcade, High Street,
Hythe CT21 5BW
Tel: 01303 260103
*Open Fri and Sat Bank holiday Mon 9.30am–5.30pm.
37 Stalls and cafe. Furniture, china and glass, jewellery,
plated brass, picture postcards, framing etc.*

Nightingales, 89–91 High Street,
West Wickham BR4 0LS
Tel: 020 8777 0335
*Over 5,000 sq ft of antiques, furniture and collectors
items, including ceramics, glass, silver, furniture and
decorative ware. Open Mon–Sat 10am–5pm (Closed
Suns except December).*

Lancashire

The Antique & Decorative Design Centre,
56 Garstang Road, Preston PR1 1NA
Tel: 01772 882078
info@paulallisonantiques.co.uk
www.paulallisonantiques.co.uk
*Open 7 days a week 10am–5pm. 25,000 sq ft of quality
antiques, objets d'art, clocks, pine, silverware, porcelain,
upholstery, French furniture for the home and garden.*

GB Antiques Centre, Lancaster Leisure Park,
(the former Hornsea Pottery), Wyresdale Road,
Lancaster LA1 3LA
Tel: 01524 844734
*140 dealers in 40,000 sq ft of space. Porcelain, pottery, Art
Deco, glass, books, linen, mahogany, oak and pine furniture.
Open 7 days 10am–5pm.*

Kingsmill Antique Centre, Queen Street,
Harle Syke, Burnley BB10 2HX
Tel: 01282 431953
antiques@kingsmill.demon.co.uk
www.kingsmill.demon.co.uk
Dealers, packers and shippers.

Leicestershire

Oxford Street Antique Centre,
16–26 Oxford Street, Leicester LE1 5XU
Tel: 0116 255 3006

Lincolnshire
St Martins Antiques Centre, 23a High Street, St Martins,
Stamford PE9 2LF Tel: 01780 481158
peter@st-martins-antiques.co.uk
www.st-martins-antiques.co.uk

London
Alfie's Antique Market, 13 Church Street,
Marylebone NW8 8DT
Tel: 020 7723 6066
www.alfiesantiques.com
London's biggest and busiest antique market. Open
10am–6pm Tues–Sat.

Covent Garden Antiques Market,
Jubilee Market Hall, Covent Garden WC2
Tel: 020 7240 7405
Visit the famous Covent Garden Antique Market. 150 traders
selling jewellery, silver, prints, porcelain, objets d'art and
numerous other collectables.

Grays Antique Markets,
South Molton Lane W1K 5AB
Tel: 020 7629 7034
grays@clara.net
www.graysantiques.com
Over 200 specialist antique dealers selling beautiful and
unusual antiques and collectables. Open Mon–Fri 10am–6pm.

Northcote Road Antique Market, 155a Northcote Road,
Battersea SW11 6QB Tel: 020 7228 6850
www.spectrumsoft.net/nam
Indoor arcade open 7 days, Mon–Sat 10am–6pm,
Sun 12noon–5pm. 30 dealers offering a wide variety of
antiques and collectables.

Palmers Green Antiques Centre, 472 Green Lanes,
Palmers Green N13 5PA Tel: 020 8350 0878
Over 40 dealers. Specializing in furniture, jewellery, clocks,
pictures, porcelain, china, glass, silver & plate, metalware,
kitchenalia and lighting, etc. Open 6 days a week, Mon–Sat
10am–5.30pm (closed Tues), Sun 11am–5pm, open Bank
Holidays. Removals and house clearances, probate valuations
undertaken, quality antiques and collectables. All major
credit cards accepted.

Norfolk
Tombland Antiques Centre, Augustine Steward House,
14 Tombland, Norwich NR3 1HF
Tel: 01603 761906 or 619129
www.tomblandantiques.co.uk
Open Mon–Sat 10am–5pm. Huge selection on 3 floors.
Ideally situated opposite Norwich Cathedral.

Northamptonshire
The Brackley Antique Cellar, Drayman's Walk,
Brackley NN13 6BE Tel: 01280 841841
antiquecellar@tesco.net
The largest purpose-built antique centre in the Midlands.
Open 7 days 10am–5pm. 30,000 sq ft of floor space, over
100 dealers.

Oxfordshire
Antiques on High, 85 High Street, Oxford OX1 4BG
Tel: 01865 251075
Open 7 days a week 10am–5pm. Sun and Bank Holidays
11am–5pm. 35 friendly dealers with a wide range of
quality stock.

Scotland
Scottish Antique and Arts Centre, Carse of Cambus,
Doune, Perthshire FK16 6HD
Tel: 01786 841203
sales@scottish-antiques.com
www.scottish-antiques.com
Over 100 dealers. Huge gift and collectors sections. Victorian
and Edwardian furniture. Open 7 days 10am–5pm.

Scottish Antique Centre,
Abernyte PH14 9SJ Tel: 01828 686401
sales@scottish-antiques.com
www.scottish-antiques.com
Over 100 dealers. Huge gift and collectors sections. Victorian
and Edwardian furniture. Open 7days 10am–5pm.

Shropshire
Stretton Antiques Market, Sandford Avenue,
Church Stretton SY6 6BH
Tel: 01694 723718
60 dealers under one roof.

Surrey
Maltings Monthly Market, Bridge Square,
Farnham GU9 7QR Tel: 01252 726234
info@farnhammaltings.com
www.farnhammaltings.com
9.30am–4.00pm first Sat of the month.

East Sussex
The Brighton Lanes Antique Centre, 12 Meeting House Lane,
Brighton BN1 1HB Tel: 01273 823121
peter@brightonlanes-antiquecentre.co.uk
www.brightonlanes-antiquecentre.co.uk
A spacious centre in the heart of the historic lanes with a
fine selection of furniture, silver, jewellery, glass, porcelain,
clocks, pens, watches, lighting and decorative items. Open
daily 10am–5.30pm, Sun 12noon–4pm. Loading bay/parking
– Lanes car park.

Tyne & Wear
The Antique Centre, 2nd floor, 142 Northumberland Street,
Newcastle-upon-Tyne NE1 7DQ Tel: 0191 232 9832
time-antiques@btinternet.com

Wales
Offa's Dyke Antique Centre, 4 High Street, Knighton,
Powys LD7 1AT Tel: 01547 528635/520145
14 dealers. Ceramics, 18th and 19thC earthenware,
stoneware and porcelain, early 20thC industrial and studio
pottery. Reference books on ceramics and general antiques.
Good antique drinking glasses. Country antiques and
bygones. 19th and 20thC paintings and drawings.
Antiquities. General antiques and collectables.

The Works Antiques Centre, Station Road, Llandeilo,
Carmarthenshire SA19 6NH Tel: 01558 823964
theworks@storeyj.clara.co.uk www.works-antiques.co.uk
Open Tues–Sat 10am–6pm, Sun 10am–5pm. Open Bank
Holiday Mondays. 5,000 sq ft 60 dealers. Ample parking.
Free tea and coffee.

Warwickshire
Stratford Antiques Centre, 59–60 Ely Street,
Stratford-upon-Avon CV37 6LN Tel: 01789 204180
Come and visit Stratford-upon-Avon. A one stop collectors
experience with 2 floors and courtyard full of shops. Open
7 days a week from 10am–5pm.

West Midlands

Birmingham Antique Centre, 1407 Pershore Road, Stirchley, Birmingham B30 2JR Tel: 0121 459 4587
bhamantiquecent@aol.com
www.birminghamantiquecentre.co.uk
Open 7 days, Mon–Sat 9am–5pm, Sun 10am–4pm. Cabinets available to rent.

Wiltshire

Upstairs Downstairs, 40 Market Place, Devizes SN10 1JG
Tel: 01380 730266 or 07974 074220
devizesantiques@amserve.com
Open Mon–Sat 9.30am–4.30pm, Sun 9.30am–3pm, closed Wed. Antiques and collectables centre on 4 floors with 30 traders.

Worcestershire

Worcester Antiques Centre, Reindeer Court, Mealcheapen Street, Worcester WR1 4DF Tel: 01905 610680
WorcsAntiques@aol.com
Porcelain & pottery, furniture, silver and dining room accessories, jewellery, period watches and clocks, scientific instrumentation, Arts & Crafts, Nouveau, Deco, antique boxes and treen, books, ephemera, militaria and kitchenalia with full restoration and repair services on all of the above.

Yorkshire

St Nicholas Antique Shops, 35 St Nicholas Cliff, Scarborough YO11 2ES Tel: 01723 365221
sales@collectors.demon.co.uk
www.collectors.demon.co.uk
International dealers in stamps, postcards, silver, gold, medals, cigarette cards, cap badges, militaria, jewellery, commemorative ware, furniture, clocks, watches and many more collectables.

York Antiques Centre, 1a Lendal, York YO1 8AA
Tel: 01904 641445

USA

Alhambra Antiques Center, 3640 Coral Way, Coral Cables, Florida Tel: 305 446 1688
4 antiques dealers that sell high-quality decorative pieces from Europe.

Antique Center I, II, III at Historic Savage Mill, Savage, Maryland Tel: 410 880 0918 or 301 369 4650
antiquec@aol.com
225 plus select quality dealers representing 15 states. Open every day plus 3 evenings – Sun–Wed 9.30am–6pm, Thurs, Fri and Sat 9.30am–9pm. Closed Christmas, Easter and Thanksgiving days. Open New Year's Day 12noon–5pm.

Antique Village, North of Richmond, Virginia, on Historic US 301, 4 miles North of 1–295 Tel: 804 746 8914
Mon, Tues, Thurs, Fri 10am–5pm, Sat 10am–6pm, Sun 12noon–6pm, closed Wed. 50 dealers specializing in Art Pottery, country & primitives, Civil War artifacts, paper memorabilia, African art, toys, advertising, occupied Japan, tobacco tins, glassware, china, holiday collectibles, jewellery and postcards.

Antiques at Colony Mill Marketplace, 222 West Street, Keene, New Hampshire 03431 Tel: (603) 358 6343
Open Mon–Sat 10am–9pm, Sun 11am–6pm. Over 200 booths. Period to country furniture, paintings and prints, Art Pottery, glass, china, silver, jewellery, toys, dolls, quilts, etc.

The Coffman's Antiques Markets, at Jennifer House Commons, Stockbridge Road, Route 7, PO Box 592, Great Barrington MA 01230 Tel: (413) 528 9282/9602
www.coffmansantiques.com

Fern Eldridge & Friends, 800 First NH Turnpike (Rte 4), Northwood, New Hampshire 03261
Tel: 603 942 5602/8131
FernEldridgeAndFriends@NHantiqueAlley.com
30 dealers on 2 levels. Shipping available in USA. Open 10am–5pm daily. Closed major holidays, please call ahead.

Goodlettsville Antique Mall, 213 N. Main St, Germantown, Tennessee Tel: 615 859 7002

The Hayloft Antique Center, 1190 First NH Turnpike (Rte 4), Northwood, New Hampshire 03261 Tel: 603 942 5153
TheHayloftAntiqueCenter@NHantiqueAlley.com
Over 150 dealers offering Estate jewelry, sterling silver, rare books, glass, porcelain, pottery, art, primitives, furniture, toys, ephemera, linens, military, sporting collectibles and much more. Open 10am–5pm daily. Closed major holidays, please call ahead.

Hermitage Antique Mall, 4144–B Lebanon Road, Hermitage, Tennessee Tel: 615 883 5789

Madison Antique Mall, 320 Gallatin Rd, S. Nashville, Tennessee Tel: 615 865 4677
18th and 19thC English antiques and objets d'art.

Michiana Antique Mall, 2423 S. 11th Street, Niles, Michigan 49120
michianaantiquemall.com
Open 7 days, 10am–6pm.

Morningside Antiques, 6443 Biscayne Blvd., Miami, Florida Tel: 305 751 2828
The city's newest antiques market specializing in English, French and American furniture and collectibles in a small setting with many different vendors.

Nashville Wedgewood Station Antique Mall, 657 Wedgewood Ave., Nashville, Tennessee
Tel: 615 259 0939

Parker-French Antique Center, 1182 First NH Turnpike (Rte 4), Northwood, New Hampshire 03261
Tel: 603 942 8852
ParkerFrenchAntiqueCenter@NHantiqueAlley.com
135 antique dealers all on one level offering a good mix of sterling silver, jewelry, glassware, pottery, early primitives. No crafts, reproductions or new items. Open 10am–5pm daily. Closed major holidays, please call ahead.

Quechee Gorge Antiques & Collectibles Center, Located in Quechee Gorge Village
Tel: 1 800 438 5565
450 dealers. Open all year, 7 days a week. Depression glass, ephemera, tools, toys, collectibles, Deco, primitives, prints, silver and fine china.

Showcase Antique Center, PO Box 1122, Sturbridge MA 01566 Tel: 508 347 7190
www.showcaseantiques.com
Open Mon, Wed, Thurs, 10am–5pm, Fri, Sat 10am–5pm, Sun 12noon–5pm, closed Tues. 170 dealers.

Tennessee Antique Mall, 654 Wedgewood Ave, Nashville, Tennessee Tel: 615 259 4077

Key to Illustrations

Each illustration and descriptive caption is accompanied by a letter code. By referring to the following list of Auctioneers (denoted by ➤), Dealers (⊞) and Clubs (§), the source of any item may be immediately determined. Inclusion in this edition in no way constitutes or implies a contract or binding offer on the part of any of our contributors to supply or sell the goods illustrated, or similar articles, at the prices stated. Advertisers in this year's directory are denoted by (†).

If you require a valuation for an item, it is advisable to check whether the dealer or specialist will carry out this service and if there is a charge. Please mention Miller's when making an enquiry. Having found a specialist who will carry out your valuation it is best to send a photograph and description of the item to the specialist together with a stamped addressed envelope for the reply. A valuation by telephone is not possible. Most dealers are only too happy to help you with your enquiry; however, they are very busy people and consideration of the above points would be welcomed.

A&J ⊞ A & J Collectables, Bartlett Street Antique Centre, 10 Bartlett Street, Bath, Somerset BA1 2QZ Tel: 01225 466689

Ada ⊞ Fountain Antiques Market, 6 Bladud Buildings, Bath, Somerset BA1 5LS Tel: 01225 339104

AH ➤ Andrew Hartley, Victoria Hall Salerooms, Little Lane, Ilkley, Yorkshire LS29 8EA Tel: 01943 816363 info@andrewhartleyfinearts.co.uk www.andrewhartleyfinearts.co.uk

AMB ➤ Ambrose, Ambrose House, Old Station Road, Loughton, Essex IG10 4PE Tel: 020 8502 3951

AMC ⊞ Amelie Caswell Tel: 0117 9077960

Ann ⊞ Annie's Dolls & Teddies Tel: 01424 882437 anniestoys@btinternet.com

ARo ⊞† Alvin's Vintage Games & Toys Tel: 01865 772409 alvin@vintage-games.co.uk www.vintage-games.co.uk

ATK ⊞ J. & V. R. Atkins Tel: 01952 810594

AUTO ⊞ Automatomania, M13 Grays Mews, 58 Davies Street, London W1K 5LP Tel: 020 7495 5259/07790 719097 magic@automatomania.com www.automatomania.com

B ➤ Bonhams, 101 New Bond Street, London W1S 1SR Tel: 020 7629 6602 www.bonhams.com

B(Ba) ➤ Bonhams, 10 Salem Road, Bayswater, London W2 4DL Tel: 020 7313 2700

B(Ch) ➤ Bonhams, 65–69 Lots Road, Chelsea, London SW10 0RN Tel: 020 7393 3900

B(Ed) ➤ Bonhams, 65 George Street, Edinburgh EH2 2JL, Scotland Tel: 0131 225 2266

B(Kn) ➤ Bonhams, Montpelier Street, Knightsbridge, London SW7 1HH Tel: 020 7393 3900

B(WM) ➤ Bonhams, The Old House, Station Road, Knowle, Solihull, West Midlands B93 0HT Tel: 01564 776151

B&L ➤ Bonhams and Langlois, Westaway Chambers, 39 Don Street, St Helier, Jersey JE2 4TR, Channel Islands Tel: 01534 722441

BaN ⊞† Barbara Ann Newman Tel: 07850 016729

BAu ➤ Bloomington Auction Gallery, 300 East Grove St, Bloomington, Illinois 61701, USA Tel: 309 828 5533 joyluke@aol.com www.joyluke.com

BBe ⊞ Bourton Bears Tel: 01451 821466 mel@strathspey-bed-fsnet.co.uk www.bourtonbears.com

Beb ⊞ Bebes et Jouets, c/o Post Office, Edinburgh EH7 6HW, Scotland Tel: 0131 332 5650/0771 4374995 bebesetjouets@u.genie.co.uk www.you.genie.co.uk/bebesetjouets

BGC ⊞ Brenda Gerwat-Clark, Granny's Goodies, Unit 3 Georgian Galleries, Camden Passage, London N1 Tel: 0207 704 2210/07774 822299

BKS See **B**

BLH See **AMB**

Bon See **B(Kn)**

Bon(C) See **B(Ch)**

BOB ⊞ Bob's Collectables Tel: 01277 650834

BR ➤ Bracketts, The Auction Hall, The Pantiles, Tunbridge Wells, Kent TN2 5QL Tel: 01892 544500 sales@bfaa.co.uk www.bfaa.co.uk

BWe ➤ Biddle and Webb Ltd, Ladywood, Middleway, Birmingham, West Midlands B16 0PP Tel: 0121 455 8042 antiques@biddleandwebb.freeserve.co.uk www.biddleandwebb.co.uk

BWL ➤† Brightwells Fine Art, The Fine Art Saleroom, Easters Court, Leominster, Herefordshire HR6 0DE Tel: 01568 611122 fineart@brightwells.com www.brightwells.com

C Christopher Littledale, The Sussex Toy & Model Museum

CAG ➤ The Canterbury Auction Galleries, 40 Station Road West, Canterbury, Kent CT2 8AN Tel: 01227 763337 auctions@thecanterburyauctiongalleries.com www.thecanterburyauctiongalleries.com

CBB ⊞ Colin Baddiel, Gray's Mews, 1–7 Davies Mews, London W1Y 1AR Tel: 020 7408 1239/020 8452 7243

CBP ➤ Comic Book Postal Auctions Ltd, 40–42 Osnaburgh Street, London NW1 3ND Tel: 020 7424 0007 comicbook@compuserve.com www.compalcomics.com

CDC ➤ Capes Dunn & Co, The Auction Galleries, 38 Charles Street, Off Princess Street, Greater Manchester M1 7DB Tel: 0161 273 6060/1911 capesdunn@compuserve.com

CGX ⊞ Computer & Games Exchange, 65 Notting Hill Gate Road, London W11 3JS Tel: 020 7221 1123

CHAC ⊞ Church Hill Antiques Centre, 6 Station Street, Lewes, East Sussex BN7 2DA Tel: 01273 474 842 churchhilllewes@aol.com www.church-hill-antiques.co.uk

CLE ➤ Clevedon Salerooms, The Auction Centre, Kenn Road, Kenn, Clevedon, Bristol, Somerset BS21 6TT Tel: 01934 830111 clevedon.salerooms@blueyonder.co.uk www.clevedon-salerooms.com

CMF ⊞ Childhood Memories Tel: 01252 793704 maureen@childhood-memories.co.uk www.childhood-memories.co.uk

CNM ⊞ Caroline Nevill Miniatures, 22A Broad Street, Bath, Somerset BA1 5LN Tel: 01225 443091 www.carolinenevillminiatures.co.uk

CO ➤ Cooper Owen, 10 Denmark Street, London WC2H 8LS Tel: 020 7240 4132 www.CooperOwen.com

COB ⊞ Cobwebs, 78 Northam Road, Southampton, Hampshire SO14 0PB Tel: 023 8022 7458 www.cobwebs.uk.com

CoC ⊞ Comic Connections, 4a Parsons Street, Banbury, Oxfordshire OX16 5LW Tel: 01295 268989 comicman@freenetname.co.uk

CRN ⊞ The Crow's Nest, 3 Hope Square, opp. Brewers Quay, Weymouth, Dorset DT4 8TR Tel: 01305 786930 peter.ledger3@btopenworld.com

CRU ⊞ Mary Cruz Antiques, 5 Broad Street, Bath, Somerset BA1 5LJ Tel: 01225 334174

CSK ⚒ Christie's South Kensington

CTO ⊞ Collector's Corner, PO Box 8, Congleton, Cheshire CW12 4GD Tel: 01260 270429 dave.popcorner@ukonline.co.uk

CWO ⊞ www.collectorsworld.net, PO Box 4922, Bournemouth, Dorset BH1 3WD Tel: 01202 555223 info@collectorsworld.biz www.collectorsworld.net www.collectorsworld.biz

CY ⊞ Carl & Yvonne Tel: 01785 606487

CYA ⊞ Courtyard Antiques Ltd, 108A Causewayside, Edinburgh EH9 1PU, Scotland Tel: 0131 662 9008

DAC No longer Trading

DN ⚒ Dreweatt-Neate, Donnington Priory, Donnington, Newbury, Berkshire RG14 2JE Tel: 01635 553553 fineart@dreweatt-neate.co.uk www.auctions.dreweatt-neate.co.uk

DOL ⊞ Dollectable, 53 Lower Bridge Street, Chester CH1 1RS Tel: 01244 344888/679195

DQ ⊞ Dolphin Quay Antique Centre, Queen Street, Emsworth, Hampshire PO10 7BU Tel: 01243 379994

DRJ ⊞ The Motorhouse, DS & RG Johnson, Thorton Hall, Thorton, Buckinghamshire MK17 0HB Tel: 01280 812280

DuM ⚒ Du Mouchelles, 409 East Jefferson, Detroit, Michigan 48226, USA Tel: 313 963 6255

EH ⚒ Edgar Horns, 46–50 South Street, Eastbourne, East Sussex BN21 4XB Tel: 01323 410419 sales@edgarhorns.com www.edgarhorns.com

FHF ⚒ Fellows & Sons, Augusta House, 19 Augusta Street, Hockley, Birmingham, West Midlands B18 6JA Tel: 0121 212 2131 info@fellows.co.uk www.fellows.co.uk

G(B) ⚒ Gorringes Auction Galleries, Terminus Road, Bexhill-on-Sea, East Sussex TN39 3LR Tel: 01424 212994 bexhill@gorringes.co.uk www.gorringes.co.uk

G(L) ⚒ Gorringes inc Julian Dawson, 15 North Street, Lewes, East Sussex BN7 2PD Tel: 01273 478221 auctions@gorringes.co.uk www.gorringes.co.uk

GAZE ⚒ Thomas Wm Gaze & Son, Diss Auction Rooms, Roydon Road, Diss, Norfolk IP22 4LN Tel: 01379 650306 sales@dissauctionrooms.co.uk www.twgaze.com

GRa ⊞ Grays Antique Markets, South Molton Lane, London W1K 5AB Tel: 020 7629 7034 grays@clara.net www.graysantiques.com

GTM ⊞ Gloucester Toy Mart, Ground Floor, Antique Centre, Severn Road, Old Docks, Gloucester GL1 2LE Tel: 07973 768452

HAL ⊞† John & Simon Haley, 89 Northgate, Halifax, Yorkshire HX1 1XF Tel: 01422 822148/360434 toysandbanks@aol.com

HarC Hardy's Collectables Tel: 07970 613077 www.poolepotteryjohn.com

HAYS ⚒ Hays & Associates, Inc, 120 South Spring Street, Louisville, Kentucky 40206, USA Tel: 502 584 4297 www.haysauction.com

HHO ⊞ Howard Hope, 19 Weston Park, Thames Ditton, Surrey KT7 0HW Tel: 020 8398 7130 howard_hope@yahoo.com www.gramophones.uk.com

HO ⊞ Houghton Antiques Tel: 01480 461887/07803 716842

HOB ⊞ Hobday Toys Tel: 01895 636737 wendyhobday@freenet.co.uk

HOLL ⚒ Holloway's, 49 Parsons Street, Banbury, Oxfordshire OX16 5PF Tel: 01295 817777 enquiries@hollowaysauctioneers.co.uk www.hollowaysauctioneers.co.uk

HRQ ⊞ Harlequin Antiques, 79–81 Mansfield Road, Daybrook, Nottingham NG5 6BH Tel: 0115 967 4590 sales@antiquepine.net www.antiquepine.net

HUM ⊞ Humbleyard Fine Art, Unit 32 Admiral Vernon Arcade, Portobello Road, London W11 2DY Tel: 01362 637793/07836 349416

HUX ⊞ David Huxtable, Saturdays at: Portobello Road, Basement Stall 11/12, 288 Westbourne Grove, London W11 Tel: 07710 132200 david@huxtins.com

HYP ⊞ Hyperion Collectables

IM ⚒ Ibbett Mosely, 125 High Street, Sevenoaks, Kent TN13 1UT Tel: 01732 456731 auctions@ibbettmosely.co.uk www.ibbettmosely.co.uk

IQ ⊞ Cloud Cuckooland, 12 Fore Street, Mevagissey, Cornwall PL26 6UQ Tel: 01726 842364 inkquest@dial.pipex.com www.inkquest.dial.pipex.com/

J&J ⊞ J & J's, Paragon Antiquities Antiques & Collectors Market, 3 Bladud Buildings, The Paragon, Bath, Somerset BA1 5LS Tel: 01225 463715

JDJ ⚒ James D. Julia, Inc, PO Box 830, Rte.201, Skowhegan Road, Fairfield ME 04937, USA Tel: 207 453 7125 jjulia@juliaauctions.com www.juliaauctions.com

JM ⚒ Maxwells of Wilmslow inc Dockree's, 133A Woodford Road, Woodford, Cheshire SK7 1QD Tel: 0161 439 5182

JUN ⊞ Junktion, The Old Railway Station, New Bolingbroke, Boston, Lincolnshire PE22 7LB Tel: 01205 480068/480087

KA ⊞ Kingston Antiques Centre, 29–31 London Road, Kingston-upon-Thames, Surrey KT2 6ND Tel: 020 8549 2004/3839 enquiries@kingstonantiquescentre.co.uk www.kingstonantiquescentre.co.uk

KOLN ⚒ Auction Team Koln, Postfach 50 11 19, 50971 Koln, Germany Tel: 00 49 0221 38 70 49 auction@breker.com

L ⚒ Lawrence Fine Art Auctioneers, South Street, Crewkerne, Somerset TA18 8AB Tel: 01460 73041 www.lawrences.co.uk

L&E ⚒ Locke & England, 18 Guy Street, Leamington Spa, Warwickshire CV32 4RT Tel: 01926 889100 www.auctions-online.com/locke

LBe ⊞ Linda Bee, Art Deco Stand L18–21, Grays Antique Market, 1–7 Davies Mews, London W1Y 1AR Tel: 020 7629 5921

MCa ⊞ Mia Cartwright Tel: 07956 440260 mia.cartwright@virgin.net

MED ⚒ Medway Auctions, Fagins, 23 High Street, Rochester, Kent ME1 1LN Tel: 01634 847444 medauc@dircon.co.uk www.medwayauctions.co.uk

MEM § Memories UK, Mabel Lucie Attwell Club, Abbey Antiques, 63 Great Whyte, Ramsey, Nr Huntingdon, Cambridgeshire PE26 1HL Tel: 01487 814753

MEx ⊞ Music Exchange, 21 Broad Street, Bath, Somerset BA1 5LN Music 01225 333963 Records 01225 339789

MFB ⊞ Manor Farm Barn Antiques Tel: 01296 658941 or 07720 286607 mfbn@btinternet.com www.btwebworld.com/mfbantiques

MLL ⊞ Millers Antiques Ltd, Netherbrook House, 86 Christchurch Road, Ringwood, Hampshire BH24 1DR Tel: 01425 472062 mail@millers-antiques.co.uk www.millers-antiques.co.uk

MP Michael Pearson

MRW ⊞ Malcolm Welch Antiques, Wild Jebbett, Pudding Bag Lane, Thurlaston, Nr Rugby, Warwickshire CV23 9JZ Tel: 01788 810 616 www.rb33.co.uk

MTMC § Muffin the Mule Collectors' Club, 12 Woodland Close, Woodford Green, Essex IG8 0QH Tel: 020 8504 4943 adrienne@hasler.gotadsl.co.uk www.Muffin-the-Mule.com

MUL ⚒ Mullock & Madeley, The Old Shippon, Wall-under-Heywood, Nr Church Stretton, Shropshire SY6 7DS Tel: 01694 771771 auctions@mullockmadeley.co.uk www.mullockmadeley.co.uk

MURR ⊞ Murrays' Antiques & Collectables Tel: 01202 309094

N ⚒ Neales, 192 Mansfield Road, Nottingham NG1 3HU Tel: 0115 962 4141 fineart@neales.co.uk www.neales-auctions.com

NOS ⊞ Nostalgia and Comics, 14–16 Smallbrook Queensway, City Centre, Birmingham, West Midlands B5 4EN Tel: 0121 643 0143

OPG Octopus Publishing Group Ltd

OTS ⊞ The Old Toy Shop, PO Box 4389, Ringwood, Hampshire BH24 1YN Tel: 01425 470180 djwells@btinternet.com www.TheOldToyShop.com

OW See **Sta**

P   See **B**

PB   See **B(Ba)**

PC   Private Collection

PEZ ⊞ Alan Pezaro, 62a West Street, Dorking, Surrey RH4 1BS Tel: 01306 743661

PF ⚒ Peter Francis, Curiosity Sale Room, 19 King Street, Carmarthen SA31 1BH, Wales Tel: 01267 233456 Peterfrancis@valuers.fsnet.co.uk www.peterfrancis.co.uk

PLB ⊞ Planet Bazaar, 149 Drummond Street, London NW1 2PB Tel: 020 7387 8326/07956 326301 info@planetbazaar.co.uk www.planetbazaar.co.uk

POLL ⊞† Pollyanna, 34 High Street, Arundel, West Sussex BN18 9AB Tel: 01903 885198/07949 903457

PrB ⊞ Pretty Bizarre, 170 High Street, Deal, Kent CT14 6BQ Tel: 07973 794537

RAND ⊞ Becky Randall, c/o 36 Highfield Road, Wilmslow, Buckinghamshire MK18 3DU Tel: 07979 848440

RAR   No longer trading

RBB   See **BWL**

RDG ⊞ Richard Dennis Gallery, 144 Kensington Church Street, London W8 4BN Tel: 020 7727 2061

RGa ⊞ Richard Gardner Antiques, Swanhouse, Market Square, Petworth, West Sussex GU28 0AN Tel: 01798 343411

ROS ⚒ Rosebery's, The Old Railway Booking Hall, Crystal Palace Station Road, London SE19 2AZ Tel: 020 8761 2522

RTo ⚒ Rupert Toovey & Co Ltd, Spring Gardens, Washington, West Sussex RH20 3BS Tel: 01903 891955 auctions@rupert-toovey.com www.rupert-toovey.com

RTT ⊞ Rin Tin Tin, 34 North Road, Brighton, East Sussex BN1 1YB Tel: 01273 672424 rick@rintintin.freeserve.co.uk

RUSS ⊞ Russells Tel: 023 8061 6664

RW   Rob Wilson

S ⚒ Sotheby's, 34–35 New Bond Street, London W1A 2AA Tel: 020 7293 5000 www.sothebys.com

S(Cg) ⚒ Sotheby's, 215 West Ohio Street, Chicago, Illinois 60610, USA Tel: 312 670 0010 www.sothebys.com

S(NY) ⚒ Sotheby's, 1334 York Avenue at 72nd St, New York NY 10021, USA Tel: 212 606 7000 www.sothebys.com

S(S) ⚒ Sotheby's Sussex, Summers Place, Billingshurst, West Sussex RH14 9AD Tel: 01403 833500 www.sothebys.com

S&NJ   Sheila & Norman Joplin

SAND   No longer trading

SJ   Sheila Joplin

SK(B) ⚒ Skinner Inc, 357 Main Street, Bolton MA 01740, USA Tel: 978 779 6241

SMAM ⊞ Santa Monica Antique Market, 1607 Lincoln Boulevard, Santa Monica, California 90404, USA Tel: 310 673 7048

SMI ⊞ Skip & Janie Smithson Antiques Tel: 01754 810265/ 07831 399180 smithsonantiques@hotmail.com

SP   Sue Pearson

SpM ⊞ Girl Can't Help It!, The Sparkle Moore & Cad Van Swankster, Alfies Antique Market, G100 & G116 Ground Floor, 13–25 Church Street, Marylebone, London NW8 8DT Tel: 020 7724 8984/07958 515614 sparkle.moore@virgin.net www.sparklemoore.com

SSF ⊞ Suffolk Sci-Fi and Fantasy, 17 Norwich Road, Ipswich, Suffolk Tel: 01473 400655/07885 298361 mick@suffolksci-fi.com www.suffolksci-fi.com

STa ⊞† Starbase-Alpha, Unit 19–20 Rumford Shopping Halls, Market Place, Romford, Essex RM1 3AT Tel: 01708 765633/01908 240365 starbasealpha1@aol.com www.starbasealpha.cjb.net

STE ⊞† Stevenson Brothers, The Workshop, Ashford Road, Bethersden, Ashford, Kent TN26 3AP Tel: 01233 820363 sales@stevensonbros.com www.stevensonbros.com

STK   No longer trading

SWO ⚒ Sworders, 14 Cambridge Road, Stansted Mountfitchet, Essex CM24 8BZ Tel: 01279 817778 www.sworder.co.uk

T&D ⊞ Toys & Dolls, 367 Fore Street, Edmonton, London N9 0NR Tel: 020 8807 3301

TAC ⊞ Tenterden Antiques Centre, 66–66A High Street, Tenterden, Kent TN30 6AU Tel: 01580 765655/765885

TBoy   See **IQ**

THE ⚒ Theriault's, PO Box 151, Annapolis MD 21404, USA Tel: 410 224 3655 info@theriaults.com www.theriaults.com

TMA ⚒ Tring Market Auctions, The Market Premises, Brook Street, Tring, Hertfordshire HP23 5EF Tel: 01442 826446 sales@tringmarketauctions.co.uk www.tringmarketauctions.co.uk

TOP ⊞ The Top Banana Antiques Mall, 1 New Church Street, Tetbury, Gloucestershire GL8 4DS Tel: 0871 288 1102 info@topbananaantiques.com www.topbananaantiques.com

TOY   No longer trading

TQA ⚒ TreasureQuest Auction Galleries, Inc, 2581 Jupiter Park Drive, Suite E 9 Jupiter, Florida 33458, USA Tel: 561 741 0777 www.tqag.com

TR   Tim Ridley

TRA ⊞ Tramps, 8 Market Place, Tuxford, Newark, Nottinghamshire NG22 0LL Tel: 01777 872 543 info@trampsuk.com

TWr ⊞ Tim Wright Antiques, Richmond Chambers, 147 Bath Street, Glasgow G2 4SQ, Scotland Tel: 0141 221 0364

UCO ⊞† Unique Collections, 52 Greenwich Church Street, London SE10 9BL Tel: 020 8305 0867 glen@uniquecollections.co.uk www.uniquecollections.co.uk

UD ⊞ Upstairs Downstairs, 40 Market Place, Devizes, Wiltshire SN10 1JG Tel: 01380 730266/07974 074220 devizesantiques@amserve.com

UNI   No longer trading

VEC ⚒† Vectis Auctions Ltd, Fleck Way, Thornaby, Stockton-on-Tees, Cleveland TS17 9JZ Tel: 01642 750616 admin@vectis.co.uk www.vectis.co.uk

VJ ⊞ Ventnor Junction, 48 High Street, Ventnor, Isle of Wight PO38 1LT Tel: 01983 853996 shop@ventjunc.freeserve.co.uk

WaH ⊞ The Warehouse, 29–30 Queens Gardens, Worthington Street, Dover, Kent CT17 9AH Tel: 01304 242006

WAL ⚒† Wallis & Wallis, West Street Auction Galleries, Lewes, East Sussex BN7 2NJ Tel: 01273 480208 auctions@wallisandwallis.co.uk grb@wallisandwallis.co.uk www.wallisandwallis.co.uk

WAm ⊞ Williams Amusements Ltd, Bluebird House, Povey Cross Road, Horley, Surrey RH6 0AG Tel: 01293 782222/ 07970 736486 adrian@williams-amusements.co.uk www.williams-amusements.co.uk

WHO ⊞ The Who Shop International Ltd, 4 Station Parade, High Street North, East Ham, London E6 1JD Tel: 020 8471 2356/07977 430948 whoshop@hilly.com www.thewhoshop.com

WI ⊞ David Winstone, Bartlett Street Antique Centre, 5–10 Bartlett Street, Bath, Somerset BA1 2QZ Tel: 01225 466689/07979 506415 winstampok@netscapeonline.co.uk

WL ⚒ Wintertons Ltd, Lichfield Auction Centre, Fradley Park, Lichfield, Staffordshire WS13 8NF Tel: 01543 263256 enquiries@wintertons.co.uk www.wintertons.co.uk

WOS ⊞ Wheels of Steel, Grays Antique Market, Stand A12–13, Unit B10 Basement, 1–7 Davies Mews London W1Y 2LP Tel: 0207 629 2813

WW ⚒ Woolley & Wallis, Salisbury Salerooms, 51–61 Castle Street, Salisbury, Wiltshire SP1 3SU Tel: 01722 424500/411854 junebarrett@woolleyandwallis.co.uk www.woolleyandwallis.co.uk

YC ⊞ Yesterday Child Tel: 01908 583403 djbarrington@btinternet.com

YO ⊞ Martin Burton, 201 Hull Road, York YO10 3JY Tel: 01904 415347 yoyomonster@jugglers.net

YT ⊞ Yew Tree Antiques, Woburn Abbey Antiques Centre, Woburn, Bedfordshire MK17 9WA Tel: 01525 872514

Picture Acknowledgments

p.17 *t* OPG/PC; *b* WL p.18 *t* OPG/PC; *b* S p.19 *t* J&J *b* HUX p.20 OPG/CSK p.21 HAL; S(NY) p.22 HAL p.23 *t* & *b* OPG/CSK *m* S(S) p.24 *t* OPG/CSK; JUN p.25 HAL; OPG/CSK p.26 *t* TQA; CBB; p.27 CBB p.28 CBB p.29 OPG/CSK p.30 OPG/CSK x 2 p.31 OPG/CSK x 2 p.32 JUN p.33 OPG/CSK x 2 p.34 OPG/CSK x 2 p.35 *r* HAL; *bl* OPG/CSK p.36 OPG/CSK p.37 OPG/CSK x4 p.38 OPG/CSK p.39 *tl* OPG/S&NJ; *tr* OPG/RW; *b* OPG/S&NJ p.40 OPG/SJ p.41 OPG/CSK p.42 OPG/PC x 3 p.43 *tl* OPG/CSK *tr* OPG/PC p.44 HUX p.45 *t* CMF *b* YO x 2 p.46 CGX x 2 p.47 *t* S(NY); *b* G(B) p.49 *t* WOS; *b* OPG/C p.50 *t* OPG/C x 2 p.52 OPG/CSK x 2; p.53 OPG/CSK p.54 *t* OPG/CSK; *b* HAL p.55 *t* OPG/C; *b* WAL p.57 OPG/CSK p.58 OPG/CSK x 3 p.59 OPG/CSK p.60 *t* and *l* OPG/CSK; *r* UD p.61 OW x 2 p.62 *tl* UNI; *r* and *b* OW x 2 p.63 SSF p.64 *tl* Bau; *tr* HOB; *b* UCO p.65 OPG/CSK x 2 p.66 *t* STa; *b* BBe p.67 *t* STa; *b* BBe p.68 CMF p.69 *t* CWO; *b* SSF p.70 UD p.71 ARo p.72 *t* OPG/MP/Trevor Jacobs; *bl* DA; *br* G(L) p.73 *t* BaN; *bl* VEC; *b r* UD p.75 OPG/MP/SP p.76 *tl* OPG/MP/SP/ *r* OPG/Peter Anderson/Chuck Steffes; *b* OPG/MP/SP p.77 G(L); p.78 HAYS; *b* UD p.79 *t* OPG/CSK; *b* UD p.80 *tl, ml,* and *bl* OPG/TR; *mb* T&D; *tr* T&D p.81 *t* T&D; *b* OPG/CSK; *br* OPG/TR p.82 OPG p.83 JUN p.84 OPG/TR

Bibliography

Bly, John. *Miller's Is it Genuine? How to collect Antiques with Confidence*, London: Octopus Publishing Group Limited, 2002.

Ellis, Phil. *Miller's Sci-fi & Fantasy Collectibles*, London: Octopus Publishing Group Limited, 2003.

Franchi, Rudy and Barbara. *Miller's Movie Collectibles*, London: Octopus Publishing Group Limited, 2002.

Higgins, Katherine. *Miller's Collecting the 1970s*, London: Octopus Publishing Group Limited, 2001.

Leibe, Frankie, Agnew, Daniel and Maniera, Leyla. *Miller's Soft Toys: A Collector's Guide*, London: Octopus Publishing Group Limited, 2000.

Luke, Tim, Solis-Cohen, Lita. *Miller's American Insider's Guide to Toys & Games*, London: Octopus Publishing Group Limited, 2002.

Marsh, Hugo. *Miller's Toys & Games Antiques Checklist*, London: Octopus Publishing Group Limited, 2000.

Marsh, Madeleine. *Miller's Collectables Price Guide Vols.14–16*, London: Octopus Publishing Group Limited, 2002–4.

Marsh, Madeleine. *Miller's Collecting the 1950s*, London: Octopus Publishing Group Limited, 1997.

Marsh, Madeleine. *Miller's Collecting the 1960s*, London: Octopus Publishing Group Limited, 1999.

Marsh, Madeleine. *Miller's Complete A–Z of Collectables*, London: Octopus Publishing Group Limited, 2004.

Miller, Judith. *Miller's Antiques Encyclopedia*, London: Octopus Publishing Group Limited, 1998.

Musters, Claire. *Miller's Antiques, Art & Collectibles on the Web*, London: Octopus Publishing Group Limited, 2000.

Musters, Claire. *Miller's Antiques, Art & Collectibles on the Web*, London: Octopus Publishing Group Limited, 2003.

Ramsay, John. *British Diecast Model Toys*, Suffolk, Swapmeet Publications, 8th Edition 1999.

Ramsay, John. *British Model Trains*, Suffolk, Swapmeet Publications, 1st Edition 1998.

Pearson, Sue. *Miller's Dolls and Teddy Bears Antiques Checklist*, London: Octopus Publishing Group Limited, 1995.

Pearson, Sue. *Miller's Teddy Bears A Complete Collector's Guide*, London: Octopus Publishing Group Limited, 2001.

Index to Advertisers

Index